Ash

Polyænus's Stratagems of war; Translated From the Original Greek, by R. Shepherd, F.R.S

POLYÆNUS'S

STRATAGEMS OF WAR;

TRANSLATED FROM

THE ORIGINAL GREEK.

POLYÆNUS'S

STRATAGEMS OF WAR;

TRANSLATED FROM

THE ORIGINAL GREEK,

BY

R. SHEPHERD, F.R.S.

LONDON.

PRINTED FOR GEORGE NICOL, BOOKSELLER TO HIS MAJESTY,
PALL-MALL

M.DCC.XCIII.

TO THE

MOST NOBLE

THE MARQUIS CORNWALLIS.

MY LORD,

THE subsequent pages having already received the approbation of so excellent a judge of the subject as the Marquis CORNWALLIS, I beg leave to place them under your Lordship's protection. The original was honoured with the patronage of two Roman Emperors, then medi-

tating

DEDICATION.

tating an expedition into Perfia: in the protection of your Lordship the translation boasts a name not less illustrious, in having terminated with the most brilliant success an Indian expedition against the ablest foe that ever disputed the British empire in the East.

And in the prefix of a name so respectable, the form of address is rendered short and easy. The author has not to amplify a character, with which the world is already so well acquainted. In this instance, to use the style of dedication would only be to anticipate the historian's pen.

For

DEDICATION.

For whether as the foldier covered with laurels, the ftatefman facrificing the pride of conqueft to his country's good, the individual exercifing uncontrolled power with unexampled humanity, or the man folicited by every temptation of accumulating wealth, yet, in character truly Horatian,

> " Ingentes oculo irretorto
> Spectans acervos,"

in whatever point of view the page of hiftory, while it records your Lordfhip's adminiftration in India, fhall perfonally regard yourfelf, it muft be panegyrick.

DEDICATION.

To that faithful page I therefore refer your Lordship's atchievements: and have the honour to be,

With great Respect,

MY LORD,

Your Lordship's most obedient

And humble Servant,

R. SHEPHERD.

ADVERTISEMENT.

THE subsequent pages, were written at a time, when the author's inclination directed his views to a military life: and the course of reading he then adopted had an aspect to that profession. While engaged in those pursuits, the collection of stratagems made by Polyænus he read with so great pleasure both as a classical and military production, that he was induced to employ some leisure hours in habiting the author in an English dress But, in respect to his line of life, changing afterwards his design, with his intended profession he laid aside the studies that attached to it. and the following translation remained more than thirty years untouched and unnoticed in his desk. Till by some means, which he can scarcely explain, it broke its confinement, and found its way to the perusal of the Marquis CORNWALLIS: who recommended the publication of it, as a work, if the translator may be permitted to use his Lordship's own words, that would prove an acceptable present to the British officers.

ADVERTISEMENT.

Since that time the extraordinary conduct of a neighbouring nation having provoked almost all Europe to arms, Great Britain of too much consequence in herself and her connections to remain an idle spectator of exertions calculated to involve the world in scenes of anarchy and confusion, found it necessary to take the field. Her navies were summoned from her ports, her armies to foreign service, her militia are embodied at home, and the country assumes a more military complection, than it hath for some time past been accustomed to wear. At this period, and in this state of things, the author hath been induced to hazard on the public the following pages.

He is aware that the world has little to do with this detail, nor at all concerned about the motives that induced him either to translate or publish but he conceives it a duty, which he owes to himself, with the work to obtrude on the public his apology for it. Lest he should appear to have misemployed his time in the prosecution of studies very different from those, which his profession might have been supposed to suggest.

His profession, as well as his disposition, leads him to wish the prevalence of universal peace. but he yet sees no characters of the time appear when we "shall beat our swords into ploughshares, and our spears into pruning hooks" a period notwithstanding, which on the sure word of prophecy he firmly trusts will come. But of that period,
which

ADVERTISEMENT.

which infinite wifdom hath predetermined, with humble patience we muft wait the approach; and in the mean time, as wife and good citizens, it is our duty to endeavour to fecure ourfelves in the poffeffion of order and peace by every means human prudence can fuggeft.

AND this he knows not by what other means, than the arm of power, is to be effected. For he is not fo wild a politician, as to fuppofe, thofe defirable objects of fecurity and peace are to be preferved to a great nation without armies: and armies he is free to acknowledge imply war. But let it be at the fame time obferved, that the term war does not neceffarily involve in it defolation, oppreffion, and diftraction. Let it be called an evil, but, in the name of common fenfe, let it be acknowledged a neceffary one. And when it is conducted by men of virtuous difpofitions, and truly great minds; the object of it is to procure the bleffings of peace. "It is that, 'fays an antient writer of the firft eminence,' for which we bear to be expofed to danger and fatigues of every kind."* The object of it, even with regard to our enemies, is no more than a conviction of injuries, an amendment of conduct, and a reparation for wrongs Refpecting ourfelves, when directed by prudent counfels, it is fecurity and peace. No wife man ever attacked his neighbour, for the fake of returning victorious from the field. And

* Polybius, L. 4. C. 1.

ADVERTISEMENT.

When war is undertaken by those that are unwise, it is a consideration that constitutes the reason, why the wise should be in a condition to repel such attacks; it forms an irrefragable argument for being prepared by military arrangements, and what the quiet speculatist may indignantly call a parade of the pride of war.

There exists an instance in the present state of Europe, to which allusion has been already made, and which exemplifies many of the above reflections. A great and powerful nation has started forth, and with a degree of boundless philanthropy undertaken the Herculean labour of reducing jarring interests to general acquiescence, harmony, and union; the one great object of her endeavours, to conciliate to the world universal peace, and *fraternize* mankind. But such is the imbecility of human nature, when they have held out the benevolent hand to *fraternize*; even that virtuous nation, big with benevolent designs, have sometimes been observed to draw it back, clinched with the full grasp of oppression.

And philosophers as they are, they have not been so unenlightened as to imagine the general blessing of peace could be promoted, or so fanciful as to form an attempt to establish it, otherwise than by force of arms. They have not been so absurd as to suppose the great cause they had in view could be accomplished by the still voice of reason, the demands of justice, or the plea of humanity. They have in arms traversed

seas

ADVERTISEMENT.

feas and land, to make profelytes to it. In foreign ftates they have thundered with their cannon, and undermined with their emiffaries. but in the great work the progrefs they have made is fmall. And even at home we obferve among them no fymptoms of the benign bleffings of peace though indeed they boaft of having laid the foundation ftone of the great work, in having *fhivered the fceptres of Princes, and overthrown the altars of God**

But though there may be fome advantage in acknowledging no power fuperiour to our noble felves, in founding our conduct on prefent utility, and laughing at the narrow prejudices, that manacle the reft of the world that line of thinking, and fo loofe a rule of acting, may have its inconveniencies too. For fuppofing there fhould be a fupreme Being, that fuperintends human actions, that rules this world with uncontroulable power, and governs every moral movement in it with adorable juftice, I muft not diffemble how far a reflection, which one of the following ftratagems hath fuggefted, carries me, and, refpecting that heroic people, how much it hath alarmed me for their fuccefs abroad, or even their fafety at home. It is the laconic harangue of Agefilaus to his little army, on his adverfary having attacked him in direct breach of oath. " Tifaphernes, ' faid the brave Spartan,' I thank for his perjury by which he has made the gods his enemies,

* Dupont's Speech in the Convention.

and

and our allies. Let us therefore, my lads, march out with becoming confidence, in conjunction with so great auxiliaries." And my author proceeds to tell me, that spirited by this short harangue the general led them forth, and obtained a compleat victory. On this little portion of antient history I leave our Gallic neighbours to make their comment.

PRELIMINARY DISCOURSE.

THOUGH the perſonal circumſtances of an author have it muſt be acknowledged little concern with his works, yet it is obſervable, that we can not intereſt ourſelves much in theſe, without wiſhing to know ſomewhat of the other. Short however is the account that hath reached us reſpecting the author of the following pages. of whom we learn little more, than that he was by birth a Macedonian, and, that the early part of his life was paſſed in arms. But, whether influenced by his love of letters, or other motives of prudence, he afterwards retired from the active ſcenes of his profeſſion; and exchanged the ſword for the gown.

IN this new ſituation his integrity and learning, his eloquence and abilities, recommended him to the notice of the Emperors Antoninus and Verus, who honoured him with a civil employ of truſt and dignity. It was then that he found himſelf at liberty to reſume his military ſtudies, and in his cloſet to contribute to the improvement of that profeſſion, for which, in his addreſs to the emperors prefixed to the

firſt

first book of stratagems, the reader will discover in him a strong predilection. Partly perhaps to gratify such his inclinations, and partly to pay a tribute of gratitude to his patrons, what leisure hours he could steal from his civil engagements, he devoted to the following collection of military stratagems

The original work has come down to us incompleat and what is still more to be regretted, in that which has reached us the text is to a very great degree mutilated and corrupted. So that much was to be supplied, even in the bare attempt at a faithful translation And, added to these defects, the brevity, with which the author relates circumstances, sometimes renders the detail apparently imperfect, and sometimes flings a shade of obscurity on it The translator has therefore every where endeavoured to explain the stratagem, as well as to translate it, and rather to give the author's meaning, than a literal version of his words, whenever the one did not clearly and fully convey the other, or where he has suspected the text to have been corrupted And, nude and unadorned as the original is, the concisenefs, the author observes in his relation of facts, besides the disadvantages above alluded to, creates also a sameness in his mode of introducing the respective detail, and an uniformity in his manner of conducting it, which has in some instances induced the translator a little to deviate from the form of narration which occurs in the original, in order to avoid as far as might be an apparent poverty of diction, and to give as much ease and variety to the stile, as matter so fettered up is capable of receiving At the same time he hath not presumed to flourish in description,

PRELIMINARY DISCOURSE.

defcription, nor to add circumftances to the general narration, which the author did not think neceffary to introduce. What the reader is to expect, the tranflator has thought it thus neceffary to apprife him.

The critic, who looks for fentiment, or defcription, will be difappointed: but he muft recollect that Polyænus wrote for military men, that facts conftituted all that was neceffary to be attended to, and that the more concifely they were to be detailed, fo much the more eafily would they be retained in memory, brought together as in a fynopfis, and be as occafion offered ready for practice. Indeed in fo vaft a collection of ftratagems had our author been more circumftantial in his relation of facts, and ftudied variety and expreffion more than was barely neceffary to elucidate them, inftead of occupying his leifure hours, the undertaking would have engroffed every hour of his time: and his work would have formed a hiftory of wars, and not, as he intended it, a collection of ftratagems.

With regard to the tranflator, if the concifenefs, which the author hath been noticed fo uniformly to obferve, has occafioned him fome little difficulties, he muft acknowledge his tafk to have been in other refpects light, in not having to contend with fome very great ones. The work exhibits no nice form of expreffion to be ftudioufly preferved, no beauties of defcription to be copied, no turn of fentiment that requires the fupport of correfpondent diction to communicate to it weight and fignificancy. The author's aim was a fimple detail of facts: the endeavour of the tranflator has been to render thofe facts with fidelity, fometimes affuming a fmall liberty in the mode of relation

c

RESPECTING the original, though the text be much corrupted, the ſtile of Polyænus is claſſical, and even elegant though he abound not in ſentiment, or deſcription, his matter is intereſting, and entertaining, and his various anecdotes, interſperſed throughout the work, are often better calculated for marking out the temper and character of the perſon reſpectively alluded to, than a regular detail of facts conducted by the hiſtorian to explain the whole ſcheme and ſyſtem of his conduct. And it appears to me ſomewhat extraordinary, that Polyænus is an author ſo little known, and one of thoſe few Greek claſſics, who have never made their appearance in an Engliſh dreſs. For this however ſome reaſons may perhaps be aſſigned. Military men generally enter too young into the profeſſion, and are too much engaged in active ſervice, to have leiſure to cultivate the ſtudy of ſo neglected a language as the Greek. And thoſe on the other hand, whoſe time is devoted to literary purſuits, have ſeldom much taſte for authors, whoſe works regard only military operations.

THE whole collection, if entire, would have conſiſted of nine hundred ſtratagems, containing the exploits of the moſt celebrated generals, of various nations, fetched from ages remote as the page of hiſtory will reach, and carried forward to our author's own time ſo wide was the field he traverſed of annals, hiſtories, and lives, in the proſecution of his deſign, ιςοδιων της ςρατηγικης επιτημης, a manual, as he terms it, of the ſcience of generalſhip And in ſo large a collection if ſome ſtratagems occur, that bear a reſemblance to each other, ſometimes with little variation employed by the ſame general, and ſometimes on differ-

ent

PRELIMINARY DISCOURSE.

ent occasions copied by others, the reader will be rather surprised that he finds so few instances of this kind, than led to have expected none. Some will strike him as unimportant, and some are not properly military stratagems. Some devices again will appear so ludicrous and absurd, as nothing but the barbarism of the times, the ignorance and superstition that in some states prevailed, will reconcile to credibility. The stratagems however that rank under those classes are few the work in general was executed with great judgment, and, as the author himself observes, he had employed upon it no small degree of pains.

POLYÆNUS was a man of eminence: and, though he might have quitted actual service in early life, for military science equally distinguished, as in his juridical character. And this collection of stratagems he considered as a work of sufficient importance, to justify his pretensions to the patronage of the emperors who honoured the author with their confidence and attention. And in so high a light was he held as a military writer, and of so great utility was the work before us esteemed, that Frontinus, a Roman knight, stimulated by the reputation it had obtained the author, published a new performance, of the same nature, and under the same title of military stratagems. Of which authors, says a very competent judge of literary merit,* whoever will take the pains to enter into a comparison, he will find it strengthen the argument of the great superiority of the Grecian to Roman writers.

SINCE the introduction of gunpowder it must be acknowledged that

* Is. Casaubonus

the art of war has undergone a material alteration. But though the manner of engaging be different, seasons, ground, forage, surprises, retreats, and all the manœuvres that flow from these subjects of military operation, are much the same as they were a thousand years ago, and still as practicable. Those antient manœuvres, which this collection records, employed in effecting retreats, are so various, that on apposite occasions, it is conceived, many of them might with some variation under the present system of war be practised with success. Stratagems also in communicating and intercepting intelligence are equally advantageous at all times, and may in some instances be as practicable now as formerly, and must be as useful too. In ambuscades the antient generals seem ever to have placed great confidence: and throughout the following stratagems it may be observed, whenever they escaped detection, they always decided the victory. A thousand or two thousand men after the enemy's lines are formed, and they are unprepared to receive them, shewing themselves at some critical period of the engagement, were found of greater effect, than three times the number from the beginning of the engagement openly marshalled against them. Woods, shrubby ground, and ditches, every one knows how to convert to those purposes. But in the course of the following stratagems we are instructed, that even plain ground will serve the purpose. and sometimes more effectually, as being by the enemy less suspected. A small eminence properly occupied has often been found effectually to shelter an ambuscade; or the banks of a river, or a piece of ground has in the course of a night been scooped out for the purpose. from whence a caution

is

PRELIMINARY DISCOURSE. xxi

is fuggefted, to reconnoitre the ground as near the time of an intended action as poffible Iphicrates, of whofe ftratagems Polyænus has recorded more than fixty, remarks that he once neglected to reconnoitre his ground, and then he narrowly efcaped being furprifed by an ambufcade.

How to guard againft mutinies in your own army, or quafh them when excited, and how to promote them in that of the enemy, how to impart confidence, refolution, and fpirit to your own troops, and imprefs the hoftile army with terror, diffidence, and difmay, how to keep your own forces together, and win over thofe of the enemy to defertion and revolts, thofe are arts in which the difference of arms, of bullets and javelins, of mortars and catapults, it is apprehended can effect no great alteration. And interfperfed throughout the work occur fo great a variety of excellent military precepts, rules, and maxims, that if not practicable in the great fcience of conducting armies under any fyftem of war, and at any day, they will at leaft be fatisfactory in the illuftration they afford of many points in the fcience of war, as it was practifed two thoufand years ago. They are the refult of the experience of the greateft generals of the world amongft nations where the glory of individuals, and at a period of time when the fafety of ftates, were centred all in military atchievements. And if to be well verfed in a fimilarity of cafes, though perhaps not exactly and in every correfponding circumftance at all times equally practicable, prepare men the better for counfel or action on emergencies, that may fuddenly prefent themfelves, fo far a general acquaintance with thofe
ftratagems

ſtratagems may ſuggeſt hints, which may be found of poſſible ſervice. Or at leaſt a knowledge of the various ſtratagems that have been practiſed, may tend to guard againſt ſimilar devices in the enemy, or modern improvements on them.

INDEPENDENT however of that military knowledge, and thoſe political maxims with which the work before us is replete, it is in other reſpects both amuſing and inſtructive. The lively repartees, and private anecdotes, which occaſionally occur, that fertility of invention in diſcovering reſources, and promptitude of mind often diſplayed in difficulties, and on ſudden emergencies, thoſe various inſtances of unſhaken reſolution under adverſity, of intrepidity in dangers, of contempt of ſufferings, with which the work abounds, intereſt the mind, entertain, and improve it. Little incidents in public characters are ſometimes noticed, which contribute to illuſtrate or explain hiſtorical facts, in the page of formal hiſtory perhaps doubtfully inſinuated, or obſcurely repreſented. The manners of the reſpective countries and times are often ſtrongly marked in the ſtratagems which refer to them, their habits, genius, ſtrength, and population are occaſionally introduced. and the policy and connections in particular of the ſeveral ſtates of Greece, their public animoſities, and the private pique of individuals, that were the ſources of continual wars, are developed. The manner in which the ſoldiers lived in camps, their fare, their employments and amuſements, the following miſcellany exhibits, and forms a valuable body of antient military hiſtory.

EVERY hero of antiquity is there brought as in review before us.

and

and in his actions we see his abilities and defects, his habit and temper of mind, more clearly and in stronger colouring, than in general descriptions of him at the head of armies, and in public scenes of life. Some characters even in those days of barbarism present themselves, whose excess of virtue we may admire but more of extreme profligacy, and disavowal of all principle, which we must detest. And it affords matter of agreeable reflection, as war is unavoidable, to compare the civilized manner, in which it is now conducted, with that in which it was carried on in antient times when oaths were used only to deceive, and savage power knew not the nice restraints of virtue Let the infidel consider this, and question his own breast, whether christianity, even as far as the interests of this world go, has done no good whether human nature be not meliorated by its influence even in that state, in which it displays most ferocity *

HAVING adverted to certain particular military operations, which it is supposed might under the present system of war admit of stratagems in assimilation to many that occur in the following collection, it may not be unacceptable to the reader, to see thrown together some

---

* This is a subject, which Paulus Oraufius hath largely discussed, and if any one should think it a point that wants evidence, he will there find it satisfactorily proved He flourished early in the 5th century, and wrote the history of the world, after the manner of Justin continuing it down from the first records of antiquity to his own time. Whether we consider the period in which he lived, when the change of manners introduced into the world by christianity might be more particularly conspicuous; or the course of studies he had pursued, and from which he must have been rendered well acquainted with the manners of the heathen world, I know none, nor can I easily conceive any, more competent to determine the point on which I refer to him.

of those general rules, as well respecting civil policy, as manœuvres in the field, which he dispersed in the following stratagems, either particularly inculcated, or plainly inferrible from them. And such brief recapitulation will perhaps serve as a clue, leading to the observation of many other articles of instruction, that will occur to the reader in the course of the volume, which without being thus sought for might elude his notice. For there is in Polyænus no regular series of history, nor in the excellent rules and maxims, he hath suggested, hath he observed any general system of detail. They are interspersed without order, and result from, the best of all lessons, experience.

AMONG the antient Greeks, their generals were their statesmen. and some hints might therefore be expected from our author, of civil as well as military import. Such is the danger he observes, and the precaution necessary, in employing foreign troops, and the little confidence to be placed in them. The danger indeed is not so great now, as in more uncivilized times but the confidence to be placed in them is pretty much, and from the nature of things ever must be, the same.

WE experience the horror of civil dissentions, and are instructed how cautious we should be to guard against the source and causes of them while we see painted as it were before our eyes, from how small circumstances such dissentions have been sometimes produced, and how easily in their infancy they might have been stifled.

IN several instances are we led to observe the difference between
treaties,

treaties, to which one party is induced by the then circumstances of the time, and peculiar exigences in their affairs, and those, which are founded on mutual disposition to cultivate them, and equal independence in the federating powers We learn from experience, with how steady an eye statesmen should look to those two points: which will instruct them, where principally to direct their caution, and where more securely to place their dependence

The stratagems, which relate to the weakening of a powerful enemy, to dissolving confederacies, gaining time by treaties, and procuring intelligence, may be considered as addressed to statesmen, as well as generals, and to pertain to the cabinet, as much as to the camp: they are not confined to particular periods, are capable of being improved on, and may be accommodated to any times and occasions.

First in the train of antient military manœuvres may be noticed the choice of ground for this camps are shifted, movements made, and a variety of subordinate manœuvres practised. And in forming this choice the general, we find, considered, not only, nor always chiefly, the position in which he may himself act with most advantage, but that, in which the enemy can act with least.

From observing in a vast variety of instances the effects of confidence, it may be concluded a matter of no small consequence, strongly to impress it on the troops. Whatever it is coolly determined to attempt; the object is half effected, in possessing your army with an assurance of being able to effect it.

From the practice of experienced generals is inferred the difference

ence of operations required, when the army is acting in a foreign country, and when the feat of war is in our own. In the latter cafe the general lies by, defends, creates obftacles, harraffes, fkirmifhes, and carries on a war of pofts. He with great deliberation weighs every circumftance, before he engages in a general action, and ventures on fo momentous an enterprife as a decifive battle. On the other hand, if the enemy's country be the fcene of action, he cautioufly rifks detachments, yet he never fuffers his troops to lie idle · he is conftantly purfuing a fucceffion of new enterprifes, by which he encourages the alacrity of his own troops, and intimidates the enemy, by the lure of hope engages to himfelf allies, and by the influence of fear detaches them from the interefts of the enemy.

The penetrating mind of able chiefs in the examples before us calls our attention to a nice inveftigation of the difpofition and character of the adverfe commander. from whence, by way of illuftration reducing the conteft as it were to fingle combat, he learns in what parts he is particularly to guard himfelf, and in what with beft effect to ftrike.

Cautions abound refpecting the impolicy of preffing a vanquifhed foe too hard, driving them by unreafonable requifitions to a ftate of defperation, and forcing them to be brave. They inftruct how to conquer, and how to ufe a conqueft, as well as another and no mean part of generalfhip, when to renounce the hopes of victory.

Instances there may be in individuals, where eafe and diffipation do not daftardife the mind. but we have no inftances, where they do not daftardife an army. The beft generals have affured us it is fo:
and

and the rules, we find laid down by them to guard againſt ſuch contamination, are to provide and promote, as well in camps, as in times of moſt profound peace, amuſements and employment that may require ſtrength and activity. In camps, where military rules and diſcipline prevail, we ſee the laurel thrive: it loves not the ſoil, in which the roſe and myrtle delight. For this truth we need but look into thoſe of Philip of Macedon, and Scipio. In ſuch camps it is, that patience in bearing fatigues, firmneſs in combating dangers, and, in a word, that courage is learned. For courage, experience aſſures us, is acquiſitious: and for that reaſon, raw and undiſciplined troops muſt ever contend at a great diſadvantage with thoſe that have lived in habits of military diſcipline, and been trained up in the ſchool of war.

Acts of cruelty to an enemy are always reprehended, as never anſwering any valuable purpoſe. On the other hand a variety of inſtances are produced: evincing that clemency is always attended with good effects.

The firſt and principal ingredient, required in the compoſition of a great general, the ſlighteſt acquaintance with the military characters that form the ſubject of the following collection will evince to be courage. Other qualifications are neceſſary to compleat the character: but courage is that principle, without which it cannot exiſt. In the great maſs courage, it has been obſerved, is acquiſitious but it is not ſo in a commander. In the former caſe, the mind is moulded into courage by habit and example in the latter character the individual ſtands alone. In his ſituation, he may give example, but can not receive it

If therefore he be deficient in courage, that defect will cling to his mind through life. Age may add to, but will not cure, it: a cool and cautious young man will never atchieve any thing that is great That coolness age will freeze into coldness, will manacle the hand of enterprise, and withold it from daring any thing, becaufe in iffue every thing is uncertain While on the other hand youthful ardour age corrects, and experience to great exploits matures it Intrepidity marks not a mind, that can not fee danger, but which feels refources, that raife the foul above it. All the admonition therefore, that intrepidity wants, is fummed up in two or three ftratagems the import of which directs, not to attempt nothing, but, as far as prudence can fee, and precaution guard, to fecure every thing, to meet in contemplation every adverfe contingency, and above all things to difcard every idea of fecurity; however great the commander's ftrength, however marked his fuperiority, to neglect nothing, which, though apparently unneceffary, had better be done, becaufe, it is a poor excufe, after a neglect has occafioned a mifcarriage, to fay " who could have thought it?" *

BUT it is not my intention to write a commentary on Polyænus My object in thofe few premifed reflections, flowing from fome of the following ftratagems, is only to evince that he is an author as inftructive, as he is entertaining and that, while he amufes one clafs of readers, he is capable of affording hints that may be purfued with advantage by another.

* See Book III. Ch. ix. Str 11.

CONTENTS

TABLE OF CONTENTS.

BOOK I.

Names	No of Stratagems	Page
Bacchus	3	5
Pan	1	6
Hercules	5	7
Theseus	1	9
Demophon	1	9
Cresphontes	1	10
Cypselus	1	10
Halnes	1	11
Temenus	1	12
Procles	1	12
Acues	1	13
Thessalus	1	13
Menelaus	1	14
Cleomenes	1	14
Polydorus	1	15
Lycurgus	5	15
Tyrtæus	1	16

Names	Strat.	Page
Codrus	1	17
Melanthus	1	17
Solon	2	18
Pisistratus	3	19
Aristogeiton	1	20
Polycrates	2	21
Istiæus	1	22
Pittacus	1	22
Bias	1	23
Gelon	3	23
Theron	2	24
Hieron	2	26
Themistocles	7	26
Aristides	1	29
Leonidas	3	30
Leotychides	1	31
Cimon	2	31
Myronides	2	32
Pericles	2	33

Cleon

CONTENTS.

Names	Strat.	Page
Cleon	1	33
Brasidas	5	34
Nicias	4	35
Alcibiades	9	36
Archidamus	5	40
Gylippus	2	42
Hermocrates	2	43
Eteonicus	1	44
Lysander	5	44
Agis	1	46
Thrasyllus	2	47
Conon	5	47
Xenophon	4	49

BOOK II.

Names	Strat.	Page
Agesilaus	33	51
Clearchus	10	61
Epaminondas	15	65
Pelopidas	3	70
Gorgias	2	71
Dercyllidas	1	72
Alcetas	1	72
Archilaidas	1	73
Isidas	1	73
Cleandridas	5	74
Pharacidas	1	75
Deiphantes	1	76

Names	Strat.	Page
Eurytion	1	76
Ephori	2	77
Hippodamas	1	78
Gastron	1	78
Megaclidas	1	79
Harmostes	1	79
Thibron	1	80
Demaratus	1	80
Erippidas	1	80
Ischolaus	4	81
Mnasippidas	1	82
Antalcidas	1	82
Agesipolis	1	83
Sthenippus	1	83
Callicratidas	2	84
Magas	2	84
Cleonymus	2	85
Clearchus Tyran.	3	86
Aristomenes	4	87
Cineas	1	89
Hegetorides	1	89
Dinias'	1	90
Nicon	1	91
Diætas	1	91
Tesamenus	1	92
Onomarchus	2	92

BOOK

BOOK III.

Names	Strat	Page
Demosthenes	2	95
Paches	1	96
Tolmides	1	97
Phormio	3	97
Clisthenes	1	98
Phrynicus	1	99
Lachares	3	100
Archinus	1	100
Iphicrates	63	101
Timotheus	17	119
Chabrias	15	125
Phocion	1	129
Chares	3	130
Charidemus	1	131
Demetrius Phal.	1	131
Philocles	1	132

BOOK IV.

Names	Strat	Page
Argæus	1	133
Philippus	22	134
Alexander	32	139
Antipater	3	153
Parmenio	1	154
Antigonus	20	154
Demetrius	12	164

Names	Strat	Page
Eumenes	5	168
Seleucus	6	170
Perdiccas	2	172
Cassander	4	173
Lysimachus	3	175
Craterus	1	176
Polysperchon	1	176
Antiochus Seleuc.	1	177
Antiochus Antioch.	1	177
Antiochus Hierax	1	178
Philippus Demetr.	2	179
Ptolemæus	1	180
Attalus	1	180
Perseus	1	181

BOOK V.

Names	Strat	Page
Phalaris	4	183
Dionysius	22	185
Agathocles	8	194
Hipparinus	1	197
Theocles	2	198
Hippocrates	1	199
Daphnæus	1	200
Leptines	2	200
Annon	1	201
Imilcon	5	201
Gescon	1	203
Timoleon		

CONTENTS

Names	Strat	Page
Timoleon	3	204
Ariston	2	205
Thrafymede	2	206
Megacles	1	207
Pammenes	5	208
Heraclides	2	210
Agathoftratus	1	211
Lycus	1	212
Menecrates	1	212
Athenodorus	1	213
Diotimus	4	213
Tynnichus	1	215
Clitarchus	1	215
Timarchus	1	216
Eudocimus	1	216
Paufiftratus	1	217
Theognis	2	217
Diocles	1	218
Chilius	1	218
Cypzelus	1	219
Telefinicus	2	219
Pompifcus Cres	6	220
Nicon	1	221
Nearchus Cres.	1	222
Dorotheus	1	223
Sofiftratus	1	223
Diognetus	1	224
Archebius	1	224
Ariftocrates	1	225

Names	Strat	Page
Ariftomachus	1	225
Charimenes	1	226
Calliades	1	226
Memnon	5	226
Philodemus	1	229
Democles	1	229
Panætius	1	230
*Pyræchmes		
*Satyrus		

BOOK VI.

	Strat	Page
Jafon	7	232
Alexander Pheræus	2	234
Athenocles	1	235
Philopæmen	3	236
Aratus	1	237
Pyrrhus	3	238
Apollodorus	2	239
Ægyptus	1	240
Leucon	4	241
Alexander Phrur.	1	243
Ariftides Eleates	1	243
Alexander Lyfimach.	1	244
Amphictyones	1	244
Samnites	1	245
Campanians	1	245
Carthaginians	5	245

Ambra-

CONTENTS

Names.	Strat.	Page.
Ambraciotæ	1	248
Phocenſians	2	249
Platæans	3	249
Corcyræans	1	251
Ægeſtæans	1	251
Locrians	1	252
Corinthians	1	252
Lampſacenians	1	253
Chalcedonians	1	253
*Ætolians	1	
*Lacedæmonians	3	
*Meſſenians	3	
*Iberians	1	
*Heracleotæ	1	
*Argives	1	
*Chians	2	
*Ambraciotæ	2	
*Buchetians	1	
*Samians	1	
*Eleans	1	
*Parians	1	
*Annibas	1	
*Theſſalians	1	
*Maſſiniſſa	1	
*Amilcar	1	
*Aſarubas	2	
*Naſamon	1	
*Hiercus	1	
Solyſon	1	254

Names.	Strat.	Page.
Alexander Theſſ.	1	255
Thraſybulus	1	255
Mentor	1	256
Anaxagoras	1	256
Pindarus	1	257
Theron	1	257
Siſyphus	1	258
Agnon	1	258
Amphiretus	1	260

BOOK VII.

	Strat.	Page.
Diocles	1	261
Alyattes	2	262
Pſammetichus	1	263
Amaſis	1	263
Midas	1	264
Cyrus	10	264
Harpagus	1	267
Crœſus	2	268
Cambyſes	1	268
Oebares	1	269
Darius	8	270
Zopirus	1	273
Artaxerxes	1	274
Orontes	5	274
Xerxes	3	276
Artaxerxes Ochus	2	277

e

CONTENTS.

Names.	Strat	Page.	Names.	Strat.	Page.
Ochus	1	278	Taurians	1	301
Tifaphernes	2	279	Pallenians	1	301
Pharnabazus	1	280	Salmatians	1	302
Glos	1	280	Tyrrhenians	1	302
Datames	7	281	Celtic Women	1	303
Cofingas	1	284			
Maufolus	2	285			
Borges	1	286	**BOOK VIII.**		
Dromichætes	1	286			
Ariobarzanes	1	287	Amulius	1	305
Autophradates	3	287	Numitor	1	306
Arfabes	2	288	Romulus	2	306
Mithridates	2	289	Numa	1	307
Mempfis	1	291	Tullus	1	308
Cerfobleptes	1	291	Tarquinius	1	309
Seuthes	1	292	Camillus	2	309
Artabazus	3	292	Mutius	1	311
Aryandes	1	293	Sylla	2	312
Brennus	2	293	Marius	3	312
Mygdonius	1	294	Marcellus	1	313
Parifades	1	295	Atilius	1	314
Seuthes	1	295	Caius	1	315
Cheiles	1	296	Fabius	4	315
Borzus	1	296	Scipio	8	317
Surenas	1	297	Porcius	1	320
Celts	1	298	Faunus	1	320
Thracians	1	299	Titus	1	321
Scythians	2	299	Caius	1	321
Perfians	2	300	Pinarius	1	322
			Sertorius		

CONTENTS.

Names	Strat.	Page.	Names	Strat.	Page
Sertorius	1	322	Pheretima	1	349
Cæsar	33	323	Axiothea	1	350
Augustus	7	332	Archidamis	1	351
Romans	3	333	Panaristes	1	351
Semiramis	1	334	Theano	1	352
Rhodogune	1	335	Deidameia	1	353
Tomyris	1	336	Artemisia	5	353
Nitetis	1	336	Tania	1	355
Philotis	1	337	Tirgatao	1	355
Clœlia	1	337	Amage	1	357
Porcia	1	338	Arsinoe	1	355
Telesilla	1	339	Cratesipolis	1	358
Chilonis	1	339	Hiereiai	1	359
Pieria	1	340	Cynnane	1	359
Polycrete	1	340	Pysta	1	360
Phocæans	1	341	Epicharis	1	360
Aretaphila	1	342	Milesians	1	361
Camma	1	342	Melians	1	361
Timoclea	1	343	Phocians	1	362
Eryxo	1	344	Chians	1	363
Pythopolis	1	345	Thasians	1	363
Chrysame	1	346	Argives	1	364
Polyclea	1	347	Acarnanians	1	364
Leæna	1	348	Cyrenensians	1	365
Themisto	1	348	Lacænians	1	365

☞ Of those, whose names have asterisks prefixed to them, the stratagems are lost.

ERRATA.

As while the preceding sheets were printing, the author being at a distance from the press, the reader's candour is bespoken to the following errors.

Page	Line	
1	15	For possibly be of service—read, be of possible service
23	13	For imperatori'—read, imperatorial
23	15	For which, after—read, when after.
20	10	For port—read, post
41	23	For eventually—read, ultimately
51	1	For stratagems, I—read, stratagems I.
52	6	For Bisander—read, Pisander
58	2	For superiourity—read, superiority
88	2	For when—read, but.
94	1	For Antonius—read, Antoninus
105	4	For Iphicrates, during—read, Iphicrates during
106	1	For superiourity—read, superiority
114	8	For left—read, left.
117	28	For Πιλαξις—read, Φιλαξι,
134	19	For to the besieged a flag of truce—read, a flag of truce to the besieged.
137	24	For however—read, yet
186	26	For as soon as—read, when
202	19	For in that—read, in the other
202	20	For the other—read, a different.
203	11	For restriction—read, astriction.
232	2	For his design—read, it.
234	20	For fire—read, torch
243	14	For inferiour—read, superiour
270	13	For Peers—read, Satraps
302	19	For auxiliares—read, auxiliaries
308	15	For rode full speed up—read, rode up full speed
317	2	(of the note) For chapters—read, stratagems.
317	2	(of the note) For Masavicius—read, Maasvicius.
340	6	For Pithu—read, Pithus.
341	11	For Bebracians—read, Bebrycians.
358	15	For form—read, from.

POLYÆNUS'S

STRATAGEMS OF WAR.

PREFATORY ADDRESS

TO THE EMPERORS

ANTONINUS and VERUS.

THE expedition, your sacred majesties, Antoninus and Verus, have undertaken against Persia and the Parthians, the gods, your own virtue, and the Roman bravery, that have ever hitherto crowned your arms with conquest, will now also attend with success. I, who am by birth a Macedonian, and have therefore as it were a national right to victory over the Persians, have determined not to be entirely useless to you at the present crisis and were my constitution robust and hale as it has been, you should not want in me convincing proofs of a Macedonian spirit. Nor, advanced as I am in years, can I bear to be left behind without some efforts of service Accept, therefore, illustrious chiefs, in a collection of stratagems employed by the most distinguished generals, this brief subsidiary of military science, which, by exhibiting as in a picture the fortitude and experience of former commanders, their conduct and operations, and the various success that attended them, may in some instances possibly be of service to yourselves,

yourselves, your lieutenants, colonels, captains, or whomsoever you may think proper to invest with military command.

FORTITUDE conquers by dint of sword, while superiour conduct by art and stratagem prevails. and the greatest reach of generalship is displayed in those victories that are obtained with the least danger * In the heat of conflict to hit upon an expedient that shall decide the contest in your favour, without waiting the issue of a regular battle, is the most infallible criterion of military capacity and this I have always conceived to be a favourite sentiment of Homer — for what else can he mean by those frequent expressions, "either by artifice or valour," but that we should first employ stratagems and device against the enemy, and if these fail, that valour and the strongest arm must carry it

IF we admit his authority, Sisyphus, the son of Æolus, was the first of the Greeks who employed stratagems in war

"With happy skill in war's devices blest,
"Those realms Æolian Sisyphus possess'd"

THE second, famed for those devices, according to the same authority, was Autolycus, the son of Mercury —

"Whose royal brows the victor's laurels grace,
"The gallant father of a valiant race,
"His stratagems in war and peace proclaim
"The warrior's wisdom, and the monarch's fame."

---

* Similar is the observation of Vegetius — "Able generals," says he, "are always attentive to stratagems because in open actions the risk is on each side equal, but the success of a stratagem throws the loss entirely on the enemy"
VEGET b. 3, c 9

PREFATORY ADDRESS.

Nor do I apprehend the fabulous account of the transformation of Proteus into animals and trees, to signify more or less than the variety of artifices he practised against the enemy.

As to Ulysses, we know he particularly valued himself on his stratagems and devices.

> " I am Ulysses, and in skill to frame
> " Deceptive wiles, unrivall'd is my fame."

To the fertility of his genius in artifice and expedients the Græcian heroes attributed the final conquest of Troy.

> " Your schemes, your plans, effected Ilium's fall,
> " And hurl'd destruction on the Trojan wall!"

And the same high compliment is paid him by others:

> " And Troy was taught more fatal far to feel
> " Ulysses' counsels than the Grecian steel."

The various stratagems he employed against the enemy Homer frequently celebrates. He represents him, " with self-inflicted wounds deformed," revolting to the enemy. The wooden horse, which Epeus by the instruction of Pallas built, was his device. Nobody also, the WINE, the FIREBRAND, and the RAM, may properly be termed stratagems, which he employed against the Cyclops. Such too were the stopping of the ears of his crew with wax, and the lashing of himself to the mast, in order to prevent the baneful influence of music. And what will you say to the beggar's purse, and the deceptions imposed on Eumæus and Penelope?

> " His was the art instruction to detail,
> " And facts inculcate, under fiction's veil."

THE boxing with Irus, the removing from the fmoak the arms of the drunken young men, and the fixing the bow at the door,—were they not all military ftratagems? But enough of thefe, and other inftances of fimilar import, adduced by Homer.

How do the tragedians reprefent that ftratagem which Ulyffes employed againft Palamedes? The Greeks, in folemn judgment, decided in favour of Ulyffes, who had fecretly depofited in the other's tent the barbarian gold and thus, over-reached by artifice and manœuvre, was that accomplifhed general falfely convicted of treafon. So far the fcenic documents of the tragedians.

BUT the following collection of ftratagems I have extracted from the faithful records of hiftory, related fuccinctly, and with what perfpicuity I could the whole comprifed in eight books, which contain nine hundred ftratagems, beginning with thofe of Bacchus.

POLYÆNUS'S

STRATAGEMS OF WAR.

BOOK I. CHAP. I.

BACCHUS

BACCHUS, in his Indian expedition, to gain admittance into the cities, inſtead of gleaming armour, habited his troops in white linen and deers' ſkins. Their ſpears were adorned with ivy, and the points of them concealed under a Thyrſus. His orders were given by cymbals and tabrets, inſtead of trumpets: and, intoxicating his enemies with wine, he engaged them in dancing.* From hence was derived the inſtitution of the orgies of Bacchus, which are only commemorations of this, and whatever ſtratagems elſe that General practiſed in his conqueſt of India, and the reſt of Aſia.

---

* This might have been effected by preſents of wine and invitations to feſtivity, or by feigned flights, and ſtores of wine purpoſely left in his camp. In rude times, and among a barbarous people, either ſtratagem might be practiſed with ſucceſs. But the former ſeems to be the deception in this place alluded to.

2. BACCHUS,

2 BACCHUS, finding his army unable to bear the exceffive heat of the Indian climate, poffeffed himfelf of the mountain Tricoryphon, one of the tops of which is called Corafibes, another Condafce, and the third Menon. On this mountain are the memorials of his birth; it is fertilized with a variety of fountains, abounds in wild beafts, produces plenty of fruit, and the air is cooled with continual fnow. His army ftationed here ufed fuddenly to fhew themfelves to the barbarians on the plains, and, fhowering down on them large flights of arrows from thofe high and craggy precipices, obtained eafy conquefts.

3 AFTER Bacchus had fubdued the Indians, with them and the Amazons he formed an alliance, and took them into his fervice. Penetrating into Bactria, whofe boundary is the river Sarunges, he found the Bactrians had poffeffed themfelves of the mountains above the river, in order to difpute his paffage. Encamping therefore on the river fide, in face of the enemy, he ordered the Amazons and his own women to ford it, expecting that the Bactrians, in contempt of the women, would quit their pofts on the mountains, and attack them; which they accordingly did. And the women retreating, were purfued by the enemy to the oppofite bank. The ftratagem fo far fucceeding, Bacchus at the head of his troops furioufly attacked, and, thus furprifed and embarraffed as they were with the water, defeated them with a great flaughter, and paffed the river himfelf without further danger.

CHAP. II.

PAN.

PAN, a general under Bacchus, was the firft who reduced to a regular fyftem the marfhalling of an army; he invented the phalanx, and ranged it with a right and left wing; from whence he is ufually reprefented with horns. Victory always fat upon the ftrongeft fword, till he pointed out the way to conqueft by artifice and manœuvre.

IN

In the midſt of a barren deſert Bacchus was by his ſcouts informed, that an immenſe army of the enemy were encamped a little above him. The intelligence was alarming, but he ſoon found himſelf relieved from his embarraſſment, by a ready expedient of Pan, who ordered the whole army, in the ſilence of the night, on a ſignal given, to ſet up a loud and general ſhout. The ſurrounding rocks, and the cavity of the foreſt re-echoed the ſound, and impoſed on the enemy an apprehenſion that his forces were infinitely more numerous than they were; and, ſeized with a general conſternation, they abandoned their camp, and fled. From the circumſtance of this ſtratagem the nymph ECHO has been feigned by the poets to be the miſtreſs of Pan; and from hence alſo all vain and imaginary fears are termed PANICS.

CHAP. III.

HERCULES

1. HERCULES, determined to extirpate the race of Centaurs from Pelium, yet inclined rather to act upon the defenſive, than commence hoſtilities, reſided a ſhort time with Pholus; where, opening a veſſel of fragrant wine, he and his companions took the charge of, and watched, it. The neighbouring Centaurs, allured by the ſmell, flocked together to the cave, and ſeized the wine. Hercules therefore, to puniſh the injuſtice of thieves and robbers, attacked and ſlew them.

2. FEARING to encounter the ſuperior ſtrength of the Erymanthian boar, Hercules had recourſe to artifice. And as the beaſt lay in a valley, which was full of ſnow, he annoyed him with ſtones from above. The boar at length enraged, rouſed himſelf, and, with great violence ſpringing forwards, ſunk into the ſnow. Thus entangled in it,

it, and unable to exert himself, he became an easy capture to the assailant.

3. HERCULES, in his expedition against Troy, as soon as he landed, advanced to give the enemy battle, at the same time ordering the pilots to put back a little to sea. The Trojan infantry soon gave way, while their cavalry pushed to the sea, in order to possess themselves of the ships; but these floating a little off from land they were not able to gain; and, finding Hercules, who had returned from the rout of the infantry, on their quarters, thus hemmed in by the enemy on one side, and the sea on the other, they fell an easy victim to the conquerors.

4. IN India Hercules adopted a daughter, whom he called Pandea. To her he allotted the southern part of India which is situate towards the sea, dividing it into three hundred and sixty-five cantons. These cantons he charged with a daily tax, and ordered each canton, by turn, on their stated day, to pay the royal stipend. So that, which ever of them first refused the tax, as it rested on the others to make it good, the queen might depend on their aid and assistance in compelling the due performance of it.

5. HERCULES, having taken the field against the Minyans, whose cavalry in a champain country were formidable, not thinking it safe immediately to hazard a battle, previously diverted the course of a river. This was the river Cephissus, which bounds the two mountains Parnassus and Hedylus, and shaping its course through the middle of Bæotia, before it vents itself into the sea, discharges its stream into a large subterraneous chasm, and disappears. This chasm Hercules filling with great stones, diverted the river upon the plain where the Minyan cavalry was stationed. The plain presently became a lake, and the cavalry thereby unserviceable. Having thus conquered the Minyans, he opened the chasm again, and the Cephissus returned to its former channel.

CHAP

CHAP. IV.

THESEUS.

THESEUS, in his battles, used always to have the fore-part of his head shaved, to prevent the enemy's advantage of seizing him by the hair. His example was afterwards followed by all the Greeks, and that sort of tonsure was from him called Theseis. But those who were particularly distinguished for this imitation of Theseus, were the Abantes, whom Homer thus characterizes.

———— " Their foreheads bare,
" Down their broad shoulders flow'd a length of hair."

CHAP. V.

DEMOPHON.

IN the custody of Demophon was kept the palladium, which had been committed to his care by Diomede. This, on Agamemnon's demanding, the real one Demophon gave to Busyges, an Athenian, to carry to Athens, and kept a counterfeit one, made exactly like the original palladium, in his tent. When Agamemnon, therefore, at the head of a large body of troops, came by force to seize it, he drew out his forces, and for some time sustained a sharp conflict with him, that so he might the more easily induce him to believe, it could be no other than the original, for which he would have so resolutely contended. After many had been wounded on both sides, Demophon's men gave ground, leaving the unsuspecting victor triumphantly to bear away the counterfeit palladium.

CHAP. VI.

CRESPHONTES.

CRESPHONTES, Temenus, and the sons of Aristodemus, agreeing to share amongst themselves the government of Peloponnesus, concluded to divide the country into three parts, Argos, Sparta, and Messena; and, while they were deliberating by what mode to proceed in assigning each his property, Cresphontes, who had fixed his mind upon Messena, advised, that he whose lot was first drawn should have Sparta, the second Argos, and that Messena should be the portion of the third. His advice was followed, and they cast lots, which was done by throwing each a white stone into a pitcher of water, instead of which, Cresphontes having moulded up a piece of clay, in resemblance of a stone, cast it into the water, where it was immediately dissolved; and the other two stones coming out assigned Argos to Temenus, and Sparta to the sons of Aristodemus, whilst Messena was allotted to him, as the determination of fortune.

CHAP. VII.

CYPSELUS

IN the reign of Cypselus the Heraclidæ engaged in an expedition against the Arcadians, from whom if they received presents of hospitality, they were warned by the Oracle immediately to conclude a peace with them. Cypselus therefore, in the harvest season, ordered the husbandmen, after they had reaped the corn, to leave it in the high way, a grateful present to the soldiers of the Heraclidæ, of which they readily availed themselves. He afterwards went out to meet them, and
offered

offered them prefents of hofpitality the favour of which, recollecting the Oracle, they declined accepting "Why this refufal? 'replied Cypfelus' Your army, in accepting our corn, has already received our prefents of hofpitality." By this device of Cypfelus were the Heraclidæ reconciled to peace, and entered into an alliance with the Arcadians.

CHAP. VIII.

HALNES.

HALNES, King of Arcadia, when the Lacedemonians were ravaging Tegæa, felected the moft able and vigorous of his troops, and pofted them on an eminence above the enemy, with orders from thence to attack them in the middle of the night. The old men and boys he ftationed as guards before the city, and commanded them, at the time he intended the attack, to kindle a large fire. Whilft the enemy, furprized at the fight of the fire, were wholly intent upon that quarter, the ambufcade fell on them, and obtained an eafy victory, thofe who efcaped the fword, fubmitting to the chains of the conquerour. And thus was accomplifhed the prediction of the Oracle.

"I give you to Tegæa to advance,
"And there in fatal fteps to lead the choral dance."

CHAP. IX.

TEMENUS.

TEMENUS and the reft of the Heraclidæ, intending an expedition againſt Rheium, difpatched ſome Locrian revolters, with inſtructions to inform the Pelopennefians, that they had a fleet at Naupactum, on pretence of ſailing to Rheium, but that their real defign was a defcent upon the Iſthmus. On the credit of this intelligence, the Peloponnefians marched their forces to the Iſthmus, and by that means gave Temenus an opportunity of taking Rheium without oppoſition.

CHAP. X.

PROCLES

WHILE the Heraclidæ, Procles and Temenus, were at war with the Euryſthidæ, who were at that time in poffeffion of Sparta, they were on a ſudden attacked by the enemy, as they were facrificing to Minerva for a fafe paffage over the mountains. Procles, little difconcerted, ordered the flutes to march on before, after whom the foldiers advancing in arms, infpired by the numbers and harmony of the mufick, preferved their ranks entire, and, eventually, defeated the enemy. From this experience of the influence of mufick, were the Lacedæmonians taught to retain flutes in their army; who, advancing before them to the field, always founded the charge. And I can from my own knowledge affert, that the Oracle had promifed victory to the arms of the Lacedæmonians, fo long as they continued the ufe of flutes in their army, and fought not againſt thoſe who did retain them. The battle

battle of Leuctra verified the prediction for there the Lacedæmonians, without the mufick of flutes, engaged the Thebans, who always ufed the flute in battle, in which inftance the God feemed directly to have pronounced the Theban victory.

CHAP. XI.

ACUES

WHEN the Lacedæmonians entered Tegæa, which was betrayed to them in the night, Acues gave his men a particular fignal, whereby to diftinguifh each other, with orders to flay all who did not know it This fignal all the Arcadians knowing, afked no queftions, but the Lacedæmonians, not being able to difcern their friends in the night, were obliged to inquire before they encountered any, whether they were friends or enemies, and, thus difcovering themfelves, were inftantly difpatched by the Arcadians.

CHAP. XII.

THESSALUS

THE Bæotians of Arna having made war upon the Theffalians, Theffalus, by a happy ftratagem, reduced them to terms of peace, without the hazard of a battle Waiting for a dark and gloomy night, he difperfed his men about the fields, with orders to light torches and flambeaus, and poft themfelves in different places on the tops of the mountains, fometimes raifing their lights above their heads, then lowering them again, thereby to afford a more doubtful and uncertain fpectacle. The Bæotians, on fight of the furrounding flames, fuppofing themfelves involved in a blaze of lightning, were thrown into confternation, and became fupphants for peace.

CHAP.

CHAP. XIII.

MENELAUS

MENELAUS, returning with Helen from Egypt, was forced to put in at Rhodes, of whose arrival Philixo, who was then mourning the unhappy fall of her husband Tlepolemus at Troy, being informed, resolved to revenge his death on Helen and the Spartan; and, at the head of as many Rhodians as she could collect, both men and women, armed with fire and stones, advanced to the ships. Menelaus, thus assailed, the wind not permitting him to put to sea, concealed the queen under deck, at the same time dressing one of the most beautiful of her attendants in her royal robes and diadem. The Rhodians, not suspecting but that she was Helen, discharged their fire and stones on the unfortunate attendant. And thus, satisfied with the ample satisfaction, as they thought, they had paid the manes of Tlepolemus, in the death of Helen, they quietly retreated, leaving Menelaus and Helen to pursue their intended voyage at leisure.

CHAP. XIV.

CLEOMENES.

IN a war between the Lacedæmonians and Argives, while the armies were encamped in front of each other, Cleomenes observed that every transaction in his camp was betrayed to the enemy, who took their measures accordingly. When he ordered to arms, the enemy armed also; if he marched out, they were ready to form against him. When he gave orders for repose, they did the same. Whenever therefore he should next issue publick orders for repast, he gave private directions

that

that the troops should arm. The publick orders were as usual conveyed to the unsuspecting Argives, whilst Cleomenes, advancing in arms, attacked them with success, unarmed, and unprepared to oppose him.

CHAP. XV.

POLYDORUS.

TWENTY years had the Lacedæmonians harassed the Messenians with a war, in which they had been continually foiled, when Polydorus, pretending a rupture between himself and Theopompus, dispatched a revolter to the enemy's camp, with information that they were at variance, and had divided their forces. The Messenians, upon this report, observed the motions of the enemy with particular attention. And Theopompus, agreeably to the information they had received, decamped, and concealed his army at a little distance from the spot, remaining in readiness to act, whenever occasion might require. The Messenians, seeing this movement, and despising the inferiority of Polydorus's army, in a body sallied out of the city, and gave him battle. Theopompus, at that moment, upon a signal given by his scouts, advancing from his ambuscade, made himself master of the empty abandoned town, and falling upon the Messenians in the rear, whilst Polydorus attacked them in front, gained a compleat victory.

CHAP. XVI.

LYCURGUS.

1. THE method Lycurgus took to enforce his laws upon the Lacedæmonians, was, on enacting any new law, by repairing to Delphos, there to inquire of the Oracle, whether it would be advantageous

to the republick to receive it, or not. The prophetefs, wrought upon by the eloquence of a bribe, always affirmed the expediency of receiving it. Thus, through a fear of offending the god, the Lacedæmonians religiously obferved those laws, as fo many divine oracles.

2. ONE command of Lycurgus, fanctioned by the Oracle, was this "O, Lacedæmonians, be not too frequently engaged in war, left by that means you also teach your enemies the military art."

3. ANOTHER advice of his was, always to give quarter to those who fled, left otherwife the enemy fhould judge it better to hazard their lives in a brave refiftance, than be fure of lofing them by running away.

CHAP. XVII.

TYRTÆUS

THE Lacedæmonians, previous to an engagement with the Meffenians, formed a general refolution either to conquer or die; and when they came to bury their dead, that they might each be diftinguifhed by their friends, had their names engraven on their fhields, which were faftened to their left arms. Tyrtæus, to make an advantage of this device, by intimidating the Meffenians with an account of it, gave private orders that frequent opportunities fhould be offered the Helots of revolting, who no fooner obferved themfelves lefs ftrictly watched, than many deferted to the enemy, whom they informed of the excefs of the Lacedæmonians' defperation. Intimidated by this report, the Meffenians, after a weak refiftance, yielded a compleat victory to the Lacedæmonians.

CHAP. XVIII.

CODRUS.

IN a war between the Athenians and Peloponnesians, victory was declared by the Oracle in favour of the Athenians, if their king fell by the hand of a Peloponesian. The enemy, informed of the Oracle, gave publick orders to every individual in the army, carefully to avoid any perfonal attack on Codrus, who was at that time king of the Athenians. He however in the evening difguifing himfelf in the habit of a wood-cutter, advanced beyond the trenches to hew wood, and there chanced to meet fome Peloponnesians, who were out upon the fame errand. With them Codrus purpofely quarrelled, and wounded fome of them with his axe; at which, exafperated, they fell upon him with their axes, and flew him; returning home to their camp, elated with the performance of fo noble an exploit. The Athenians, feeing the Oracle thus far fulfilled, as having now nothing further to wait for, with new courage and refolution advanced to battle, having previously difpatched a herald into the enemy's camp, to requeft the body of their dead king. And when the affair was difcovered to the Peloponnesians, they immediately abandoned their camp and fled. The Athenians afterwards paid divine honours to Codrus, who, by his voluntary death, had purchafed fo compleat a victory.

CHAP. XIX.

MELANTHUS.

IN a war between the Athenians and Bæotians, for the poffeffion of Melænæ, a tract of country bordering upon Attica and Bæotia, it was by the Oracle thus declared.

C " Xanthus,

"Xanthus, Melænæ's fair and fertile plain
"Melanthus shall by stratagem obtain"

Which was thus verified. Melanthus, general of the Athenians, and Xanthus, of the Bæotians, agreed to decide the victory by their own swords. As soon as they were engaged, Melanthus called out, "Thus to bring a second against a single man is unfair;" upon which, Xanthus turning about to see who this second was, Melanthus seized the opportunity, and, thus unguarded, run him through with his spear. The victorious Athenians, in memory of this succesful stratagem, instituted an annual festival, which they call APATURIA.

CHAP. XX.

SOLON.

THE Athenians, tired out with a tedious war, in which they had been engaged against the Megarensians, for the island Salamis, enacted a law, that made it death for any one to assert, the city ought to endeavour the recovery of it. Solon, undaunted by the severity of the prohibition, devised means to supersede the law. He counterfeited madness, and, running into the assembly, repeated an elegy he had composed for the occasion, and with this martial poem so spirited up the Athenians to war, that, instigated by Mars and the Muses, singing hymns and shouting, they advanced to battle, and, in an obstinate engagement, entirely routed the Megarensians. Thus Salamis again relapsed into the jurisdiction of the Athenians: whilst Solon was held in universal admiration, who by madness could repeal a law, and by the power of musick conquer in battle.

2. In the course of the war between Athens and the Megarensians, for the island Salamis, Solon sailed to Colias, where he found the women performing sacrifice to Ceres. He immediately dispatched to the Megarensians

renfians a person, who, pretending himself to be a renegade, should advise them to seize the Athenian women, an enterprize which might easily be executed, if they made all possible sail to Colias. The Megarenfians instantly manned a ship, and put to sea. Solon, in the mean time ordered the women to retire, and some beardless youths, dressed in female attire, with garlands upon their heads, and privately armed with daggers, to dance and wanton near the shore. Deceived by the appearance of the youths, and their false dresses, the Megarenfians landed, and eagerly endeavouring to seize them, hoped to find an easy capture. But the youths, drawing their swords, by the slaughter that ensued soon convinced them of the difference between men and women, and of their fatal mistake. And immediately embarking for Salamis, they made themselves masters of the island.

CHAP. XXI.

PISISTRATUS.

PISISTRATUS, in an expedition from Eubæa into Attica against Pallenis, falling in with a body of the enemy, defeated and slew them. Advancing farther, he met the remaining part of the army; whom he ordered his men not to attack, but to crown themselves with garlands, and signify to them that they had already made a truce with the party they had first met. On the credit of this assertion, they formed an alliance with Pisistratus, and admitted him into the city. When mounting his chariot, with a tall beautiful woman by his side, whose name was Phyfa, accoutred in the armour of Pallas, he impressed the Athenians with a belief that Pallas was his protectress and guide, and by this means obtained the sovereignty of Athens.

2. HAVING formed a design to disarm the Athenians, Pisistratus commanded all to appear at the Anacæum, in arms. And as soon as they

were assembled, he stepped forth, under pretence of haranguing them: but begun in so low a tone of voice, that, not being able to hear him, the people desired him to go to the porch, where they might all hear him more distinctly; and even there not raising his voice so as distinctly to be heard, while the people were with great attention listening to him, his associates went privately out, and, carrying off all the arms, carried them to the temple of Agraulus. The Athenians, after finding themselves naked and defenceless, too late perceived that Pisistratus's weak voice was only a stratagem to despoil them of their arms.

3. SOME private jealousies subsisting between Megacles and Pisistratus, Megacles being magistrate on the part of the rich, and Pisistratus of those of the lower order, after having, in a publick assembly insulted and menaced Megacles, Pisistratus abruptly retired; and, slightly wounding himself, went the next day into the forum, and publickly exposed to the Athenians his wounds. Fired with rage and resentment at seeing what he had suffered in their defence, the people assigned him a guard of three hundred men, for the protection of his person. By means of these guards, who used always to appear armed with clubs, he possessed himself of the sovereignty of Athens, and after his death left it to his sons.

CHAP. XXII.

ARISTOGEITON.

ARISTOGEITON, when put to the torture to extort from him a confession of his associates, confessed none of them, but in their stead named all the friends of Hippias. And when by Hippias's order they had been put to death, Aristogeiton reproached him with his cruelty to his innocent friends, and the success of his own stratagem.

CHAP. XXIII.

POLYCRATES

WHEN Polycrates, the Samian, infested the Græcian seas, he made no distinction in his depredations between friends and foes: observing, that in case his friends should re-demand such part of his seizures as was their property, he would have an opportunity of obliging them with the restitution of it, and thus engage them the more closely to his cause. But if he took nothing from them, he considered he should have nothing wherewith to oblige them.

2. UPON a publick sacrifice offered by the Samians in the Temple of Juno, which was attended with a parade of men in arms, a great quantity of arms being collected on the occasion, Polycrates gave the conduct of the train to his brothers Sylofon and Pantagnoftus. As soon as the sacrifice commenced, the greatest part deposited their arms upon the altar, and addressed themselves to prayer, whilst those about Sylofon, and Pantagnoftus, who had been previously apprized of the design, waiting in arms for the signal given, set upon the rest, and slew them, each dispatching his man. In the mean time Polycrates, at the head of his associates, possessing himself of the most advantageous places in the city, was joined by his brothers and their party, who had, with all expedition, forced their way to him from the temple. With these he fortified and defended himself in the tower, called Aftypalæa, till, having received an enforcement from Lygdamis, the tyrant of Naxos, he obtained the sovereignty of Samos.

CHAP. XXIV.

ISTIÆUS.

WHILST Iſtiæus, the Mileſian, reſided at the court of King Darius, in Perſia, he formed a deſign of engaging the Ionians to revolt, but was at a loſs how ſafely to tranſmit a letter, the ways being every where poſſeſſed by the king's guard. Shaving the head of a confidential ſervant, in inciſions on it he thus briefly wrote "Iſtiæus to Ariſtagoras, ſolicit the revolt of Ionia." And as ſoon as his hair was grown again, he diſpatched him to Ariſtagorus. By this means, he paſſed the guards unſuſpected, and, after bathing in the ſea, ordered himſelf to be ſhaved, and then ſhewed Ariſtagoras the marks which, when he had read, he proſecuted the deſign, and effected the revolt of Ionia.

CHAP. XXV.

PITTACUS.

PITTACUS and Phrynon agreed by ſingle combat to decide the right to Sigæum, then in conteſt between the Athenians and Mytelenians: and it was propoſed that they ſhould fight with equal weapons; and ſuch to appearance they were. But Pittacus under his ſhield had privately concealed a net, which caſting over Phrynon, he eaſily drew him, thus entangled, within his reach, and killed him. It was afterwards pleaſantly ſaid, that he had fiſhed for Sigæum with a linen line. This ſtratagem of Pittacus it was, which gave riſe to the uſe of the net in the duels of the gladiators.

CHAP. XXVI.

BIAS.

CRÆSUS, King of Lydia, intending an expedition against the islands, was deterred from his design by Bias, the Prienian, who told the king, that the islanders had bought up a great number of horses, that they might be able to bring into the field a formidable cavalry against him. " Would to Jupiter, ' said the king, with a smile,' I could catch those islanders on the continent !" — " True, ' replied Bias,' and what think you they could wish, rather than to catch Cræsus upon the seas?" This repartee of Bias had its effect in dissuading the king from his intended expedition.

CHAP. XXVII.

GELON.

GELON, the Syracusan, the son of Dinomenes, was appointed commander in chief, in a war against Himilcon, the Carthagenian: and after having by his gallant behaviour defeated the enemy, he went into the assembly, and gave up the accounts of his imperatorial commission, the expences of the war, the time, arms, horses, and ships. For all which, after great encomiums were bestowed upon him, he stripped himself, and, advancing naked into the midst of them, " Thus naked, ' said he,' I present myself to you, that now, whilst you are all armed, if I have ever injured or oppressed any individual amongst you, I may feel the just resentment of your weapons." He was answered by the acclamations of all present, styling him the most gallant, the best of generals. To whom he replied, " Then for the future always

ways let it be your care to elect such another."—" Such another, 'answered they,' we have not" He was therefore a second time elected general, which paved the way for him to the sovereignty of Syracuse.

2. WHEN Himilcon, King of Carthage invaded Sicily, Gelon, who then possessed the sovereignty there, took the field against him: but not venturing to hazard a battle, he in his own robes habited Pediarchus, who commanded the archers, and much resembled himself both in person and looks, and ordered him to march out of the camp, and attend a sacrifice on the altars. The band of archers followed him, dressed in white vestments, carrying myrtle branches in their hands, and bows privately concealed under them, which they were instructed to make use of against Himilcon, as soon as they perceived him in the same manner advancing to sacrifice. Matters thus disposed, Himilcon entertaining no suspicion of design, came forward also, and sacrificed when a sudden shower of darts immediately dispatched him, while he was officiating at the ceremonies, and offering libations.

3. GELON, in order to subvert the empire of the Megarensians, invited over to Sicily whoever of the Dorians were willing to remove, and at the same time imposed on Diognetus, Prince of Megara, an enormous fine which, not being able himself to discharge it, he levied on the citizens, who, to avoid compliance with the tribute, removed into Sicily, and there subjected themselves to the power and authority of Gelon.

CHAP. XXVIII.

THERON.

THERON, in an engagement with the Carthagenians, had put the enemy to flight. when the Sicilians, pouring into the camp, immediately fell to plundering the tents, and, whilst in that disorder, were

attacked

attacked by the Iberians, who, advancing to the affiftance of the Carthaginians, made great havock among them. Theron, perceiving the carnage that was likely to enfue, difpatched a party to wheel round the camp; with orders to fet fire to the tents that were fartheft behind. The enemy, feeing the camp on fire, and being themfelves deftitute of tents, betook themfelves, with precipitation, to their fhips, which, however, being clofely purfued by the Sicilians, few of them were able to gain.

THERON, THE SON OF MILTIADES.

2. THE Selinuntines having been defeated by the Carthaginians, and the field ftrewed with their dead, while the enemy preffed fo clofe upon them that they dared not venture forth to bury them, and yet were fhocked to fee them lie neglected and expofed, in this emergency, Theron engaged, if they would provide him with three hundred men who could cut wood, to march out with them, burn the dead, and bury them. " But if we fail in our attempt, ' continued he,' and fall victims to the enemy, the city will not fuffer much from the lofs of one citizen, and the price of three hundred flaves " The Selinuntines embraced his propofal, and gave him his choice of the number of flaves he defired Accordingly, felecting thofe he judged moft active and ftout, he led them forth, armed with wood-bills, hatchets, and axes, under pretence of cutting wood for the funeral pile But after they had advanced fome little diftance from the city, Theron prevailed on them to fhake off their fervitude, and late in the evening marched them back when, making themfelves known to the guard, they were readily admitted Theron no fooner entered, than he difpatched the guard, and, having flain in their beds fuch citizens as were moft likely to thwart and fruftrate his defigns, he poffeffed himfelf of the city, and the fovereignty of Selinuntum.

D CHAP.

CHAP. XXIX.

HIERON

HIERON, finding the enemy prepared to difpute his paffage over a river, pofted his heavy armed troops at the place where he intended to ford it, ordering the horfe and light-infantry to advance higher up, under colour of paffing it above. The enemy obferving this motion, marched their forces alfo higher up, in order to defeat his fuppofed intention. Hieron, in the mean time, effected a paffage with his heavy armed troops, eafily bearing down the fmall party of the enemy who were left to oppofe him. And as foon as he had gained the oppofite fide, he hoifted a fignal to the horfe and light-infantry, who immediately returning paffed the river at the firft port, whilft Hieron, with his heavy armed forces, fuftained the enemy's attack.

2. WHENEVER Hieron, in his wars with the Italians, took prifoners any of eminence, or who had great connexions in the ftate, he would not permit them to be immediately ranfomed, but always retained them fome time with him, treating them politely, and with the firft honours of his houfe. He afterwards received the ranfom, and courteoufly difmiffed them. From fuch diftinguifhing marks of favour, they ever after became fufpected by their fellow citizens of having their affections warped, and fecretly favouring the caufe of Hieron.

CHAP XXX.

THEMISTOCLES

THE Athenians, difpirited at the import of an Oracle, in thefe words delivered,

" Thou,

" Thou, Salamis divine, to Pluto's reign
" Shalt many a youth affign, untimely flain."

THEMISTOCLES artfully interpreted it againſt their enemies, " Since, ' ſaid he,' never could the Oracle ſtyle Salamis DIVINE, if it were to prove the cauſe of deſtruction to the youth of Greece." The happy turn thus given to it revived the courage and reſolution of the Athenians. and this interpretation of an alarming Oracle having been ſo ſatisfactory, the people were directed by Themiſtocles in his explanation of another, equally enigmatical and obſcure.

" May Jove to Athens give a wall of wood."

For when moſt of the people were for fortifying their towers, Themiſtocles bade them man. their ſhips, " for theſe, ' ſaid he,' O! Athenians, are your wooden walls" His words had their effect. The Athenians concurred with him, embarked, engaged their enemy, and overcame them.

2 WHILE the fleet was ſtationed near Salamis, the Greeks were almoſt unanimous in adviſing a retreat which Themiſtocles as violently oppoſed, preſſing them to hazard an engagement in the ſtrait ſeas But not being able to prevail, he in the night diſpatched Sycinnus, an eunuch, who was tutor to his ſons, privately to inform the king of the intention of the Greeks to give him the ſlip, " but, ' added he,' prevent it, and engage them." The king followed the eunuch's advice, and attacked the Græcian fleet; where, by the ſtraitneſs of the ſeas, the vaſt number of his own ſhips was rendered rather of diſſervice, than uſe to him. Thus by a happy ſtratagem of their commander, the Greeks obtained a victory, even againſt their own inclinations.

3. THE Greeks, after their conqueſt at Salamis, reſolved upon failing to the Helleſpont, there to deſtroy the bridge, and cut off the

king's

king's retreat. This Themistocles opposed, alledging, that if the king were precluded a retreat, he would immediately renew the battle and despair is frequently found to effect what courage fails in encountering Again therefore he dispatched Arsaces, another eunuch, to inform the king that unless he made a speedy retreat, the bridge over the Hellespont would be demolished. Alarmed at this information, the king by expeditious marches reached the Hellespont, and passed the bridge, before the Grecian army had executed their design, leaving Themistocles to enjoy his victory, without the hazard of a second engagement.

4. When the Athenians first applied themselves to fortify their city with walls, it gave great umbrage to the Spartans, whom Themistocles found means to deceive by this happy stratagem he was deputed ambassador to Sparta, and there confidently denied that the walls were raising. "But, ' added he,' if you be not satisfied with my declaration, send whom you please of credit and eminence to enquire the truth, and in the mean time let me be your prisoner." This they complied with when Themistocles privately dispatched a messenger to the Athenians, with strict charge to detain those who were sent to Athens for intelligence, till their walls were raised, and after that, not to permit them leave the city, till the Spartans had released him. The stratagem succeeding, the walls were raised, Themistocles then returned, the delegates were set at liberty, and Athens fortified, to the great mortification of the Lacedæmonians.

5. In the war with the Æginates, Themistocles prevented the Athenians from their purpose of dividing amongst themselves a hundred talents, the produce of the silver mines, and proposed that a hundred of the most opulent citizens should contribute each a talent to the fund. engaging, that if the city were satisfied with the use to which he should recommend the money to be applied, it should be placed to the publick account, if not, the contributions should be returned. The proposal was embraced, the hundred citizens vying with each

other

other in expedition, every one fitted out a handsome vessel and the Athenians saw themselves on a sudden furnished with a powerful fleet; which they employed not only against the Æginates, but against the whole power of Persia.

6. When the Ionians, in alliance with the Persians, fought under Xerxes, Themistocles ordered the Greeks to have this inscription placed on their walls " O, impious Ionians, thus to war against your fathers!" This memorial created in the mind of the king an indelible suspicion of their disaffection.

7 Themistocles, in order to elude the resentment of the Athenians, without making himself known to the master of the ship, embarked for Ionia But the vessel being forced by a storm upon Naxos, which was at that time invaded by the Athenians, afraid of being apprehended, he went up to the master, and discovered to him who he was, at the same time threatening, if he suffered him to be taken, to accuse him to the Athenians of having been bribed to transport him to Ionia For the common safety of them both, he therefore proposed that no one should be permitted to set foot on shore. Terrified by these menaces, the master obliged every one to continue on board, and put out again to sea as expeditiously as he was able.

CHAP. XXXI.

ARISTIDES

ARISTIDES and Themistocles, most inveterate enemies, were each at the head of opposite factions in the state: but upon Persa's expedition against the Athenians, they amicably went out of the city together, and, grasping each other's hand, protested, " Here we deposit our former animosities, and lay aside our mutual enmity, till we have put an end to the war in which we are engaged against Persa."

After

After this solemn protestation on both sides, loosing their hands, they filled the ditch by which they stood, as if they had there buryed their animosity, and acted unanimously through the whole course of the war. This harmony in the conduct of the generals, distressed the enemy, and secured to themselves the victory.

CHAP. XXXII.

LEONIDAS.

LEONIDAS engaged the Persian army, at Thermopylæ, the straitness of the place making the great superiority of the enemy's forces of little service to them

2 A LITTLE before an engagement, Leonidas observing the clouds look thick and lowering, turned about to his officers, and bade them not be surprized at the thunder and lightning, which from the appearance of the heavens, he observed must be very soon expected. The army of Leonidas, thus forewarned of the phænomenon which soon appeared, confidently advanced to battle But the enemy, terrified and dispirited at the menaces of the elements, afforded an easy conquest to the Spartans

3 HAVING made an irruption into the enemy's territories, Leonidas in the night dispatched small parties different ways, with orders, upon a signal given, to fell the trees, and set fire to the villages. At sight of this, they who were in the city imagining the enemy's forces to be much more numerous than they were, ventured not out to give them battle, but suffered them to carry off the spoil unmolested.

CHAP. XXXIII.

LEOTYCHIDES.

OBSERVING the Athenians, engaged in a naval war about Mycale, were alarmed at the great superiority of the enemy's forces, Leotychides devised means to detach the Ionians from the interest of the Medes; in which he knew they were engaged, more through fear, than inclination. He pretended an express was arrived, with information of a victory obtained by the Greeks over the Persians, at Platæa. Encouraged by this assurance, the Ionians joined the Greeks, and fortune afterwards gave the sanction of truth to this stratagem, in realizing the pretended victory.

CHAP. XXXIV.

CIMON.

AT the river Eurymedon, Cimon having conquered the king's lieutenants, and taken many of his ships, manned them with Greeks, who, dressed in Median habits, sailed to Cyprus. The Cyprians, deceived by the barbarian dress, readily received the fleet as friends and allies. But no sooner were they safe on shore, than they too plainly proved that they were Greeks; and made themselves masters of the island, more by the sudden consternation into which the Cyprians were thrown, than the force that was employed against them.

2. CIMON having carried off from Sestos and Byfantium many captives and rich spoil, was, at the request of the allies, appointed to divide them. The captives alone composed one share of the division, and the other was made up of robes, vestments, bracelets, and other trinkets.

trinkets. The allies chose the ornaments, and the Athenians contented themselves with the naked captives. Cimon was ridiculed for having made, as was thought, so unequal a division, and assigned a choice of so much the better portion to the allies. Shortly after came the friends and relations of the captives from Lydia and Phrygia, and redeemed them at very great ransoms. The forecast of Cimon, and the advantageous disposition he had made, then appeared; and the Athenians retorted their ridicule upon the allies.

CHAP. XXXV

MYRONIDES

THE Athenians and Thebans having formed against each other; Myronides, the Athenian general, ordered his men, as soon as the signal for battle was given, to begin the charge from the left. They did so, when Myronides, after having for a short time engaged at the head of them, hastily advanced to the right wing, calling out aloud, "We are victorious in the left." Upon mention of the word VICTORIOUS, the Athenians received a fresh accession of courage, and charged the enemy with redoubled fury. The Thebans, on the contrary, dispirited with the news of their defeat, abandoned the field to the enemy.

2. WHEN Myronides led the Athenians against Thebes, and was advancing to the field, he ordered them to ground their arms, and take a view of the country round. They did so, when addressing them, "Observe, 'said he,' what a spacious plain this is, and what a number of horse the enemy have in it. If we run away, the cavalry will most undoubtedly overtake us; But if we stand like men, there are the fairest hopes of victory." By this concise harangue, he convinced them of the necessity of maintaining their ground, and penetrated even to the territories of Phocis and Locri.

CHAP. XXXVI.

PERICLES

WHILST the Lacedæmonians were ravaging Attica, in order to divert their operations, by carrying the war into their own country, Pericles fitted out fome Athenian galleys with orders to lay wafte the maritime parts of Sparta and thus retaliated the injuries the Athenians had fuftained, by committing greater upon the Lacedæmonians

2 WHEN Archidamus, who had been formerly a friend and acquaintance of Pericles, invaded Attica, Pericles, who was very rich, and had large eftates, fufpecting, that on account of their former intimacy, Archidamus might not fuffer his property to fhare the general ravage, to fecure himfelf from the fufpicion of the Athenians, before the devaftation was begun, went into the affembly, and made a publick donation to the city of all his poffeffions

CHAP. XXXVII.

CLEON.

CLEON, by means of a lucky difcovery, betrayed Seftos to the Abydenians without the expence of a battle Theodorus, a friend of his, who had the command of the watch in the city, having an intrigue with a woman in the fuburbs, obferved a narrow acqueduct, which was continued through the walls By pulling up a ftone, through this pafs he ufed to vifit his miftrefs, and at his return, replacing the ftone as ufual, he continued his amour undifcovered. At an hour, when wine and mirth had opened his mind, he confeffed his intrigue to his friend Cleon, who immediately communicated it to the Abydenians. and, waiting for a dark night, when Theodorus had pulled up the ftone, and was amusing himself with his mistress, he introduced a party of the enemy through the aqueduct. These, after they had slain the watch, opened the gates to the rest of the army, and easily made themselves masters of Sestos.

CHAP. XXXVIII.

BRASIDAS.

BRASIDAS was attacked near Amphipolis, and upon a rough craggy hill hemmed in by the enemy, who, to prevent his escape by night, raised round the hill a high wall of stone. The Lacedæmonians were instant with their general to lead them out to battle, and not let them stay to be cooped up, and perish with famine. But Brasidas, without regarding their solicitations, told them, he best knew the proper time for engaging. After the enemy had extended their wall round the greatest part of the hill, one place only being left open, like a pass into a spacious lawn, he gave orders for battle, adding, that this was the time to shew their spirit. Then making a vigorous sally, they forced a passage with great slaughter of the enemy, and little loss to themselves. For the straitness of the place was no inconvenience to the small number of their forces, whilst the wall secured them from an attack upon their rear. Thus were the enemy's numbers rendered useless, and the Lacedæmonians effected a safe retreat.

2. AMPHIPOLIS, which was under the Athenian protection, having been betrayed into the hands of Brasidas, he ordered the gates to be shut: and, taking the keys, threw them over the walls, that thus not having it in their power to open their gates again to the enemy that had invested it, they might place all their confidence in a vigorous defence.

3. WHEN Brasidas, who had with great secrefy advanced to Amphipolis, found every thing there in confusion, not judging it prudent to

hazard

hazard a battle with an enemy, actuated by defpair, he iffued a proclamation, promifing fecurity to the Athenians, if they would agree to a truce with him, and retreat with their own property And to the Amphipolitans he made another propofal, that they fhould enjoy the freedom of the ftate, if they would enter into a ftrict alliance with the Lacedæmonians The terms of the proclamation were accepted by the Athenians, who drew off their forces, and the Amphipolitans became allies to Lacedæmon

4 BRASIDAS, intending to fail to Sicyon by night, ordered a trireme * to be manned, and fail before him, whilft himfelf followed in a light floop. That in cafe the trireme was attacked by a larger veffel, the floop might come up to its affiftance; but if it were equally engaged, he in the mean time might arrive fafe at Sicyon.

5. THE enemy in a narrow defile hanging upon the Lacedæmonians' rear, Brafidas ordered his men to cut down great quantities of wood as they marched, and pile it in heaps, which being fet on fire, and the flame fpreading wide, he thus fecured his rear, and effected a fafe retreat.

CHAP. XXXIX.

NICIAS.

NICIAS failed by night to that part of Corinth, where is the mountain Solyges, and after he had there landed his Athenian forces, and a thoufand other troops, and pofted them in ambufcade, at different places, he returned to Athens. and on the next morning, as foon as it was day, openly embarked for Corinth. The Corinthians advanced with alacrity to oppofe him, and difpute his landing When the ambufcade fuddenly difcovered themfelves, and furioufly falling upon the enemy, gave them a total defeat.

2. THE

---

* A fhip containing three benches of oars.

2 The Athenians being encamped about Olimpius, Nicias ordered wooden spikes in the night to be fixed in the ground, which extended on a level before the camp, and on the next day, when Ecphantus, general of the Syracusan horse, advanced with his cavalry, he was entirely routed, the spikes sticking into the horses' hoofs every step they advanced. And many of them not being able to make good their retreat, were cut to pieces by the heavy armed troops, that were provided with hard stiff shoes for the purpose.

3 Nicias, with a few men, was left to defend a town, whilst the main body of the army lay at Thapsus. But the Syracusans having possessed themselves of the outworks, where was deposited a great quantity of wood, Nicias, finding himself unable any longer to defend the town, set fire to the wood, which continuing to burn fiercely, repelled the enemy, till the army returned from Thapsus, and relieved him.

4 Nicias, when closely pursued by Gylippus, and very near being taken, dispatched a herald to him, with a proposal to surrender on whatever conditions he would offer him: at the same time desiring that some one might be sent to ratify the treaty. Gylippus, not distrusting the herald, immediately encamped, and, desisting from further pursuit, sent back Nicias's herald, and with him one commissioned to conclude the treaty. But Nicias, having in the mean time possessed himself of a more advantageous post, continued the war, after he had by this imposition of the herald made good his retreat.

CHAP. XL.

ALCIBIADES

TO make trial of the affection of his friends, Alcibiades contrived the following device—In a dark place in his house he shut up the statue of a man; and discovering it to his friends separately, as a person, whom he had

had murdered, he begged their affiftance in contriving means to conceal the fact They all excufed themfelves from having any concern in an affair of that nature, except Callias, the fon of Hipponicus, who readily offered to receive the pretended corpfe, and feciete it from a difcovery. In Callias, therefore, he difcovered a faithful friend, who ever afterwards held the firft place in his affections.

2. In a foreign expedition, Alcibiades landed his forces in the enemy's country by night and waited their attack the next day. But finding them not difpofed to venture out of the city, and hazard a battle, he planted an ambufcade, and, after burning his tents, weighed anchor from thence, and failed back As foon as from the city they had feen him embark, they confidently opened their gates, and in little parties ftraggled up and down the country when the ambufcade, fallying out upon them, took many prifoners, and no inconfiderable booty. Alcibiades immediately appeared on the coaft again, and taking on board both the fpoil and the captors, failed back to Athens

3. While the Lacedæmonians laid fiege to Athens, Alcibiades, in order to excite vigilance in the centinels, who were pofted at the Piræum, and the long walls which extended to the fea, gave notice, that three times every night he would hold out a torch from the tower, and that whoever of the guard did not anfwer him, by holding up their's at the fame time, fhould be punifhed for neglect of duty. The ftratagem had its effect, for all were particularly careful to be in readinefs, to anfwer their general's fignal

4 In an expedition againft Sicily, Alcibiades touched at Corfica, where, as his army was numerous, he divided it into three parts, that it might the more eafily be fupplied with forage and advancing to Catane, when he found the Catanæans determined not to admit him, he difpatched an embaffy to them, defiring that he might be permitted to enter their city alone, and to communicate to them what he had of confequence to propofe. This requeft being complied with, he left

orders

orders with his generals, whilst the citizens flocked from all quarters to the assembly, to make a vigorous attack upon such gates as were weakest. Accordingly, whilst Alcibiades was haranguing the Catanæans, they found the Athenians in possession of the city.

5 AFTER Alcibiades had possessed himself of Catane, he retained in his service, and found means to attach to him, a faithful Catanæan, who was well known at Syracuse. Him he dispatched thither, under pretext of being charged with a commission to the Syracusans by some of their friends in Catane, which was, to inform them that the Athenians devoted their time to pleasures and festivity, and accustomed themselves to stroll from the camp, secure and unarmed, and that therefore if early in the morning they could surprize the camp, the Athenians they would find an easy capture, unarmed, and indulging themselves in the city. The Syracusan chiefs easily credited him, and gave orders immediately for an embarkation of their whole army for Catane. They accordingly landed at Corsica, and, advancing to Catane, encamped at the river Symæthus. As soon as Alcibiades perceived them advancing, manning his triremes with all expedition, he embarked and sailed directly to Syracuse, where he arrived without opposition, and entirely demolished their fortifications.

6 ALCIBIADES being ordered from Sicily, to take his trial for defacing the statues of Mercury, and a prophanation of the mysteries, hired a light-built vessel, to carry him to Lacedæmon. He there advised the state to send speedy succours to the Syracusans, and to fortify Decelæa, which if neglected, they could receive from thence neither the product of the soil, nor of the silver mines. and cautioned them, that they must also expect the revolt of the islanders, as soon as they saw themselves besieged. These his transactions at Lacedæmon induced the Athenians to pass his recall from exile.

7 IN an action between the Athenians and Syracusans, Alcibiades observing a great quantity of dry fern between the two armies, while a

brisk

brisk wind blew full on the backs of the Athenians, and against the enemy's faces, ordered the fern to be set on fire: and the wind driving the smoak into the enemy's eyes, they found themselves unable to make any stand, and a general rout ensued *

8. ALCIBIADES, when so pent up by Tyribasus that there was but one way by which he could secure his retreat, while the enemy, who would not hazard a general engagement, hung upon his rear, encamped in a place well covered with wood, where he ordered a quantity of timber to be cut down, and piled in different heaps this in the night he set on fire, and privately decamped. The barbarians, seeing the fire, never suspected the Græcians of having struck their tents. and as soon as the stratagem was discovered, and Tyribasus prepared to follow him, he found his march so interrupted by the fire, that he was obliged to desist from the pursuit.

9 ALCIBIADES privately dispatched Theramenes and Thrasybulus with a large squadron to Cyzicum, to cut off the enemy's retreat to the city, whilst he himself, with a few triremes, advanced to offer them battle. Mindarus, conceiving a contempt for his little fleet, instantly prepared for the engagement: when no sooner had they closed, than the Athenian fleet counterfeited flight, and the Lacedæmonians, as if victory had declared in their favour, eagerly pursued them. But Alcibiades, as soon as he approached that part of his fleet which sailed under the command of Theramenes and Thrasybulus, hoisted his flag, and, tacking about, stood to the enemy Mindarus then endeavoured to sheer off, and make for the city, but was prevented by the movement of Theramenes. Cut off from that resource, he directed his course to a point of Cyzicum called Cleros, but from thence also he was repulsed by the army of Pharnabazus. Alcibiades in the mean

---

* A similar stratagem Hannibal is reported by Frontinus to have employed against the Romans at Cannæ.

time closely pursued him, shattering his ships, by running foul of them with his beaks, and hauling them off with his grappling-irons, as often as they attempted to land whilst those who, effected a landing, were cut to pieces by Pharnabazus. And the death of Mindarus finally completed to Alcibiades a brilliant and glorious victory.*

CHAP. XLI.

ARCHIDAMUS.

ON the night before a battle, in which Archidamus was to command the Lacedæmonian army against the Arcadians, to spirit up the Spartans, he had an altar privately erected, adorned with two suits of bright armour, and directed two horses to be led round it. In the morning, the captains and subalterns, observing those new suits of armour, the prints of two horses' feet, and an altar raised as it were of itself, persuaded themselves that Castor and Pollux had been to assure them of their assistance. The soldiers, thus inspired with courage, and impressed with enthusiastick notions of divine assistance, fought gallantly, and obtained the victory.

2 At a time when Archidamus laid close siege to Corinth, the rich citizens and the poor were divided into separate factions, the one party inclined to deliver up the city to the enemy, and the other to establish in it an oligarchy. Archidamus, receiving intelligence of these divisions, flackened the siege. He no longer advanced his machines to the walls, no longer marked out his lines of circumvallation, no longer employed himself in levelling the ground. The rich men therefore, suf-

---

* I have in this stratagem followed the original, in which, however, there is an undoubted error, for Pharnabazus never was an ally of the Athenians. It is probable therefore that the fleet, which Alcibiades is said to have dispatched under the command of Theramenes and Thrasybulus to Cyzicum, landed there a body of troops under Thrasybulus and that the true reading, instead of Pharnabazus, is Thrasybulus.

pecting

pecting that he had gained over the other faction to betray the city to him, determined to be before hand with them, and difpatched an embaffy to Archidamus with the furrender of it. ftipulating for their fafety by the fanction of a future alliance.

3 At Lacedæmon happened a violent fhock of an earthquake, by which five houfes only were left ftanding Archidamus, feeing the men wholly bufied in faving their effects, and fearing left they fhould themfelves ftay to be buried in the ruins, ordered the trumpet to found an alarm on which the Spartans, imagining an enemy was advancing againft them, immediately repaired to him. The houfes in the mean time fell, but the men were thus happily preferved

4. The Arcadians, after a victory obtained over the Spartans, being left mafters of the field, Archidamus weak, and difabled with his wounds, fent to petition a truce, to bury their dead, while there yet remained any to perform the office *

5. Archidamus marched his army by night to Caræ, through a long tedious road, rough and craggy, and incommoded with waters He endeavoured, as much as poffible, to keep up the fpirits of his men, haraffed as they were with a fatiguing and laborious march, both by example and exhortation encouraging them to perfevere By this forced march, they furprized the enemy, and, unprepared as they were for fo fudden an attack, entirely defeated them, and plundered the city When afterwards, exulting in their victory, they were banqueting in the captured town, Archidamus afked them, at what particular time the city appeared to them to be taken. Some anfwered, when they began the clofe attack, others when they came within the reach of their javelins. " Neither, ' replied he,' but when we continued our march through that tedious dreary fwamp: for perfeverance and refolution eventually conquer every thing"

* The ftratagem is left imperfect, and fhould be thus fupplied,—" The nature of the " requeft impreffed the Arcadians with horror at the carnage it conveyed, induced them to " fheath the fword, and, inftead of a truce, enter into an alliance with the Spartans "

CHAP. XLII.

GYLIPPUS

GYLIPPUS, ambitious of being invested with the chief command of the Syracusan army, convened the other generals to a council of war where he communicated to them a design of possessing themselves of a hill which lay between the city and the Athenian Camp. With this proposal after they had signified their concurrence, he by night dispatched a revolter to inform the enemy of the design, who took advantage of the intelligence, and immediately possessed themselves of the mountain. Upon this Gylippus pretended great indignation, as if his plan had by some or other of the generals been discovered to the enemy. To prevent therefore any such communication of intelligence in future, the chiefs of Syracuse committed to Gylippus the sole management of the war.

2. The eminence, of which the Athenians had possessed themselves, Gylippus finding it necessary to recover, out of a great number of vessels selected twenty which he manned, and had frequently manœuvred. These, as soon as he had compleated his compliment of men for the rest of the fleet, he ordered to put to sea early the next morning. The enemy no sooner perceived them under sail, than they also embarked, and advanced to give them battle. But whilst they edged off, and the Athenians were briskly pursuing them, Gylippus also, having manned the rest of the fleet, put to sea. And the attention of the Athenians being thus engaged in a naval action, the few troops, they had left behind, were easily dislodged by Gylippus's infantry, who afterwards possessed themselves of the post.

CHAP. XLIII.

HERMOCRATES.

AN infurrection taking place in Syracufe, and a great band of flaves being collected together, Hermocrates fent ambaffador to Sofiftratus, their leader, one Daimachus, a captain of horfe, and formerly a particular friend and acquaintance of Sofiftratus who told him from the generals, that from particular regard for the fortitude he had difplayed, they had agreed to give the men their freedom, furnifh them with arms, and allow them a military ftipend, and that they alfo admitted him to the rank of general, and defired that he would forthwith come and join them in their deliberations on public bufinefs. Relying on the friendfhip of Daimachus, Sofiftratus attended the generals, with twenty of his beft and ableft men · who were all immediately feized, and thrown into chains, whilft Hermocrates marched out with fix thoufand picked men, and having taken prifoners the reft of the flaves, he engaged to them on oath, that they fhould receive no ill treatment from him, provided they would return to their refpective mafters to which they all agreed, except three hundred, who revolted to the Athenians.

2 THE Athenians, having fuffered in a naval engagement with the Syracufans off Sicily, refolved to withdraw their forces from the ifland in the night, whilft the Syracufans lay buried in wine and fleep after their triumphal facrifices Hermocrates fufpected the defign, but not venturing to hazard an engagement with troops drowfy and inebriated as his were, he difpatched a revolter who told Nicias, his friends, who were ever vigilant in watching all opportunities of information, apprized him, that if he attempted to make his retreat that night, he would inevitably fall into the enemy's ambufcade. The intelligence

obtained

obtained credit with Nicias, who waited for the next day, before he decamped. The next morning, Hermocrates ordered the Syracusans to arms, who were by that time well refreshed, and had slept off the fumes of the last evening's debauch and possessing himself of the posts at the passes of the rivers, and the bridges, he defeated the Athenians with great slaughter.

CHAP. XLIV.

ETEONICUS

CONON, the Athenian, had besieged Eteonicus, the Lacedæmonian, in Mitylene, when a light-horseman arrived express with news of Callicratidas, the Spartan admiral, having defeated the enemy at Arginusæ. Eteonicus commanded the express to retire out of the city privately by night, and the next day to return, crowned with chaplets, and hymning victory, and he himself offered sacrifice for the auspicious news, while Conon and the Athenian army, struck with consternation, raised the siege. Eteonicus, exerting himself with redoubled vigour, fitted out a fleet for Chios, and marched the army to Methymna, a city then in alliance with Lacedæmon.

CHAP. XLV.

LYSANDER.

LYSANDER, having promised his Milesian friends to reduce the people to their subjection, for that purpose went to Miletum And in his harangues, whilst he severely animadverted on the innovators, he promised the citizens his endeavours to secure to them their liberty, and to protect them in it. The people, not doubting his sincerity,

readily

readily embraced his offers, and put themselves under his protection When, unprepared for an attack, at a signal given, his friends fell upon the unsuspecting citizens, and having slain the leaders of the opposition, Miletum relapsed into the power of his friends

2. At the Ægospotamos the Athenians several times put to sea, and bearing down upon the enemy offered them battle, which Lysander always declined whereupon they returned to their station, exulting in their success, and hymning victory The Lacedæmonian at last sent two sloops to observe them, the captains of which, as soon as they perceived the enemy landing, hoisted a brazen shield as a signal to Lysander, who immediately advanced with the rest of the fleet, crowding all the sail he could, and came up with the Athenians, just after the forces were landed Some of them were gone to rest, and others employed, part on one thing, part on another · when the Lacedæmonians on a sudden attacking them, a regular force against a confused rout, obtained an easy victory. They took the whole fleet, both men and ships, except one galley only, which escaped to carry the ungrateful news to Athens

3 Lysander used to say, " Boys were to be cheated with dice, but an enemy with oaths "

4. After Lysander had made himself master of Thasos, knowing that many of the citizens, who were in the Athenian interest, had concealed themselves through fear, convened the Thasians to the temple of Hercules Where, in a gracious and conciliating harangue, he signified to them how readily he forgave all those who might have concealed themselves in consequence of this revolution of affairs, and hoped they would dismiss all fears of his resentment. On the assurance he gave them, in so sacred a place as the temple, and that too in the city of his ancestor Hercules, and captivated by this specious address, the Thasians, who had before concealed themselves, began to venture o it, and appeared publickly. whom Lysander, after forbearing two or three

days

days to take any notice of them, that so they being less fearful, might also be less circumspect, ordered to be suddenly seized and executed.

5. When it was debated by the Lacedæmonians and their allies, whether they should not endeavour the entire destruction of Athens, Lysander urged many arguments against it and particularly the consideration, that Thebes, which was a neighbouring state, would thereby be rendered more powerful, and a more formidable enemy to Sparta. Whereas, if they could preserve the dependence of Athens, under the government of tyrants, they might through its vicinity, watch the motions of the Thebans, whose affairs must of course decrease Lysander's advice was approved, and they were prevailed on to give up the design of destroying Athens.

CHAP. XLVI.

AGIS

In a war between the Peloponnesians and Lacedæmonians, the latter were reduced to great scarcity of provisions, when Agis gave orders that the oxen for one whole day should be kept from their feeding. And to conceal from the enemy their distress, he sent over some revolters to inform them, that the next night a great reinforcement was expected at the Lacedæmonian camp. All the day the mouths of the cattle were muzzled, and loosed as soon as night came on. The hungry oxen thus set free, and turned loose into the pastures, leaping about and bellowing, raised a terrible noise, which the cavities between the hills did not a little contribute to increase He ordered the soldiers at the same time to disperse themselves abroad, and kindle several fires. The Peloponnesians, alarmed at the bellowing of the oxen, and the shouts they heard, as well as the fires which they observed, concluded the enemy to be strongly reinforced, struck their tents, and precipitately retreated

CHAP. XLVII.

THRASYLLUS.

TO conceal from the enemy the number of his ships, Thrasyllus ordered the pilots to link two together, expanding only the sails of one. And by this stratagem only one half of his fleet was discernible by the enemy.

2. THRASYLLUS, having laid close siege to Byzantium, and vigorously carried on the attack, struck such a general terror into the minds of the Byzantines, left their city should be carried by storm, that they capitulated with him for the surrender of it within a limited time, and gave hostages for their observance of the articles. Thrasyllus accordingly raised the siege, and embarking his army sailed for Ionia; but returned secretly by night, and made himself master of the defenceless city.

CHAP. XLVIII.

CONON.

CONON, in danger of being deserted by his allies, dispatched a revolter to the enemy with information of their intended retreat, of the time when they intended to strike their tents, and of their rout. who took their measures accordingly, and placed an ambuscade to intercept them. He then informed the allied army of intelligence he had received, that an ambuscade was planted to intercept them, of which he was happy in an opportunity of apprizing them, that they might be upon their guard, and the more safely effect their retreat. As soon as they were satisfied of the truth of Conon's intelligence

ligence, and difcovered the ambufcade, won with his generofity, they returned back to the camp, and continued with him till he had put an honourable end to the war.

2. CALLICRATIDAS, with a fleet double to the enemy, falling in with Conon, gave chafe, and purfued him almoft to Mitylene. when obferving the Lacedæmonian fhips widely feparated in the purfuit, Conon hoifted up the purple flag, which was the fignal for battle to the other commanders. They immediately ftood to, and forming a line, furioufly engaged the Lacedæmonian fleet, which, being thrown into confufion by this fudden attack of the enemy, were moft of them either fhattered to pieces, or funk. And Conon obtained a compleat victory.

3. WHEN Agefilaus was laying wafte Afia, Conon, being fent to the affiftance of Pharnabafus, advifed the Perfian to let his gold circulate amongft the orators of the Græcian ftates. "Of which, 'faid he,' when they have once tafted, they will at your requeft influence their country, not only to make a peace with you, but to turn their arms againft the Spartans" The advice was followed, and fucceeded. for the Corinthian war prefently broke out, in confequence of which the Spartans were obliged to recall Agefilaus from Afia

4. CONON when blocked up in Mitylene by the Lacedæmonians, feeing it neceffary to give the Athenians notice of it, and yet diftreffed how to do it undifcovered, manned two of his fwifteft failing floops with able feamen, and having furnifhed them with every thing neceffary, he ordered them to lie by till the evening. As foon as the day clofed, and he obferved the guard ftraggling about the fhore, and varioufly employed, fome in dreffing their wounds, fome piling the wood, and others lighting the fires, he commanded them to fet fail, and fteer different courfes. that in cafe one was taken, the other might efcape. But they both arrived fafe, the enemy being either too neglectful to obferve, or too indolent to purfue them.

5. JUST

5. Just before a naval engagement, Conon, having received intelligence by a revolter, that a choice detachment of the enemy's fleet had determined, as their principal aim, to take the ship in which he sailed, fitted out a trireme exactly like his own. And investing the captain of it with the admiral's robes, he ordered it to the right wing and also commanded, that the whole fleet should receive their signals from it. This the enemy observed, and forming a line of their best ships, immediately attacked the supposed admiral's vessel, while Conon vigorously engaging them with the rest of his fleet, sunk part, and put the rest to flight.

CHAP. XLIX.

XENOPHON.

XENOPHON, in his famous retreat from Persia, when he found Tisaphernes's cavalry continually attacking his baggage, advised that their carriages, with all that was not absolutely necessary either for war, or the conveyance of their stores, might be left behind, lest the Greeks should defeat all possibility of a retreat, by sacrificing their lives in the defence of their property.

2 As the enemy kept continually galling his rear, Xenophon formed his little army into two fronts, placing his baggage in a hollow square in the middle, and in this disposition he prosecuted his march, covering his rear with the cavalry, slingers, and targeteers, who repulsed the frequent incursions of the barbarians.

3 Xenophon, observing that the barbarians had possessed themselves of a defile through which his route necessarily lay, favoured by a high mountain with an extensive view of the country, discerned an accessible hill, but defended by a party of the enemy. At the head of a detachment, such as he judged sufficient for the purpose, thither he marched;

marched, and diflodging the forces that were pofted there, difcovered himfelf to the enemy below who feeing the advantageous pofition of the Greeks, abandoned themfelves to flight, and thus opened a fafe paffage for the Græcian army

4 THE barbarian cavalry being drawn up on the oppofite fide of a river, which Xenophon was obliged to crofs, and ready to difpute his paffage over it, he felected a thoufand men, whom he detached to ford the river a little above, whilft he himfelf, to engage the obfervation of the enemy, made a feint, as if intending to crofs it directly againft them. In the mean time the detached party gained the oppofite fide, and appearing above the enemy, engaged them whilft Xenophon fafely paffed it with the remaining part of his army.

PREFATORY

STRATAGEMS OF WAR.

PREFATORY ADDRESS.

WITH this second book of Stratagems, I beg leave to present your most sacred majesties, Antoninus and Verus, who are yourselves well qualified to judge at what expence of labour and time I have made this collection, ever studious of your service though the honourable post, I hold under you at the bar, allows me few leisure hours for the prosecution of other studies.

BOOK II. CHAP. I.

AGESILAUS.

1 AGESILAUS took the field against the Acarnenfians about seed-time, but finding that at that season they intended sowing their lands, against the remonstrances of the Lacedæmonians, he marched back his army alleging, that after they had sown their corn, in order to preserve it, they would be more inclinable to peace "For then, 'said he,' peace they must have, or suffer us to reap the fruits of their labour"

2 THE Lacedæmonians, advancing to an engagement against the united force of Thebes and Athens, though the light-armed troops could be of no service, Agesilaus ordered the whole phalanx to the attack Chabrias, general of the Athenians, and Gorgidas of the Thebans, observing the number of the enemy, commanded their respective corps not to advance, but with their shields fixed on their knees, and their spears couched, in that posture to remain, and receive the enemy's charge.

charge Agesilaus, struck with the firm disposition of their battle, judged it the province of a general rather to retreat, than hazard so unpromising an engagement.

3. AGESILAUS appeared at Coronæa with a force superiour to what he had ever commanded before when an express arrived with intelligence that Bisander, the Lacedæmonian admiral, had by Pharnabazus been defeated and slain Lest the army should be dispirited by this ill news, Agesilaus gave orders to the heralds to proclaim the contrary. that the Lacedæmonians had been victorious by sea. And to favour the deceit, he himself appeared crowned, offered sacrifices on account of the auspicious news, and sent portions of the victims round to his friends These demonstrations of victory so inspirited his troops, that they marched out to battle with confidence and alacrity

4. AGESILAUS, after his victory at Coronæa, being told that the Athenians had fled for refuge to the temple of Minerva, replied, "Let them go wherever they are inclined, for nothing can be attended with greater danger, than an engagement to which the enemy is forced by despair."

5. AGESILAUS, in his Asiatick expedition, to inspire his men with a contempt for the barbarians, whom they had been used to regard with terror, ordered some Persian captives to be stripped, and exposing them naked before the army, he bade the Greeks observe their delicate and puny frames, occasioned by the luxurious lives in which they were trained up; and on the other hand, how rich and costly was their apparel. laconically adding, "Those are our enemies, and these the rewards of victory"

6. IT was a constant maxim with this general, always to leave the enemy a door open for flight.

7. UPON a complaint of the allies, that the Lacedæmonians brought into the field fewer forces than themselves, Agesilaus commanded them to sit down by themselves, and the Spartans to do the same.

that

that so the matter might be brought to a proof. Thus seated, a herald made proclamation for all the potters to rise of the allies a great number did so. Upon the second proclamation, which was for the smiths to rise, many more stood up. All the carpenters, who were a large body, were next ordered to rise. And, in the same manner, all other handicraftmen and mechanicks, in their order. So that amongst the allies, there were scarce any left seated. But of the Lacedæmonians, not a man was seen standing; for they are by their laws restricted from practising any mechanick employment. Thus were the allies taught, that though they contributed, towards carrying on the war, more men; yet the Lacedæmonians brought into the field more soldiers.

8. WHEN Agesilaus, having marched his army into Asia, continued ravaging the territories in that part of the king's dominions, Tisaphernes proposed to him a truce for three months: which time was employed in intrigues to win over to the king's interest the Græcian cities, that were in Asia. And at the same time, while the Greeks, refraining from action, quietly waited for the expiration of the truce, the Persian was indefatigable in augmenting his force, and, contrary to his own engagements, on a sudden attacked them. Unexpecting an enemy, and unprepared to resist, a general tumult and consternation pervaded the Græcian camp; when Agesilaus, with a composed and tranquil countenance, or rather with looks expressive of joy, thus addressed his troops. "Tisaphernes I thank for his perjury, by which he has made the gods his enemies, and our allies. Let us therefore, my lads, march out with becoming confidence, in conjunction with so great auxiliaries." Spirited by this short harangue, the general led them forth, and obtained a compleat victory.

9. UPON his march to Sardis, Agesilaus dispatched persons to propagate a report, that his march was only a pretence to deceive Tisaphernes: for though the expedition seemed professedly against Lydia, yet his real design was against Caria. Tisaphernes, informed of this,

directed

directed all his attention towards the defence of Caria; whilst the Lacedæmonian made an impression upon Lydia, and enriched himself with the spoil of that defenceless territory.

10. WHEN Agesilaus invaded Acarnania, and the Acarnanians had retired to the mountains, he halted in the plain country, and contented himself with destroying the wood in the adjacent places, by grubbing up the trees. The Acarnanians despised his apparent inertion, whilst he seemed wholly occupied in destroying their trees, and ventured down from the posts they possessed in the mountains, to the cities which were situated on the plains. This movement of theirs invited Agesilaus to action who, by a forced march of a hundred and sixty furlongs in the night, early the next morning surprized them, made prisoners all the men he could pick up, and retreated with a great quantity of cattle, and other booty.

11. AGESILAUS, having heard that the Thebans had secured the pass at Scolos, ordered all the embassies from Greece to continue at Thespiæ, and commanded them to store there the forage for the army. The Thebans, informed of this, marched their forces, which were posted at the pass at Scolos, against Thespiæ, in order to intercept whatever might be intended for that station. Whilst Agesilaus after a two days march found the post at Scolos deserted, which he passed undisputed.

12. THE Thebans, when Agesilaus was ravaging their country, possessed themselves of a hill, by Nature almost inaccessible, called the Seat of Rhea where he could not engage them but at a great disadvantage, nor penetrate any further into the country, till he had dislodged them. He made a feint therefore of drawing off his forces, and marching directly against Thebes which was at that time quite evacuated The Thebans, afraid for their city, abandoned their advantageous post, and hasted to the defence of it, whilst Agesilaus passed the hill without opposition

13 AT

13 At the battle of Leuctra, many of the Lacedæmonians having thrown down their arms, and deserted their ranks, that so great a body might not be branded with infamy, Agesilaus procured himself to be appointed a temporary legislator In that capacity, not venturing to unhinge the constitution so far as to establish any new laws, he only for the time dispensed with the execution of the old ones, leaving them after the battle of Leuctra to remain in full force

14. A sedition happening at Sparta, and a great part of the soldiery having possessed themselves of the sacred mountain of Diana Issoria nigh Pitane, while the united forces of the Thebans and Arcadians at the same time pressed hard upon them, a general consternation took place amidst the tumults of war and sedition, Agesilaus, whose resolution and promptitude of thought in the most general confusion never forsook him, considered, that to endeavour to force them to obedience, would in their present circumstances be dangerous, and to supplicate and intreat them, a diminution of his authority. Going therefore to the mountain alone and unarmed, with an intrepid and unsuspecting countenance, he called out, "My lads, you have mistaken my orders, you therefore to that mountain, ' pointing to another place,' and you post yourselves there take your respective stations, and rest on your arms" Supposing him ignorant of their intention of mutiny, they obeyed, and marched to the several stations he assigned them But as soon as night came on, he disposed of twelve of the ringleaders in different places, and thus quashed the sedition

15 The army being in great distress, and numbers every day deserting, to conceal from the rest of the army the number of deserters, Agesilaus sent men in the night through the different quarters of the camp, with orders to gather up all the shields that were cast away, and bring them to him left the shield being found, should betray the desertion of its master. By this means, no shields being afterwards seen, the

the defertion of the troops was not perceived, and the army refumed their courage

16 AGESILAUS lay a long time before Phocis, without being able to carry the city, nor could he well difpenfe with the lofs of time, the fiege was likely to coft him The Phocian allies on the other hand were no lefs weary of the fiege, than he was. He therefore ordered his army to ftrike their tents, and retreated. Upon this retreat of the enemy, the allies gladly received their difcharge: of which Agefilaus having notice returned, and made an eafy conqueft of the city thus evacuated by the allies.

17 HAVING occafion to march through Macedonia, Agefilaus fent an embaffy to king Æropus, to treat with him for a free paffage But the Macedonian, who had received intimation of the weaknefs of the Lacedæmonian cavalry, refufed to enter into any treaty with him. and, ordering his own cavalry to take the field, returned anfwer, that he would meet him in perfon. Agefilaus therefore, to make a greater fhew of cavalry than he really had, ordered the infantry to form the firft line, and behind them he placed all the horfe he could mufter up, difpofing them in a double phalanx. and increafing the number with affes, mules, and fuch horfes as, being paft fervice, were ufed only for drawing the baggage. Soldiers mounted upon thefe, and equipped in compleat horfe armour, gave the appearance of a numerous cavalry. And ftruck with fo formidable a force, Æropus concluded a league with the Lacedæmonians, allowing them a free paffage through his dominions.

18 WHILE the army was encamped in Bæotia, Agefilaus obferving the allies averfe to an engagement, and continually flipping away, difpatched private orders to Orchomenus, a city in the alliance, whither they withdrew themfelves, to admit none of the allies into their city, without orders from him. Finding therefore no place of refuge, they no longer confulted for their fafety by flight, but victory.

STRATAGEMS OF WAR.

19. In an engagement with the Lacedæmonians the Thebans being hard preffed endeavoured to cut their way through the Lacedæmonian phalanx. The engagement continued obftinate, and the carnage on both fides was great: when Agefilaus commanded his troops to act upon the defenfive, and open their ranks: which gave the Thebans an opportunity of breaking through, who immediately betook themfelves to flight. Agefilaus then fell upon their rear, and, without further lofs to himfelf, obtained a compleat and cheap victory over the flying foe.

20. In another engagement with the Bæotians, obferving the allies to be on the point of giving ground, Agefilaus ordered a retreat which was made through a narrow defile of mountains, the Lacedæmonians leading the van: there he halted, and the enemy falling upon his rear, the allies had no alternative but to conquer, or die.

21. AGESILAUS having invaded Bæotia, ordered the allies to deftroy the timber, and lay wafte the country: but obferving their negligence and remiffnefs in executing his orders, he commanded them to defift from further ravages, at the fame time removing his camp three or four times a day. In confequence of thefe manœuvres, they became obliged to cut down wood for the purpofe of erecting their tents: And thus were they compelled by neceffity to do what their general's orders, and the injury the enemy would thereby fuftain, could not prevail upon them to effect.

22. AGESILAUS, acting in Egypt as an ally to Nectanebus, they were in a little fpot of ground hemmed in, and blockaded. The Egyptian, impatient at feeing himfelf thus immured, was inftant with Agefilaus to hazard an engagement. But he continued inflexible to his purpofe, waiting till his little army was furrounded with a wall and trench, one fmall gap only remaining, which looked like a gateway into the inclofure. Agefilaus then calling out, "Now is the time for courage!" fallied out at the portal, vigoroufly attacked, and

routed

routed the enemy, the enclosure serving as a fortification to prevent them from being surrounded by superiority of numbers

23. A BATTLE was fought between the Lacedæmonians and Thebans, in which the victory was doubtful, the night only determining the dispute. Agesilaus dispatched in the night a party of soldiers, on whom he could depend, with orders to bring off from the field, or secretly bury, all the Spartans they could find; which having accomplished they retired into the camp before day. The enemy perceiving by day-light, that almost all the dead were Thebans, lost their spirits and alacrity, presuming they had received a signal defeat.

24. AGESILAUS, returning from his Asiatick expedition, marched through Bæotia, when the Thebans, endeavouring to harrass him in his march, possessed themselves of the defiles through which he was obliged to pass. Upon this he formed his army into a double phalanx, and in that disposition gave publick orders to direct their march to Thebes. Terrified lest he should surprise the city in their absence, the Thebans instantly quitted their posts, and returned with all the expedition they could to protect it. leaving Agesilaus to pursue his march unmolested.

25. THE Thebans, to prevent the irruption of Agesilaus into their territories, fortified their camp. on either side of which was a narrow defile. Agesilaus, forming his army into a square and hollow column, advanced against the pass on the left. on which having drawn the enemy's whole attention, he privately detached small bodies of troops from his rear, who possessed themselves of the other pass without opposition. and through that he entered the Theban territories, and ravaged them at discretion.

26. WHILE Agesilaus was encamped against Lampsacum; there came to him some sick revolters from the mines. who told in the camp, that the Lampsacenians had destined to the mines all the prisoners they should take. This so enraged the army, that they advanced

to

to the very walls of the city, determined to storm and plunder it. Agesilaus, unable to repress their fury, and yet inclined to save the city, pretended to join in the general resentment, and ordered his troops immediately to destroy all the neighbouring vineyards, as being the property of the principal citizens. While the troops were thus employed, he found means to apprise the Lampsacenians of their danger, and to put them on their guard against the intended attack.

27. WHILE the Lacedæmonians and Thebans were encamped against each other on opposite sides of the Eurotas, Agesilaus finding the Lacedæmonians eager to pass the river, and dreading the superiour force of the enemy, industriously propagated a report, that the oracle had declared, the army would be routed, that first crossed the river. Thus restraining the ardour of the Lacedæmonians, he left a few of the allies under the command of their general Symmachus the Thasian, to guard the passage of the Eurotas, at the same time ordering him, as soon as the enemy attempted to cross the river, to retreat with precipitation, directing his rout to some hollow ways, where he had placed an ambuscade: himself in the mean time taking a strong position with the Lacedæmonian veterans. The Thebans, observing the small force that was left under Symmachus to dispute their passage, assumed confidence, and crossed the river; and while they pursued the troops, that according to their instructions fled before them, they fell into the ambuscade, and lost six hundred men.

28. AGESILAUS having marched into Messenia, dispatched a spy, who returned with intelligence, that not only the Messenians had quitted the city, resolved to oppose him, but even their wives and children, and the slaves, who were manumitted on the occasion. He therefore gave up the enterprise, observing, that men in desperation would always fight with most determined courage.

29. WHEN the Lacedæmonians were blocked up in their city by the Thebans, indignant at being cooped within their walls with

the women, determined to sally out, and by a glorious attempt either conquer, or die. Agesilaus dissuaded them from the rash design, reminding them, that they once had thus blocked up the Athenians: who, instead of throwing away their lives in such a wild attempt, manned their walls, and defended the city, till wearied out with opposition and delay, they had themselves been compelled to raise the siege, and evacuate the country.

30. AGESILAUS, returning from Asia with great spoils, was harassed by the enemy, who annoyed him with their arrows and darts. He therefore flanked his army with the prisoners, whom unwilling to sacrifice, the barbarians desisted from future attacks.

31. THE city Menda, which was in the interest of the Athenians, Agesilaus surprised by night, and possessed himself of the strongest part of it. The Mendensians enraged, and determined to dispute the post with him, "What occasion," said he, standing up and haranguing them, "for so much rage and resentment? one half of you are in the conspiracy, that betrayed the city to me." The Mendensians thus made to suspect each other, submitted to the victor's terms without further resistance.

32. IT was the practice of Agesilaus, to restore without ransom to their countries those captives, who had powerful connections in their respective states; in order to lessen their consequence and power to excite innovations, by creating a suspicion of their fidelity in the minds of their fellow citizens.

33. IN the embassies Agesilaus received, he always made it a requisition, that the enemy should depute persons of the first consequence in the state. When living with them on terms of friendship, and politely treating them, among the common people he raised suspicions of their disaffection, and thus promoted sedition in their respective cities.

CHAP.

CHAP. II.

CLEARCHUS

CLEARCHUS at the head of a numerous army having advanced to a river, in one place so easily fordable that the water would not reach higher than the knees, and in another so deep as to be breast-high, endeavoured first to effect a passage where the water was shallowest. But finding it roughly disputed with slings and arrows, he marched his heavy-armed troops to the spot, where the river was deepest. The greatest part of their bodies being there concealed beneath the water, and that which was above covered with their shields, they crossed it without loss, and forced the enemy to retreat, while the remaining part of the army passed the shallow ford without opposition.

2. AFTER the death of Cyrus, Clearchus retreating with the Grecian forces encamped in a neighbourhood that abounded with provisions. Thither Tisaphernes sent ambassadors, assuring them of his permission to continue unmolested there, on giving up their arms. Clearchus pretended so great attention to the embassy, as induced Tisaphernes, depending on a treaty taking place, to disband part of his army, and send his troops into quarters. After which the Greeks struck their tents in the night, and in an unremitted march of a day and night got so far start of the Persian, that before he could collect his dispersed troops, they were entirely out of his reach.

3. CLEARCHUS requested Cyrus not to expose himself to danger, but to post himself at a distance, as a spectator of the engagement representing to him, that a single man by mere bodily strength could be of little consequence in determining an action, whereas if he fell in battle, they must all fall with him. He then advanced slowly with the Greeks in a close firm phalanx, the exact order of whose march struck

terror into the enemy. And as soon as they approached within reach of their javelins, he ordered them, as fast as they could run, to close. And by this manœuvre the Greeks were superior to the Persians in every action.

4. AFTER the death of Cyrus, the Greeks were left in possession of a large and rich tract of country, which was so surrounded by a river, that, but for one narrow isthmus, it was perfectly insular. Clearchus finding it difficult to prevent them from encamping in the peninsula, dispatched to the camp a pretended deserter, who informed them that the king had it in contemplation to draw a wall across the isthmus, and hem them in. The Greeks took the alarm, acceded to Clearchus's measures, and encamped without the isthmus.

5. RETURNING from an expedition with great treasures, Clearchus was surprised by a superiour force on a mountain, upon which he had posted himself. While the enemy were drawing a trench round the mountain, he was inceffantly importuned by his officers to engage, before they were quite blocked up. Have a little patience, replied the chief. And as soon as the evening approached, in the most incompleat part of the trench he depofited his baggage and booty; and on that, as a narrow pass, engaged the enemy, thereby defeating the advantage which their superiourity of numbers gave them.

6. CLEARCHUS returning with the spoils he had taken from Thrace, and not being able to make good his retreat to Byzantium, encamped near the Thracian mountains: and expecting that the Thracians would from thence pour down and attack him in the night, he ordered his troops to lay on their arms, and in the course of the night frequently to rouse themselves. In order to make trial of their readiness to receive a sudden attack, he chose a very dark night, and in the midst of it at the head of a small detachment appeared before his own camp, his men brandishing and striking their arms against each other in the Thracian manner. His troops, taking them for the enemy, immediately

ately formed, to receive them. The Thracians in the mean time in reality advanced, in hopes to surprise them asleep who being drest and in arms, received the assailants, and, unprepared as they were for so ready and vigorous a resistance, defeated them with great slaughter

7. AFTER the revolt of the Byzantines, Clearchus, though condemned by the Ephori, prosecuted the expedition against the Thracians, and with four ships arrived at Lampsacum where he apparently lived in a loose and dissipated manner To him the Byzantines applied for assistance against the Thracians, by whom they were closely pressed. Pretending a severe fit of the gout, it was three days before he admitted the Byzantine ambassadors to an audience when he told them, he was very sorry for their situation, and assured them of the assistance they required Accordingly manning two ships, besides the four he had with him, he set sail for Byzantium There he debarked his own troops, and addressing himself to an assembly of the people, advised them to embark on board his ships all their cavalry and effective men, and, in order to divert the attention of the enemy from the city, to fall upon their rear. At the same time he directed the masters of the vessels, as soon as they saw him give the signal for battle, immediately to weigh anchor. The troops embarked, and the signal given, the vessels were immediately under sail when Clearchus, pretending to be thirsty, and observing a tavern close by, desired the Byzantine generals to step in with him. And posting a party of his men at the door, he massacred the generals, and enjoined the master of the tavern, on risk of his life, not to suffer the transaction to transpire, till taking advantage of the absence of the citizens, who were busied in forwarding the embarkation, he introduced his own troops, and made himself master of the city

8. THE Thracians sent ambassadors to Clearchus, who had carried terror and devastation through their country, to solicit peace. But averse to it on any terms, as an inexpedient measure, he ordered the

cooks

cooks to cut in pieces two or three Thracian bodies, and hang them up enjoining them, if any Thracians asked what it meaned, to tell them they were to be got ready for Clearchus's supper. Struck with horror at such acts as that, the Thracian ambassadors took their leave, without ever opening their commission.

9. CLEARCHUS, finding his infantry much galled by the enemy's horse, formed his army into platoons*, each platoon covering a more than usual space, and ordered them, lowering their shields, under cover of them, with their swords to dig ditches as large as they readily and conveniently could. As soon as this was effected, he advanced beyond the ditches into the plain that lay before them, directing his troops, as soon as they were pressed by the enemy's cavalry, to retreat behind the ditches they had made. The horse pushing eagerly after them, fell one over another into the ditches, and became an easy sacrifice to the troops of Clearchus.

10. WHEN Clearchus was in Thrace, his army was harrassed with groundless apprehensions of nocturnal attacks: to re-establish therefore that tranquillity in his camp, which was thus disturbed by continual tumults and confusion, he ordered, that if any tumult should arise, not a man should stir, and if any one rose and left his tent, that he should be killed as an enemy. These orders effectually dissipated all apprehensions of a nocturnal surprise, and quiet and tranquillity again took place.

---

* I have ventured thus to translate the Greek πλινθιον, though perhaps the platoon may not exactly answer to the πλινθιον, which signifies a brick or tile: a quadrilateral figure, whose opposite sides were equal, its length extended towards the enemy, and exceeding its depth.

CHAP. III.

EPAMINONDAS.

PHÆBIADES, prefect of the tower, conceived a paffion for the wife of Epaminondas, who informed her hufband of the advances he had made to her. Epaminondas directed her to diffemble with the lover, and to invite him to fupper. defiring him at the fame time to bring fome friends with him, to whom fhe promifed to introduce ladies as eafy and complying as herfelf. According to engagement Phæbiades and his company came, and found every thing agreeable to their wifhes. After having fupped, and drank freely, the ladies defired leave to retire, in order to attend an evening facrifice, and promifed to return. The requeft was complied with, and the porters were ordered again to introduce them. They accordingly left the company, and gave their drefs to fome beardlefs youths, whom one of the women attending back to the porters, they, after a fhort converfation with her, introduced to the company. The young men, according to their inftructions, immediately difpatched both Phæbiades and his companions*.

2 WHEN Epaminondas advanced to Leuctræ, the Thefpians difcovered a difinclination to engage which he plainly obferved, but to avoid any confufion in the army by their defertion, at the inftant of attack, ordered proclamation to be made, that whoever of the Bœotians wifhed to leave the field, fhould have liberty to do it. The Thefpians, armed as they were, took advantage of the proclamation,

---

* This whole relation has many marks of fpurioufnefs. It is no ftratagem of war, but a pretended anecdote of Epaminondas. It mentions the wife of that illuftrious chief, who was never married as well as the ignoble death of Phæbiades, who died gallantly fighting againft the Thebans

... ... while Epaminondas with the determined troops, that remained with him, obtained a glorious and splendid victory.

2. Epaminondas having made an irruption into Peloponnesus, found the enemy encamped at Mount Onæum. A violent storm of ... happened at the time, which greatly intimidated the army. The augur declared against engaging. "It is the very time," said Epaminondas ... the thunder, plainly signifying the confusion of the army ... That ... the general gave to the phænomenon, inspired confidence in the soldiers, who with eagerness advanced to the attack.

3. In the engagement at Leuctra, Epaminondas commanded the Thebans, and Cleombrotus the Lacedæmonians. Victory remained long in suspence: when Epaminondas called on his troops, to give him one step more, and he would ensure the victory. They did so: and obtained it. The Spartan king Cleombrotus was killed in the action, and the Lacedæmonians left the enemy masters of the field.

5. In a successful expedition against the Lacedæmonians, Epaminondas had it in his power to have taken Lacedæmon: but retreated from before the city without availing himself of the advantage he possessed. His colleagues threatening to bring him to account for his conduct, he shewed them the Arcadians, the Messenians, the Argives, and other Peloponnesians. 'If,' said he, 'we were to extirpate the Lacedæmonians, all these would become our enemies, who are now our allies, not for the sake of aggrandising Thebes, but to check the Spartan power.'

6. Epaminondas used to encourage the Thebans to try their strength with the Lacedæmonians, who lived amongst them, in wrestling and boxing: and in those exercises easily mastering them, they conceived a contempt for the people, and thus learned to meet them in the field with confident superiority.

7. While in Peloponnesus, Epaminondas constantly drew up his army as for action at sun-rise: thereby impressing the enemy with a

persuasion

persuasion that he meant to try it openly with them in the field. Deceived by this feint, he attacked them in the night, quite unprepared to receive him.

8. At the memorable action between the Lacedæmonians and their allies, commanded by Cleombrotus, and the Thebans under the conduct of Epaminondas, the Theban general contrived by two devices to support the spirit of his troops, alarmed at the superior force of the enemy, whose army amounted to forty thousand men. When they marched out of the city, he prepared a man to meet them, an entire stranger, with a garland on his head, and dressed with ribbands, who told them he was commissioned by Trophonius to inform them, that the victory would be their's, who began the attack. The Thebans, religiously impressed with this declaration of the oracle, Epaminondas then ordered to pay their vows at the temple of Hercules: after having previously instructed the priests to open the temple by night, take out the rusty arms that lay there, furbish them up, and place them before the statue of the god, after that with their attendants to quit the place, and apprise nobody of what was done. No sooner had the soldiers and their officers entered the temple, which they found open, without any servant attending, and the old rusty arms new furbished, bright and gleaming, than they raised their acclamations to the god, and advanced to battle, in confidence that they fought under the auspices of Hercules. The event corresponded with the confidence they had assumed: and with a fifth of the number, they defeated an army of forty thousand men.

9. To prevent an irruption that Epaminondas attempted into Lacedæmonia, a body of Spartans were detached to secure the pass by the Onæan mountains: before which Epaminondas halted, and pretended immediately to attempt to force it. The Lacedæmonians continued all night under arms, ready to receive him: who on the contrary, giving orders to his men to refresh and repose themselves, deferred his attack

till

till the next morning, when striking his tents, he engaged the enemy sleeping and weary for want of the night's rest, easily defeated them, and forced the pass.

10. Epaminondas once attempted by an assault in the night to possess himself of the city of Lacedæmon, in the absence of the Lacedæmonian forces. But Agesilaus, by some deserters being informed of his design, by a forced march threw himself with a body of troops into the town, and being there prepared to receive the enemy repulsed them with great loss. Amidst the confusion that ensued in the Theban army, routed by night and vigorously pressed by the Lacedæmonians, many threw away their shields, which Epaminondas observing, in order to conceal their disgrace, directed the troops to deliver up their shields to the keepers of the baggage, and themselves to attend the general only with their swords and spears. This ingratiated him with those who had thrown away their arms, and who, in return for that act of favour, were most alert in executing his commands.

11. In an engagement between the Thebans and Lacedæmonians, night coming on, and the victory remaining undetermined, both armies retreated to their respective camps. The Lacedæmonians, who encamped in regular order, with their proper regiments, and companies, missing their comrades, became acquainted with their loss, and went under great discouragement and concern to rest. Epaminondas, on the contrary, ordered the Thebans, without regard to their particular regiment, or company, to sup as quick as they could, in whatever tent they happened to gain, and to supply each other with such provisions as they found at hand. Immediately after supper, they repaired to sleep, which was the sounder, as not being disturbed by the known loss of their comrades. The next morning they marched to the attack, well refreshed and in full spirits, and obtained an easy victory over the enemy, faint and dispirited by the loss of their friends, and like an army that had already suffered a defeat.

12. When Epaminondas took the field against the Lacedæmonians and

and their allies, whose army amounted to forty thousand men. observing his troops, as might be expected, alarmed at the great superiourity of the enemy, by various stratagems he endeavoured to keep up their spirits. There was in the temple of Pallas at Thebes a statue of the goddess holding a spear in her right hand, and before her knees lay a shield. In the night he introduced an artist into the temple, who altered the statue, and made her in her left hand hold the handle of the shield. In the morning, before the troops marched out, he ordered the temples to be all thrown open, on pretence of performing some offices of religion, before he went to battle. The soldiers remarked with astonishment the change in the goddess's appearance, which they considered as an assurance of her immediate protection. In a studied harangue on the occasion, Epaminondas used every argument to support the impression and the Thebans engaged with such confidence of success, that closing with the enemy sword in hand, they obtained against a great advantage in numbers, a compleat and brilliant victory.

13. WHILE the Thessalians were drawn up on the opposite side of the river Sperchius in order to dispute the Theban's passage over the bridge, Epaminondas, observing in the morning a cloud rise from the east of the river, commanded his men to carry every one of them two faggots of wood, one green and the other dry, and at midnight to set fire to the dry one, and lay the green one at the top of it. The night, the clouds, and the smoke so obscured the air, that Epaminondas marched his army over the bridge undiscovered, nor till the smoke and clouds were dispersed, did the Thessalians know the Theban army had crossed the bridge, who then presented themselves in order of battle on the open plain.

14. To gain the advantage of ground against the Lacedæmonians, Epaminondas ordered his general of the horse, with sixteen hundred of the cavalry, to ride up and down, advancing a small distance before the army. Having by this means raised a cloud of dust, which prevented

the

the enemy from observing his motions, he filed off, and took possession of the higher ground. His position soon explained to the Lacedæmonians, what before they could not account for, the advanced movements of the cavalry.

15. To excite the Thebans to a vigorous attack on the Lacedæmonians, Epaminondas produced a great snake, and before the army, bruising its head, 'Crush but the head,' said he, 'and you see how impotent is the rest of the body. Thus let us but bruise the head of the confederacy, that is the Lacedæmonians, and the power of the allies will be insignificant.' The Thebans felt the force of his observation, attacked and routed the Lacedæmonian troops, and the whole body of the allies immediately gave way and fled.

CHAP. IV.

PELOPIDAS

PELOPIDAS advanced against two fortified towns of the Magnesians, distant about an hundred and twenty furlongs from each other. Upon approaching one, he ordered some horsemen, with chaplets on their head, on full speed to ride up to him, and inform him that the other city was taken. This intelligence as soon as he received, he desisted from his present enterprise, and marched to the city which was supposed to have been taken. As soon as he came before the walls of it, he directed a great fire to be kindled, the smoke of which being seen in the other city, confirmed the people in their suspicion of that city being taken, and burnt; and therefore to avoid the same calamity on the return of Pelopidas, they opened their gates, and surrendered the city to him. With the forces he took in that town, he then advanced against the other, who, convinced of the fate of that already taken, ventured to hold out no longer, but surrendered theirs also to the conquerour.

2 PELO-

2. PELOPIDAS, not having time to cross a river in his retreat from Theffaly, the enemy preffing fo clofe upon his rear, encamped by the fide of it, and in front of the enemy entrenched himfelf as ftrongly as the time would permit. Then directing a great quantity of wood to be cut down, and laid in the trenches, he ordered his troops to reft About midnight he fet the wood on fire, which burning very brifkly, interrupted the purfuit of the enemy, and gave him an opportunity of paffing the river unmolefted

3 A LACEDÆMONIAN garrifon having been impofed on Thebes, the commander of it fixed his quarters in the tower It happened to be the feaft of Venus which the women celebrate with great feftivity, while the men as fpectators attend To do honour to the goddefs, the captain of the garrifon ordered fome proftitutes to be introduced among whom entered Pelopidas, with a dagger concealed under his veft, flew the captain of the garrifon, and delivered Thebes from the tyranny of the foe.

CHAP. V.

GORGIAS

GORGIAS was the perfon, who firft inftituted the facred band. It confifted of thirty*, devoted to each other by mutual obligations of love And fuch was the effect of the paffion, they had conceived for each other, that they were fcarcely ever known to fly but either died for each other, or gallantly conquered

2 GORGIAS, who commanded a detachment of cavalry, having fallen in with a body of heavy-armed troops under the command of Phæbidis on a confined piece of ground, ordered a retreat, as if

* It fhould be *three hundred*, which is the number of the *facred band*.

unable

unable to suftain the attack of the heavy-armed troops. The enemy continued to prefs clofely on him, till he had at laft drawn them to an open plain. When Gorgias, hoifting up a helmet on the top of a fpear, gave a fignal to his troops to face about. The impreffion of the cavalry, as foon as they had room to act, the heavy-armed troops were no longer able to fuftain, but abandoned themfelves to flight many were flain in the rout, and Phœbidas amongft others, with difficulty efcaped to Thefpia.

CHAP. VI.

DERCYLLIDAS.

DERCYLLIDAS pledged himfelf with an oath to Medias the tyrant of Scepfis, that if he would come forth to a conference with him, he fhould have free liberty to return into the city. The tyrant accordingly advanced to meet him. At that conference Dercyllidas ordered him on peril of his life to direct the gates to be opened. Thus intimidated, he gave the orders impofed on him, and the gates were thrown open. "Now," faid Dercyllidas, "return into your city: for that I engaged to you. But I and my army will enter too."

CHAP. VII.

ALCETAS.

ALCETAS the Lacedæmonian, having planned an expedition from Iftiæa, in order to conceal his ftrength, embarked part of his forces on board one trireme, which he ordered to manœuvre in fight of the enemy. When taking his opportunity, he privately failed with

his

his whole force, consisting of three triremes, and possessed himself of all the enemy's stores.

CHAP. VIII.

ARCHILAIDAS.

ARCHILAIDAS the Lacedæmonian pursuing his rout through a suspicious country, where he thought it very probable ambuscades might be formed to intercept him, though he had received no intelligence of any, signified it to his army as a fact, of which he had been apprised, and ordered them therefore to march in order of battle. His apprehensions were eventually verified, a strong force having been placed in ambush to surprise him. whom he instantly attacked, and unprepared to receive the Lacedæmonians, as not suspecting any preparation for action on their side, easily cut to pieces.

CHAP. IX.

ISIDAS.

IN consequence of the fatal battle at Leuctra, the Thebans having placed a garrison at Gythium, a port of the Lacedæmonians, Isidas associated with him a hundred youths of his acquaintance; who oiling* themselves, bound chaplets of olive on their temples, and, concealing under their arms a dagger, run naked upon the plain, Isidas being first, and the rest following him. And while the Thebans, deceived by their appearance, supposed they were only entertaining themselves with

* It was a practice both with the Greeks and Romans, previous to exercises of agility, such as running, wrestling, &c. to oil their limbs, in order to render them more pliant and flexile.

spot, the Lacedæmonians with sword in hand fell upon them, killed some, and, expelling the rest from the town, regained the possession of Gythium.

CHAP. X.

CLEANDRIDAS

IN an expedition against Terenus, Cleandridas marched his army under cover of a hollow way, in order to surprise the city. But the Terenensians, apprised by deserters of his design, marched out, and shewed themselves on the eminences above him. His troops were disheartened at the advantageous position, when Cleandridas called out, "Courage, my lads," and then ordered a herald to proclaim aloud, "Let those of the Terenensians, who can, answer the signal agreed on, and they will be safe." The Terenensians, induced by this proclamation to suppose themselves betrayed, precipitately retreated, in order to secure the city, leaving Cleandridas to pursue his march in safety, who, after having ravaged the country, retreated without molestation.

2. CLEANDRIDAS, the Thurian, after having defeated the Leucanians, led the Thurians to the field of battle, and there observed to them, on the spot where they had been posted, the close and compact manner in which they fought, and to which he told them they owed the victory; while the enemy, quitting their posts, and loosening their ranks, were not able to sustain their united shock. While he was thus haranguing them, the Leucanians had rallied, and with a considerable accession of force were advancing against him. Cleandridas retreated to a confined and narrow spot, where the enemy's superiority of numbers was rendered useless, and his own troops extended a front equal to theirs. By this manœuvre the Leucanians received a second defeat.

3. To increase the suspicions, that were entertained by the Tegeates against

against their chiefs, as being secretly in the interest of the Lacedæmonians, Cleandridas, when he ravaged the country, from all devastation scrupulously exempted their estates. Distinguished by such marks of the enemy's attention, they were immediately charged with treason and, finding the resentment of the people run high against them, for fear of being punished by a false imputation of treason, became really guilty of it, and betrayed to him the city: thus necessitated for their own preservation to realize a false suspicion.

4. IN the Leucanian war, Cleandridas, after having defeated the enemy with half their number, apprehensive that he should not be able again to bring them to an action, if they knew his strength, presented a narrow front, forming the phalanx in depth. The Leucanians, despising the supposed inferiority of his numbers, thought of nothing but how to prevent the escape of the enemy: and accordingly extended their ranks, in order to surround them. After they had by this motion precluded their own retreat, Cleandridas ordered his officers to extend their cohorts as wide as they could, and thereby surrounded the Leucanians, who were all cut to pieces, except a few, who basely saved themselves by flight.

5. CLEANDRIDAS always dissuaded a regular engagement against a superiour force: observing, that when the lion's skin was not sufficient, it was necessary to sew to it the fox's tail.

CHAP. XI.

PHARACIDAS.

THE Carthaginians having declared war against the Syracusans, Pharacidas fell in with a Carthaginian squadron, and took nine ships, which, having the enemy's main fleet, of much superiour force, to pass, he manned with his own troops and sailors. The Carthaginians, knowing the ships, and supposing them their friends, suffered them to pass unmolested into the haven of Syracuse.

CHAP. XII.

DEIPHANTES.

DEIPHANTES directed the Dorians, in order to bring the Argives to an action, to ravage their country, and himself at the same time embarked a detachment, with which he landed near a mountain in the vicinity of the Argive camp. A scout was dispatched to give information to the Argives of the depredations the Dorians committed who immediately marched out to engage them. Deiphantes, with his detachment, in the mean time sallied out from his ambuscade, and in the absence of the army took possession of their camp. The parents, children, and wives of the Argives, having thus fallen into the hands of the enemy, to redeem them, they delivered up to the Dorians the country and cities of which they had dispossessed them.

CHAP. XIII.

EURYTION.

EURYTION, King of Sparta, finding the war in which he had engaged against the Arcadians protracted beyond his expectation, in order to throw the city into factions, dispatched a herald to inform them, the Lacedæmonians would raise the siege, if they would banish the guilty. under which term he distinguished those, who had been

concerned

concerned in the destruction of Ægina. Those, accordingly, who had been instrumental in the massacre committed there, apprehensive left they should be sacrificed by the people for the purchase of peace, banded together, on promise of freedom associated with them the slaves, and put to the sword all whom they thought inimical to their party. The city thus divided into two factions, they, whose object was peace, assembled in a particular quarter of the town by themselves, and threw open the gates to the enemy who by the Mantinæan faction obtained what they were unable to effect by force of arms.

CHAP. XIV.

EPHORI.

THE Ephori, having been apprised of a conspiracy, formed by Cynadon, and not thinking it adviseable to seise him in the city, privately dispatched a party of horse to the borders of Lacedæmon, where it was contrived, Cynadon, attended by two soldiers, should be invited to a private conference. As soon as he arrived on the spot, the horse, who had been dispatched for that purpose, seised him, and by torture made him confess the rest of the conspirators. His confession was sent to the Ephori, who ordered them to execution, which, a previous form or trial not being required, was attended with no tumult or confusion.

2. HAVING learned that a riot was intended, the signal of which was to be a cap thrown up in the midst of the forum, the crier was ordered to make this proclamation: "All who are for the cap being thrown up, quit the forum." Accordingly all who were concerned in the intended riot, finding their design was discovered, desisted from the execution of it.

CHAP XV

HIPPODAMAS

WHILE Hippodamas was blocked up by the Arcadians in Praise, and reduced to great straits for want of provisions, the Spartans dispatched to him a courier, whom the Arcadians intercepted, and conducting him to the walls, gave him permission to deliver his dispatches there, but would not suffer him to enter the city. Hippodamas from the walls instantly called out to him, "Tell the Ephori to deliver us from the woman, that is bound in the temple of Chalciœcus." The Arcadians could make nothing of the injunction but the Lacedæmonians understood the deliverance he required, to be from famine. For there hung in the temple of Chalciœcus a picture of Famine, a woman pale, and emaciated, with her hands tied behind her. Thus did Hippodamas so contrive his information, as to keep it secret from the enemy, but render it plain to those for whom it was intended.

CHAP XVI.

GASTRON.

IN the Persian war, Gastron the Lacedæmonian commanding in Ægypt, previous to a battle, made the Græcians and Egyptians change their arms and dress. The Græcians appeared in the Egyptian habit, and the Ægyptians in that of Greece. He drew up the Greeks in the front, and the Ægyptians formed behind, to support them. The Greeks with their accustomed resolution maintained the post of danger,

and

and opening the way before them, the Ægyptians, animated by their example, advanced boldly to the charge. The Persians seeing this, and supposing them also to be Greeks, gave way, and a general rout ensued.

CHAP. XVII.

MEGACLIDAS

MEGACLIDAS, in his retreat before a superiour force, posted himself on a rough and woody mountain, where being closely pressed by the enemy, he divided his army: directing the most cumbrous and useless part of it, to endeavour to make their escape through the woods, knowing the enemy would be apprised of the attempt. And, while they were engaged in pursuit of the fugitives, he with the choicest part of his troops took a different rout, and made good his retreat.

CHAP. XVIII.

HARMOSTES.

HARMOSTES the Lacedæmonian being closely besieged by the Athenians, and having no more than two days provision left, the Spartans dispatched a herald to him: whom the Athenians conducted to the walls, but would not permit him to enter the city. The herald from thence proclaimed aloud, "The Lacedæmonians bid you persist, for you will soon receive relief." To this Harmostes replied, "Tell the Lacedæmonians to be in no hurry, for we have yet six months provision in store." The Athenians, as winter now approached, not caring for a tedious winter campaign, raised the siege, and disbanded their army.

CHAP.

CHAP. XIX.

THIBRON.

THIBRON, having attacked a fort in Asia, prevailed on the governor to meet him, and try if they could negotiate a truce, in which, if they failed, he engaged by oath to reconduct him into the fort. The governor accordingly met him, and the conference was begun during which, the garrison being more remiss through expectation of a truce taking place, the besiegers took advantage of it, and in a vigorous attack carried the fort by storm. Thibron, agreeably to his oath, reconducted the governor to the fort, and there ordered him to be executed.

CHAP. XX.

DEMARATUS

THE intelligence, which Demaratus communicated to the Lacedæmonians, concerning Xerxes's army, he engraved on a tablet, which he afterwards covered with wax: that, if intercepted, no characters might appear.

CHAP. XXI.

ERIPPIDAS.

AS soon as Erippidas arrived at Trachinian Heraclæa, he summoned an assembly, which he surrounded with armed troops, and ordered

dered the Trachinians to be seated by themselves. He then demanded of them an account of their iniquitous practices, as the laws of Sparta in criminal cases required. This done, he ordered the soldiers to chain the offenders, carry them out of the city, and execute them.

CHAP. XXII.

ISCHOLAUS.

ISCHOLAUS observing at Ænos the Athenian fleet in strong force hovering near the coast, and suspecting their intention to cut out some of his ships from the harbour, ordered them to be secured by their masts to a tower, that stood near the ramparts, the ships nearest the strand being fastened immediately to the tower, and the rest to each other. In the night the Athenians made the attempt that Ischolaus suspected: of which the people of Ænos informed by the guard immediately sallied forth, and made great havock among the Athenians both by sea and land.

2. ISCHOLAUS's rout lying through a country, in one part steep and craggy, and full of precipices, while in the other the enemy had advantageously posted themselves on a mountain that commanded the plain below, when the wind was very high, he ordered a quantity of wood to be set on fire. The enemy by the smoak and fire driven from their post, Ischolaus took the advantage, and passed them without loss or danger.

3. ISCHOLAUS, when in Dryes besieged by Chabrias, who was advancing the ram to the walls, himself gave orders for a part of the wall to be demolished: supposing that it would be attended with this double effect, that it would engage his own soldiers to fight more reso-

lutely,

lutely, when they found themselves no longer protected by the wall; and also discourage the enemy from carrying on their works, when they saw how little the besieged depended on their fortifications. And so effectually the stratagem succeeded, that the enemy would not venture to enter a city, where the inhabitants appeared actuated by desperation.

4. HAVING been informed that some of the guard intended to betray the city, then invested by the Athenians, to the enemy, Ischolaus ordered a mercenary to be added to every sentry. And by this manœuvre, without the appearance of suspicion, he prevented the execution of any traiterous design.

CHAP. XXIII.

MNASIPPIDAS.

THE enemy having come up with Mnasippidas, who had a very inferiour force, attacked him in the night. when he ordered his light-armed troops and trumpets to wheel round, and after they had turned the enemy's flank, to sound the charge, and fall upon their rear with a shower of darts. Finding themselves thus attacked both in front and rear, they made a precipitate retreat, apprehending they were in danger of being hemmed in by a numerous army.

CHAP. XXIV.

ANTALCIDAS.

ANTALCYDAS finding, while he lay with a superiour fleet at Abydos, that the Athenian vessels at Tenedos would not venture to join Iphicrates at Byzantium, who, he was informed, had attacked the
Chalce-

Chalcedonians, his allies, gave orders to sail to Chalcedon: but weighing anchor, he took his station near Cyzicum. When the movement of Antalcydas was known at Tenedos, it was determined immediately to sail and join Iphicrates at Byzantium. And as soon as they approached the enemy's fleet, which crowded into a bay were not at a distance discovered, Antalcidas sailed out, and vigorously attacked them: sunk some, and made capture of the rest.

CHAP. XXIV.

AGESIPOLIS.

AT the siege of Mantinæa, which was conducted by Agesipolis, the Lacedæmonian forces were joined by their allies, who, though well affected to the Mantinæans, were obliged to attend the Lacedæmonians in that expedition, as being masters of Greece. Agesipolis having received intelligence, that the allies secretly supplied the besieged with whatever they occasionally wanted, to prevent such intercourse in future, let loose a number of dogs about the camp, and particularly about that part of it, which fronted the city. This stopped the correspondence, no one venturing to pass between the camp and the city, for fear of being discovered by the barking of the dogs.

CHAP. XXVI.

STHENIPPUS.

STHENIPPUS the Lacedæmonian, pretending resentment at having been fined by the Ephori, retired to the Tegeates, who readily received him. And while he resided there, he found means to bribe a party, that were inimical to Aristocles the prince, and by their assistance, when he was going to attend a sacrifice, fell upon him, and slew him.

CHAP. XXVII.

CALLICRATIDAS.

CALLICRATIDAS the Cyrenæan desired the præfect of the tower of Magnesia, to receive four of his sick which request being complied with, four persons in compleat armour, and with swords under their vests, laid themselves down upon beds, and twenty young men, with arms concealed, carried the litters As soon as they were introduced within the walls, they fell upon the centinels, and slew them, and made themselves masters of the fort

2. When Callicratidas was besieged at Magnesia, and the enemy were proceeding to advance the battering-ram; at a place, least accessible to the assailants, he directed a breach to be made in the walls and while the enemy's attention was engaged in the quarter where they directed the attack, he passed the breach, and in a vigorous sortie falling on their rear, repulsed them with great loss, and made no small number prisoners After his return to the city, he repaired the breach he had directed to be made in the walls of which the enemy had been too warmly engaged to take advantage.

CHAP. XXVIII.

MAGAS.

WHEN Magas left Cyrene, to proceed on a foreign expedition; he committed to his friends the charge of the city. But the darts and
other

other weapons of war he fecured in the tower, and difmantled the walls That, in his abfence if any innovations fhould be attempted, he might fecure an eafy entrance into it on his return.

2 MAGAS, having made himfelf mafter of Parætonium, directed the watch to kindle fires in the light-houfe both in the evening, and early in the morning, as if he were there And by this deception he penetrated unmolefted into the country, as far as the place that is called Chius.

CHAP. XXIX.

CLEONYMUS.

CLEONYMUS, King of Lacedæmon, at the fiege of Trœzenes, pofted againft different parts of the city expert dartfmen, and ordered them to hurl into the town javelins with this infcription "I am come to affert the liberties of Trœzenes" The Trœzenians alfo, whom he had taken prifoners, he fent home without ranfom. that they might communicate to their fellow citizens the happy intelligence Eudamidas, however, an officer of experience, and of indefatigable attention, warmly oppofed his interefts And while the different factions were engaged in animofities and contention within the gates, Cleonymus fcaled the walls, made himfelf mafter of the city, and impofed on it a Spartan garrifon.

2. AT the fiege of Edeffa, when a breach was effected in the walls, and the fpear-men, (whofe fpears were fixteen cubits long) fallied out upon the affailants, Cleonymus deepened his phalanx, and ordered the front line to ufe no arms, but with both hands to feize the enemy's fpears, and hold them faft, while the next rank immediately advanced, and clofed upon them. Their fpears thus feized, the men retreated;

retreated, but the next rank, preffing on them, either took them prifoners, or flew them. By this manœuvre of Cleonymus the long and formidable fpear was rendered ufelefs, and became rather an incumbrance, than a weapon of offence.

CHAP. XXX.

CLEARCHUS.

IN order to procure a tower to be erected in Heraclæa, Clearchus directed the mercenaries to fteal out by night, and to plunder, rob, maim, and do all the mifchief they could. Under thofe injuries the citizens complained to Clearchus, and begged his protection who told them, it was impoffible to prevent the depredations of the troops otherwife than by confining them within walls, a meafure he wifhed to recommend to them. They confented to his propofal, and marked out a part of the city, where he raifed a wall, and erected a tower which however were no protection to them, but fecured to him a power of committing every irregularity he pleafed.

2. CLEARCHUS, tyrant of Heraclæa, gave out, that he intended to difmifs his guards, and reftore the republic into the hands of the THREE HUNDRED who accordingly met at the fenate houfe, to make their acknowledgments to him for the reftoration of their liberty. Thither he repaired, and, placing an armed force at the fenate door, directed the crier to call them out and, the foldiers feizing them one by one, he ordered them all to be conveyed to the tower.

3. CLEARCHUS, fufpecting the number of citizens too great for the fafety of his government, and having no pretence to rid himfelf of them, undertook an expedition againft the city Afticum in the midft of the dog-days, compleating his levies, of youths from fixteen years of age to twelve. On approaching Afticum, he encamped the citizens

on

on a flat morafs, full of dead and ftagnated waters, and ordered them to watch the motions of the Thracians: while he himfelf with the mercenaries, as if intending to fuftain all the danger of the fiege, took his poft on an eminence, fhaded with wood, and refrefhed with rivulets. In this pofition he protracted the fiege, till he loft all the citizens: the ftagnate waters at that hot feafon neceffarily producing in the camp fatal difeafes. Having thus effected his purpofe, he raifed the fiege, and pretended the citizens died by an infectious difeafe.

CHAP. XXXI.

ARISTOMENES.

ARISTOMENES the Meffenian once ferved in a naval engagement as an ally to Dionyfius: when opening his lines a little, and finding fome of the enemy's fhips in the midft of his divifion, he called out to his officers, "Let them fly." The enemy hearing this, and fuppofing the defeat general, gave up the action, and abandoned themfelves to flight.

2. AFTER three fplendid* victories obtained over the Lacedæmonians, Ariftomenes general of the Meffenians, difabled with wounds, was with many others taken prifoner. They were fentenced by the Lacedæmonians to be all thrown down the precipice, the reft naked, but Ariftomenes, in refpect to his bravery, in arms. The others underwent the fentence, and were killed on the fpot: but the broad fhield of Ariftomenes, being in fome meafure fupported by the air, let him gently down upon the ground. Looking up, he faw nothing above,

* The original is, τρις εκατομφονια θυσας. A literal tranflation would have founded aukwardly in Englifh: but the meaning is, that he had three times facrificed to Mars for having by his own hand flain in an action a hundred of the enemy.

but inacceffible precipices, yet, poffeffing a mind above the pregravation of defpair, he did not relinquifh all hopes of safety. when examining the mountain round, he at laft perceived a cleft, and into it fome foxes enter When breaking off from a dead body a bone, he caught one of the foxes by the tail, and, though feverely bitten by it, would not quit his hold but following it into the cleft, and clearing away the rubbifh with the bone he held in his other hand, he efcaped through the mountain, and arrived at the Meffenian camp, juft as they were going to try the iffue of another battle He immediately armed, and put himfelf at their head The Lacedæmonians, feeing Ariftomenes, whom they had thrown from the precipice, a punifhment from which no one ever efcaped with life, leading the enemy's troops againft them, and again engaging in battle, precipitately quitted the field, flying before him, as a being more than human

3. ARISTOMENES, another time prifoner with the Lacedæmonians, and bound with cords, went fo clofe to a fire that was in the prifon, as to burn the cords, then fell upon the guards, and flew them. And privately entering Sparta, he fixed up their fhields in the temple of Chalciœcus with this infcription, "Ariftomenes has efcaped from the Lacedæmonians unhurt." after which he returned to Meffena

4. UPON the day when the Lacedæmonians made their annual facrifice to Caftor and Pollux, Ariftomenes and a friend, mounted on two white horfes, and ornamented with gold ftars on their heads, as foon as night came on, fhewed themfelves at a little diftance from the Lacedæmonians, who with their wives and children were celebrating the feftival on the plain without the city. They, fuperftitioufly believing them to be Caftor and Pollux, the more freely indulged in wine and paftime. when the two fuppofed deities, alighting from their horfes, advanced with fword in hand amongft them, and, after leaving many dead on the fpot, remounted their horfes, and made their efcape.

CHAP.

CHAP. XXXII.

CINEAS.

IN an engagement between the Thebans and Mantinenfians, both fides claimed the victory: the Mantinenfians however propofed to fend heralds to the Thebans, afking leave to carry off their dead. But Cineas the Athenian, whofe brother Demetrius lay dead in the field, oppofed the propofition: declaring, he would fooner leave his brother without a fepulchre, than give up the honour of the victory to the enemy: " for," added he, " to prevent the enemy from erecting trophies on our's and our country's difgrace, my brother facrificed his life." Moved by the refolution of Cyneas, the Mantinenfians relinquifhed their defign.

CHAP. XXXIII.

HEGETORIDES.

WHILE the Thafians were clofely befieged by the Athenians, and numbers daily perifhed by war and famine, none venturing to propofe a treaty with the enemy on account of a law then in force, which made it a capital offence to propofe a treaty with the Athenians. Hegetorides, putting a rope about his neck, entered the affembly, and thus addreffed them, " Fellow citizens, you will difpofe of me as you think proper, and as may ferve your intereft beft; but in pity to the reft of the citizens, who have hitherto furvived the havock, that famine and the fword have made among us, repeal the law that precludes all deliberations concerning peace." The Thafians took his advice, abfolved Hegetorides, and repealed the law.

CHAP. XVII

DINIAS.

DINIAS the son of Telesippus, by birth a Pherœan, removed to Cranon a city of Thessaly, where he supported himself by catching birds on the lakes and rivers, and there advanced himself from that low station to the sovereignty by the following devices. The Cranonians for the watch and guard of the city used to pay by agreement a certain stipend a year. Dinias took it upon stipulated terms, and for three years performed his office so diligently, that the citizens could walk out more secure in the night, than by day. His conduct in this office gained him great reputation, and to ingratiate himself further with the people, he hired more watchmen, in order to keep every thing in greater security. The collectorship of the tenths of corn being vacant, he persuaded his younger brother, who had then never held any publick office, magnifying it as a very lucrative employment, to hire it. His brother, thus appointed collector, associated with him a number of young men proportionate to the different tracts of land, from whence he was to collect the corn. and on the celebration of a festival, which is called Tænia, when the Cranonians give themselves up to banqueting and merriment, Dinias uniting to his own dependents, the watchmen, the gatherers of corn, that were connected with his brother, with this band of sober men he attacked and easily defeated those who were drunk, slew more than a thousand of the citizens, and assumed the sovereignty of Cranon.

CHAP. XXXV.

NICON.

NICON, a free-booter from Pheræ in Peloponnesus, having in frequent irruptions committed great depredations on the Messenians, Agemachus, their general, at last surprised, and took him. Being brought before their assembly, he engaged to the Messenians, if they would spare his life, to put them in possession of Pheræ To this they agreed: when fixing on a dark night, he took with him a few attendants, with bundles of straw on their shoulders, directing a greater number at a short distance to follow him. About two o'clock in the morning he arrived at the gates, called to the centinels, and gave them the word. Knowing his voice, as well as the word, they instantly opened the gates. and Nicon and his party entering, each threw down his bundle, and drawing their swords slew the centinels, and the rest, rushing in, made themselves masters of the city.

CHAP. XXXVI.

DIÆTAS.

DIÆTAS general of the Achaians, finding himself unable by a regular siege to carry the city of the Heræenses, contrived by stratagem to effect what he had in vain attempted by force of arms. By large bribes he won over some of the citizens to his purpose, who took frequent opportunities of attending the centinels to the gates. and familiarly conversing with them, and treating them with entertainments, they found means to take an impression of the keys, which they sent to Diætas, who had keys made exactly to the pattern. These he sent back to the confederates, directing them to fix a night, when they would open their gates to him. By the device of the keys having with a select body of troops entered the city: Diætas found it necessary to support that device with another. For after the Heræenses had been alarmed, and apprised of what had happened, they sallied forth in great numbers, with the advantage of being well acquainted with every part of the city. Diætas, seeing the appearance of a formidable opposition, dispersed his trumpets in various parts of the city, directing them every where to sound the attack. The Heræenses, hearing the sound of the enemy's trumpets from all sides, and from thence supposing them in possession of every quarter of the town, abandoned the city, and fled. They afterwards sent an embassy to Diætas, requesting permission to return to their own country, and engaging to the Achaians future subjection.

CHAP. XXXVII.

TESAMENUS.

TESAMENUS in his march observing a number of birds hovering over a particular spot, without ever settling, supposed some men in the place, which kept them on the wing. On reconnoitring the ground, he found the Ionians in ambush; whom he attacked, and cut to pieces.

CHAP. XXXVIII.

ONOMARCHUS.

ONAMARCHUS the Phocian, when Elatia was besieged by the Bœotians, ordered all the inhabitants out of the town, and locked the gates.

gates In one rank he placed the fathers, mothers, children, and wives And, ranged before them, he formed in order of battle all that could bear arms. Pelopidas concluding, from such appearance of desperation, that they were determined either to conquer, or die, retreated without hazarding an engagement.

2. WHEN Onomarchus commanded against the Macedonians, he covered his rear with a steep and craggy mountain, and on the tops of it placed in ambush a number of men expert in throwing stones, furnished with huge stones and pieces of jagged rocks for the purpose He then advanced, and formed his army on the plain. The Macedonians began the attack with their javelins, which the Phocians pretending themselves unable to sustain, retreated half way up the mountain. The Macedonians briskly pursued them, till they came within reach of the ambuscade: who then discovered themselves, and with huge stones annoyed the Macedonian phalanx. Onomarchus then gave the signal for the Phocians to face about, and renew the charge. The Macedonians vigorously attacked by the troops next to them, and grievously annoyed by those above, with great difficulty made good a precipitate retreat. on which occasion, Philip king of Macedon is said vauntingly to have cried out, " We do not fly, but retreat like rams, to renew the attack with greater power."

POLY.

POLYÆNUS'S
STRATAGEMS OF WAR.

PREFATORY ADDRESS.

To your moſt ſacred majeſties, Antonius and Verus, I addreſs this Third Book of Stratagems: from whence I truſt ſome advantage may be derived as well by the ſtateſman, as the ſoldier. For to know how to negotiate advantageouſly with an enemy, and to preſerve good government at home, are as much in the province of imperatorial ſcience, as conduct in the field. This is a truth, yourſelves illuſtrate, who, veſted with imperatorial power, and ſovereigns of the world, are ever forming deſigns for the glory and happineſs of your ſubjects, and in the boſom of peace planning operations of war. Your real exploits in the field I forbear to mention; they are known to all the world.

BOOK III. CHAP. I.

DEMOSTHENES.

DEMOSTHENES, finding Pylos, a city of the Lacedæmonians, ſtrongly garriſoned, directed his march to Acra. The Lacedæmonians apprehending what he intended as a feint to be his real deſign, quitted Pylos,

Pylos, and marched with all expedition to Acra, hoping to surprise Demosthenes immediately on his landing. But on their approach thither, Demosthenes expeditiously returned to Pylos, of which evacuated by the garrison he easily made himself master.

2. DEMOSTHENES, when he commanded the Acarnanians and Amphilochians against the Peloponnesians, encamped in front of the enemy, a large torrent parting the camps. Observing the enemy greatly to out-number him, and apprehending their object would be to surround him, in a hollow place aptly formed for an ambuscade he concealed a body of heavy armed troops, with three hundred of the allies: directing them, if the enemy attempted to surround him, to sally forth and fall upon their rear. The Peloponnesians, as he expected, extended their lines, endeavouring to surround the allies: when the ambuscade sallying forth, fell upon their rear, and with ease decided the victory.

CHAP. II.

PACHES.

PACHES, having laid siege to Notium, proposed to Hippias, general of Pissithnus, a conference, engaging to him by oath, that if he would come out and meet him, he should be reconducted into the city alive and safe. Hippias accordingly advanced to meet him: when Paches, leaving him to the care of a guard, took the city by storm, then directed Hippias to be conducted into it, agreeably to his engagement, alive and safe, and afterwards to be executed.

CHAP. III.

TOLMIDAS

THE Athenians, to enable Tolmidas to man a fleet, voted him a compliment of a thousand men, with permission to chuse them. When going up to each of the youths, he told him that he intended to make choice of him, but that it would have a better appearance, if he would give in his name, and offer himself as volunteer. Three thousand accordingly gave in their names. From those therefore, who did not give in their names, Tolmidas chose the thousand, the state had allotted him · and with the three thousand, that had turned out as volunteers, was enabled to man fifty ships with an addition of four thousand men, instead of one thousand.

CHAP. IV.

PHORMIO.

PHORMIO had invaded Chalcis, and brought off some booty, with which he afterwards landed at Cyros. Thither the Chalcidensians sent an embassy to him, demanding a restitution of what they had lost. Having with secresy and dispatch fitted out a tender,* as if just arrived from Athens, he pretended that the people had ordered him immediately home: made full restitution to the ambassadors of whatever they demanded, and instantly got under sail, but dropped anchor at a little

---

* The υπηριτικαι, which I have translated "Tenders," were light ships fitted for particular uses, sometimes built for victualling ships to supply the main fleet with provisions, and sometimes for expedition, to carry expresses, and to observe the enemy's motions.

island, no great distance off. And while the Chalcidensians, seeing their property restored, and supposing Phormio to have sailed for Athens, neglected to post guards either in the city, or the country, he surprised them, unprepared for defence, was very near making himself master of the city, and brought off from the country immense booty.

2. PHORMIO with only thirty sail resolved to face the enemy, whose force consisted of fifty: and forming his little force into five lines, wore away before the adverse fleet under an easy sail. The enemy feeling their superiority, and eager to engage, crowded all the sail they could, to come up with them: by which means the swiftest sailing vessels left the rest at a distance. Phormio, observing this want of order in the enemy, kept his lines. and vigorously attacking the ships that came first into action, sunk them; and then bore down upon those that were next. The other captains, in their respective lines, observing the same manœuvre, gave the enemy no time to form, and left them no hope of safety, but in flight.

3. PHORMIO in a single ship, being attacked near Naupactum by two, took the advantage of a heavy merchantman that lay at anchor deeply laden, and doubling round her, directed his beak with full force against the stern of the slowest sailer, and funk her before the other could come up to her assistance: after which he easily defeated the other.

CHAP. V.

CLISTHENES.

WHILE Clisthenes lay before Cirra, the oracle declared, the city should be invincible till the sea reached the sacred land. The Cirrenses looked upon themselves as perfectly safe in this assurance, the sacred land, to which their city was contiguous, being situated far distant from the

the ocean. But Clisthenes, informed of the oracle, immediately devoted to Apollo both the city and the country; so that every thing being thus made sacred, the oracle was fulfilled, and the sea that washed the country of Cyrra, washed the sacred land. Clisthenes afterwards succeeded in his enterprise, and reduced the place; when the country was consecrated in form to the god.

CHAP. VI.

PHRYNICUS.

WHEN Phrynicus commanded in Samos, he formed a design to betray the city, but being charged with it, before the plot was ripe for execution, conscious of the intention, and afraid of conviction, he changed sides and betrayed the enemy, apprising the Samians of all their movements before they took place. In such a part, where the wall was weakest, he told them, they would direct all their force; but come, said he, let us fortify it before they arrive. They did so, and compleated their works in time. After which the operations of the enemy were conducted, just as Phrynicus had informed them they would be. Alcibiades, who commanded them, suspecting the duplicity of Phrynicus afterwards sent letters to the Samians, informing them of the intended treason. But the Samians were too much prejudiced in favour of Phrynicus, from the good measures he had advised, to pay any regard to the letters of an enemy.

CHAP. VII.

LACHARES

LACHARES, after Athens was taken by Demetrius, in the habit of a slave, with his face blacked, and on his arm a basket of money covered with dung, slipped out through a little gate, and mounting his horse, with all possible expedition endeavoured to make his escape. But a party of Tarentine horse being dispatched after him, when close at his heels, Lachares scattered the golden Darius's on the road. The men dismounted, to pick up the money: and the pursuit by that means interrupted gave Lachares time to make his escape into Bœotia.

2. WHEN Thebes was taken, Lachares hid himself in the common sewers: and after remaining there three or four days, he ventured out in the night, got safe to Delphos, and from thence to Lysimachus.

3. WHEN the enemy had made themselves masters of Sestos, Lachares concealed himself some days in a pit: having with him just provision enough to support Nature. It fortunately happened, that a woman's burial passed close by, when throwing a woman's gown round him, with a black veil on his head, he mixed among the mourners, and thus escaped out of the gates, and safely reached Lysimachia.

CHAP. VIII.

ARCHINUS.

THE Argives had ordered new arms to be made for all the citizens at the publick expence and Archinus was appointed superintendant of the work. He accordingly gave out to each of the citizens their new arms,

arms, and received of them their old ones in return; upon pretence of dedicating them to the gods according to the Argive decree. Inftead of which, he armed with them a banditti of ftrangers, and lodgers, the profligate, the poor, and defperate, and by their affiftance feized on the fovereignty.

CHAP. IX.

IPHICRATES.

IPHICRATES, after having formed his lines, and ready to engage, obferving feveral trembling, and pale, and in their countenances expreffing every fymptom of fear, ordered a herald to make proclamation, that whoever had left any thing behind him, might go back and fetch it, and immediately return and join the army. Of this proclamation the cowards all gladly took advantage, and left the field. As foon as they were gone, Iphicrates called out "Now, my lads, is the time for action, as we have got rid of our incumbrances. The rewards of courage and refolution will now be their's only, who deferve them." From this harangue the army derived new confidence, and engaging in the abfence of thofe, who had fkulked away, obtained a glorious victory.

* 2. After routing the enemy, Iphicrates never fuffered his lines to be broken in the ardour of purfuit, continually calling out to the light-armed troops to beware of ambufcades. It was alfo a general rule with him, never to prefs his enemy too clofe in their rout, if there were any narrow paffes, or rivers behind them. For thus to hem them in, is often to force them through defperation to rally and fight. Neither did he conceive it a point of good generalfhip, to purfue the enemy to their walls and battlements: for a victory gained, and rafhly fol-

---
* This is not fo properly a ftratagem, as a ftring of military inftructions.

lowed

lowed up within javelin's reach of the walls, has often been snatched away, and the conquerours in their turn with disgrace and loss, have been forced to relinquish their conquests.

3. IPHICRATES, having made himself master of a town in the night, while the people assembled in great bodies, and poured into the forum, ordered the gates to be thrown open, thereby giving the inhabitants an opportunity to escape, that he might with the greater security keep possession of the place.

4. Upon an irruption which Iphicrates had made into Thrace, while his troops were flying before the enemy as if struck with a panick fear, he ordered proclamation to be made, that whoever would inform of any man, that had thrown away his arms, he for his information should have them. The proclamation had the intended effect, the men recovered their spirits, and resolutely sustained the enemy's shock.

5. IPHICRATES, finding it necessary to pass the enemy in the night, directed his trumpets to an extremity of their lines, with orders to sound the charge on which alarm the enemy advanced to the post, where the trumpets sounded, while Iphicrates marched his army unmolested along the opposite extremity, the pass being left quite open.

6. AFTER a defeat Iphicrates had sustained, with the remains of his army he halted in a rough piece of ground, that was covered with wood. And being closely pursued by the enemy, to secure a retreat, he found it necessary to pass them. To effect this, he ordered his troops in the night with noise and tumult to put themselves in motion in one quarter; where having drawn the enemy's attention, he directed his march without opposition by a different one *

7. IPHICRATES, though his army was much more numerous than that of the enemy, and the augurs had pronounced success, to the equal

---

* This stratagem with a small variation is a repetition of the preceding one.

fur-

surprise of both armies still declined an engagement. The augury of my own mind, says he, determines me against engaging: for where an army is very numerous, they can neither charge, nor sing the Pæan,* together; and when I order them to close, I hear more of the chattering of their teeth, than of the clang of their arms.

8. WHILE the two armies lay encamped against each other, Iphicrates, whose object was to avoid an engagement, gained a three days march of the enemy, before they knew that he had struck his tents. And this he effected by directing fires to be supplied with dry wood, and green wood to be continually thrown on them, which occasioned a constant smoak, and so darkened the air, that the armies could not perceive what was going forwards in each other's camp.

9. WHENEVER the augurs declared against engaging, without implicitly submitting to their direction, Iphicrates used to change his ground, and vary his movements: and then order the sacrifices to be repeated. And this he did, in order to gain time maturely to consider a matter of so great importance, as the good or ill success of a battle.

10. IPHICRATES, once commanding against the Lacedæmonians, had a great variety of applications, from one for the command of five hundred men, from another for the command of one hundred, and from another for a company: all which he at the time rejected. But, on a future day, hastily drawing up his army, he gave private instructions to his generals to throw it into confusion, and raise a panick among the troops, as if the enemy were advancing in force to attack them. In this general confusion the timorous fled, and the brave advanced against the supposed foe. Iphicrates then smiled, and told them, the panick was of his own raising, to try the merit of their dif-

* The Pæan previous to the charge was a hymn to Mars. The Pæan after a victory was a hymn to Apollo.

ferent

ferent pretenfions. To thofe, who had maintained their ground, he gave commands, and ordered thofe, who had retreated, to follow their leaders.

11. HAVING fixed on his ground, Iphicrates before he encamped detached a body of troops, to fecure a poft at a confiderable diftance from the army. His officers, furprifed at the movement, afked the reafon of his taking fo diftant a pofition. To prevent, replied Iphicrates, the after-reflection of, "Who would have conceived fuch a movement neceffary?" Implying, that in war every precaution ought to be taken, and as little as poffible left to hazard.

12. IPHICRATES having been brought to an engagement in an open plain, where the enemy were much fuperiour in numbers, drew up his army, firft opening a trench on his rear; thereby fhewing them, that by thus having cut off all hopes of retreat, they had nothing left but to conquer or die.

13. WHEN Iphicrates had to engage with new-raifed troops, he did not, immediately on forming, begin the attack, but wearied them by various manœuvres, before he commenced the engagement. But if he commanded new raifed troops againft an army of veterans, he immediately engaged, giving all poffible efficacy to the firft attack.

14. WHENEVER Iphicrates had forced a flying enemy into a narrow pafs, he always contrived to open a way for them, and give them time and opportunity to efcape, without endeavouring to oblige them to force a way by victory. faying, there was no reafon to compel an enemy to be brave.

15. IPHICRATES, on a profecution againft him for a capital offence, placed in court fome youths, with fwords in their hands; who fhewed the hilts of them to the judges, and thereby fo intimidated them, that juftice fhut her eyes, and Iphicrates was abfolved.

16, IPHI-

16. IPHICRATES in the palace of his father in law* went up to him, and shewed him his coat of mail "You see, 'said he,' I am always in exercise and on my guard†"

17. IPHICRATES, during truces always fortified his camp observing, that it was not the part of a good general, to say, "I could not have thought it"

18. THE enemy having encamped in great force against Iphicrates, he found it necessary to attempt a retreat And as they closely watched his motions, he cut down all the wood that was near him, and fixing it up in the camp, hung shields, helmets, and spears upon it · which the enemy observing supposed him still in camp, while he had secretly evacuated it, and effected a safe retreat

19. WHEN Iphicrates out-numbered the enemy, and wished to conceal his strength from them, in order to make them, from his supposed weakness, the more ready to engage, he used to make two soldiers sleep on one bed, taking it in turns to lye down to rest, and alternately to place their arms upon each other's. And on the contrary, if his force was small, and he wished to impress the enemy with an idea of his numbers being greater than they really were, he ordered every soldier to make two beds · then shifted his ground, and encamped in a different place. Thus the enemy, from the number of

---

* Cotys, King of Thrace, whose daughter Iphicrates had married and whom he suspected of entertaining secret designs against him, and, according to an intimation of Demosthenes in his oration against Aristocrates, not without reason

† The words are μιλιτω φυλαττισθαι, which it is difficult literally to translate Μιλιτω has a reference to the rudiments of military science and young men, on their first entrance into the service, in the initiatory studies of their profession were said μιλιταν, to exercise And in those studies a fundamental rule was φυλαττισθαι to be on their guard To this application of the words Iphicrates seems in the above passage to allude jocosely observing, and at the same time seriously intending the point of his observation to Cotys, "You see I do not forget the rudiments of my profession, I am always in exercise, and on my guard."

O   beds

beds they obſerved, confident in their own ſuppoſed ſuperiourity advanced raſhly to the charge, or diſpirited by the appearance of his, reluctantly commenced the engagement

20 THE Thebans had formed a deſign to ſurpriſe Athens by night; of which Iphicrates being appriſed, ſummoned the people at a particular ſignal in the night to aſſemble in the forum He then told them, he had a party at Thebes, who were ready to betray the city to them " Let us, 'ſaid he,' therefore march quietly out, we may make ourſelves maſters of the city without ſtriking a blow " As ſoon as the Thebans by their emiſſaries at Athens were informed of this council, and the object of it, they thought no more of ſurpriſing Athens, directing their attention to the conſervation of their own city

21 BEING very inferiour in force to the enemy, and his troops on that account diſpirited, Iphicrates at ſupper called to him the captains of companies* and leaders of bands †, and bade them raiſe from their reſpective corps whatever gold, ſilver, or trinkets, they could: on pretence that he had bribed a party in the enemy's camp, to betray the

---

* The ταξις, which I have tranſlated "Company," conſiſted of 128 men· the commander of which was denominated ταξιαρχος,

† The λοχος, or band, conſiſted of 16 men and the leader of it was ſtiled λοχαγος

The diſtinction of the terms αρχος, and αγος, may perhaps be in ſome meaſure explained by the ranks in our army, diſtinguiſhed by commiſſioned, and warrant officers though it muſt be acknowledged, they do not exactly correſpond Nor does the organization of our army exactly aſſimilate to that of the ancient Greeks They had their leaders of 16, 10, and even 5 men But then it is to be obſerved, that their actions were always decided hand to hand in which thoſe leaders were of great uſe, ſetting the example, and obſerving that their reſpective corps did their duty Whereas the battles of the moderns are generally determined by ordinance and muſquetry But when it comes to the puſh of the bayonet, in which caſe the innate valour of the Britiſh troops generally bears the palm of victory, perhaps a leader of 10, or 12, might be an improvement in our military arrangements and if thought ſo, might be eaſily conſtituted by the addition of three or four corporals to every company

army

army to him, and that to make good his engagement, he wanted every affiftance that could be fpared him. And as foon as he had received the contributions of the army, he told them, he fhould immediately proceed to action. The officers accordingly brought to him, what they had been able to raife which he took, and made an offering from it to PROPITIOUS MERCURY, as if in purfuance of the agreement between him and the confpirators: and after a fhort interval drew up his army, and advanced to the attack. The troops recovered their fpirits, and pufhed boldly on, in confidence that the enemy's army would be betrayed to them.

22. IPHICRATES ufed to refemble an army marfhalled for action to the human body. The phalanx he called the breaft, the lightarmed troops the hands, the cavalry the feet, and the general the head. If any of the inferior parts were wanting, the army he faid was defective: but if it wanted a general, it wanted every thing.

23. IPHICRATES propagated a report at Mitylenæ, that he intended fhortly to provide a number of fhields, to be fent to the Chian flaves. The rumour gaining credit among the Chians, fearful of a rebellion among the flaves, they immediately fent him prefents, and entered into an alliance with Athens.

24. WHEN preparations were making by the Athenians for the fiege of Sicyon, the Lacedæmonian general, who was ordered to relieve it, directed the ambaffadors, which came to folicit affiftance, to plant an ambufcade, and endeavour to furprife the enemy. This they accordingly did. And Iphicrates, who took the direct way to the city, had paffed it. But fome youths from the walls audacioufly calling out to him, on his prefenting himfelf before the place, "Now however you will meet your punifhment," it occurred to him, there muft be fomething particular, on which they depended. He therefore immediately marched back, but took a different rout, and with a felect

body of his best troops, resolved to explore the country when in a close covert way he discovered the ambuscade, which he cut to pieces. On this occasion he acknowledged his error, in not reconnoitring the ground: though he had immediately availed himself of his suspicions, and thereby defeated the purpose of the enemy's manœuvre.

25. When preparing for an engagement with the barbarians, to animate his men, Iphicrates called out, "Those barbarians seem not to know the terror, the arms of Iphicrates carry with them but, by your assistance, my lads, I will now teach them to know it, and to tell the tale to others" When the armies were drawn up, some one observed, the enemy cut a formidable appearance. "Therefore, 'replied Iphicrates,' we must be so much the more formidable."

26. Iphicrates on a particular occasion conjured his men by all the glorious exploits they had performed under his command, in this one request to indulge him, to advance briskly, and begin the attack · confident that if he did not instantly bear down upon the enemy, they would do it upon him, and that whichever army attacked, the other would find it difficult to sustain the charge

27. Iphicrates told his men, he would insure them the victory; if mutually animating each other, upon a certain signal he should give, they would advance but a single pace At the crisis, when victory hung in equal suspense, he gave the signal. the army returned it with acclamations, advanced a pace, and defeated the enemy

28. When Iphicrates commanded at Corinth against the Thebans, and was much pressed by his troops to bring the enemy to an action, observing, that they out-numbered him, and were also flushed with their late victory at Leuctræ, he refused to hazard an engagement "But, 'said he,' I have formed you to that height of military glory, which has taught you to despise the Thebans now let some abler officer take the command, and lead you to the charge" By this mild reprimand he

won

won the Athenians from their purpose, and repressed an ill-timed ardour, that would probably have terminated in a defeat.

29. IPHICRATES at the instance of Aristophon and Chares was prosecuted for treason against the state, in not bringing the enemy to an action at Embata, when he had it in his power to have destroyed their fleet. Finding the charge strongly supported against him, instead of proceeding farther in his defence, he stopped short and shewed the judges his sword: who, in fear lest the court might be surrounded by his confederates in arms, acquitted him. Some one intimating, after the cause was over, that he had intimidated the judges by menacing violence, "I should be an idiot indeed, ' replied Iphicrates,' if I could fight for the Athenians, and could not do the same for myself."

30. AT a time when the Athenians for some particular purpose were in great want of money, Iphicrates advised them, to pull down the publick buildings, that fronted the streets, and sell them. But as the demolition of those buildings would have been a great detriment to the houses that were built up against them, the owners of them, as Iphicrates foresaw, paid the sums that were wanted, to have the buildings preserved.

31. THE booty that was taken after an action Iphicrates distributed among the troops, according to each individual's particular deservings. But the contributions raised on cities, where no engagements had taken place, he divided not to each man singly, but to each separate corps, by companies, and bands. And, while the troops were respectively arming themselves, his practice was, after silence had been proclaimed, to promise to distinguish, in the distribution of the booty, every man in the different corps of cavalry, heavy, or light armed troops, that should particularly signalise himself. And at all festivals, and publick meetings, the

men,

men, who had displayed most courage, he always honoured with the first seats.* By these devices he promoted courage and emulation.

32. IPHICRATES used to exercise his troops in all those various manœuvres, that might be necessary in action, sham sallies, sham ambuscades, proditions, revolts, surprises, and panics: so that when any of them were really practised by the enemy, or required from his own troops, they were in either case experienced and ready.

33. THE enemy having formed, about five furlongs distant from the Athenian army, on an elevated post near the sacred mount, with the sea on their rear, and only one pass in front, so narrow as not to admit two men a-breast, and the approach towards the sea steep and craggy. Iphicrates with a body of resolute, strong men, oiling, and properly equipping, themselves, took the advantage of a still night, skirted the mountain, and swimming over particular places where the sea was deepest, landed on the rear of the enemy, cut the centinels to pieces, and secured the march of his army through the defile. Then, while it was yet night, attacking the enemy unprepared to receive him, he with little loss obtained a compleat victory, those, who escaped the sword, being made prisoners.

34. IN a winter campaign, when the Athenian army were ill-cloathed and fed, Iphicrates saw the present moment the proper instant for engaging, but observed his troops, from the hardships they experienced, ill-affected to the service. Habited therefore in a mean dress, and thinner cloathed than the rest, he went round the camp, exhorting the troops

---

* Great stress was formerly laid on the honours of the table. See Homer's Iliad, l. 12. v 310 a poem, which abounds in military documents.

Γλαῦκε, τίη δὴ νῶι τετιμήμεσθα μάλιστα
Ἕδρῃ τε, κρέασίν τε, ἰδὲ πλείοις δεπάεσσιν, &c.

Glaucus, why claim we at the festive treat
The table's honours, and the highest seat?—&c.

imme-

immediately to draw out, and advance to the attack who, seeing then general thus meanly dressed, and without shoes, sacrificed ease and convenience to the publick good, and readily followed him to the charge.

35. IPHICRATES, when his military chest was low, used to march his troops to sea coasts and unfrequented places, where their expences would be small. But when his finances were in good plight, he quartered them in cities and rich countries, where having quickly squandered away their money, their poverty might excite them to some great enterprise. But he never suffered them to be idle. When they were not engaged in actual service, he always appointed them to some employment · ordering them either to scoop the earth, to sink trenches, to cut down wood, to shift their camp, or to repair their baggage, considering idleness, as the parent of plots and mutinies

36. IPHICRATES, after ravaging Samos, sailed to Delos: whither the Samian ambassadors repaired, to purchase the property he had taken from them: all which he promised should be restored to them. And secretly fitting out a tender, which he pretended was just arrived from Athens, and had brought him letters of recall, he took a friendly leave of the Samians, and ordered the captains of his fleet to weigh anchor, and get under sail He then steered to an uninhabited island, and anchored there a day and night The Samians, as soon as they heard that Iphicrates had courteously received their ambassadors, left Delos, and was recalled home, abandoned themselves to a false security both in the city, and in the country. But while enjoying themselves in parties, and strolling abroad, he again landed at Samos, and carried off a greater booty, than he had done before. The same stratagem Phormio practised against the Chalcidensians.

37. WHEN Iphicrates, who acted as arbitrator between the Lacedæmonians and Thebans, then at war with each other, found that the Argive and Arcadian allies of the Thebans prevented a reconciliation

between

between them, he ordered a body of troops to ravage Argolis. The Argives complaining of such an incursion, he said the ravages were committed by their own revolters, against whom he pretended to march, in order to punish them: and, as if succefsful in his expedition, restored to the Argives the property of which they had been plundered. Won by such an act of generous retribution, they looked on Iphicrates as their benefactor and friend, and persuaded the Thebans to agree to the proposed conditions of peace

38. WHEN Iphicrates, in the service of Persia, had with Pharnabazus carried the war into Ægypt, there being in that part of the world no havens, he directed the captains of the veffels every one to take with him forty facks. And when they brought to land, he ordered all the facks to be filled with fand, and from the sides of the ship to be fuspended in the water. Under the stay of this counterbalance they rode safe. which served them in place of an harbour.

39. AT Epidaurum Iphicrates drew up his army near the sea, but not being in a condition to engage, he advanced to a thick, shady wood: where he called aloud for the ambush to shew themselves. The enemy, fearing a numerous ambuscade, wheeled about and retreated to their ships.

40. IPHICRATES, when in Thefialy, and Jafon the tyrant, having encamped against each other near a river's side, agreed to terminate the contest by a treaty. They accordingly met under the bridge without arms, to settle the terms of it, having been previoufly searched by each other's officers. After they had formally bound themselves by oath to adhere to the conditions that should be settled, Iphicrates mounted the bridge, and Jafon begun a facrifice to the river, with a sheep he had taken from a neighbouring flock. Iphicrates then leaping down, feized a knife, with which though he did not murder Jafon, he awed him into such terms in making the treaty, as he thought fit to prescribe.

41 IPHI-

41. Iphicrates in the Thracian war, when the enemy were encamped near him, directed a wood, which lay between the two camps, to be set on fire in the night, and leaving his baggage, and a great store of cattle, under cover of the night, rendered by the smoak more dark than it really was, retreated to a place thick and shady, and covered with underwood. As soon as day appeared, the Thracians advanced against the camp, which they found abandoned, and immediately fell to plundering the baggage, and the live stores. Thus engaged and separated, Iphicrates advancing in good order, fell suddenly upon them; defeated them, and recovered his baggage.

42. In his attack on a particular place by night, Iphicrates ordered the trumpets, dispersed in various parts, to sound the charge. The enemy intimidated at the sound of the different trumpets endeavoured to escape, some one way, and some another; while he, having cut off the few that opposed him, easily made himself master of the place.

43. While Iphicrates was at Corinth, the Lacedæmonians advanced against the city. He did not however venture immediately to hazard a battle; but learning that there were strong posts about the city, he privately possessed himself of them, and then ordered those who were within the walls to join him. The whole body of the people advancing in one firm compact band, so intimidated the Lacedæmonians with their numbers, and the advantageous position of their allies, that they raised the siege, and retreated, without striking a blow.

44. Iphicrates, when at war with the Abydenians he lay at Cherronesus, having posted himself on an advantageous spot, pretended to be afraid of Axibidius the Lacedæmonian general, and threw up a wall round his camp. The Abydenians seeing him raising a wall, and from thence presuming on his supposed weakness, ventured out of the city, and made excursions into the country, as their occasions required.

Iphicrates obferving them thus thrown off from their guard, detached a part of his army by night into the territories of the Abydenians, ravaged their country, made many prifoners, and carried off booty to a confiderable amount.

45. WHEN Iphicrates lay at Corinth, having learned, that thofe who fupported the oppofite faction had refolved in the night to admit into the city mercenaries from Lacedæmon, he muftered his troops, left a fort of them in the city as a garrifon, marched the reft out, and drew them up without the gates. Then haftening to the gate, which the Lacedæmonian faction had opened for the admiffion of the mercenaries, he threw himfelf in with them upon their rear: and a confufed engagement fucceeding, unexpected on the part of the mercenaries, many of them fell in the night, and in the morning many more were cut to pieces, who had taken refuge in the temples.

46. IPHICRATES, in an expedition into Thrace, being encamped with eight thoufand men, and hearing that the Thracians intended to attack his camp in the night, evacuated it in the evening, and pofted himfelf in a valley about three furlongs diftant, where he lay unobferved by the enemy. They accordingly attacked his camp, which they found evacuated, and plundered it ridiculing the Greeks, as an enemy who had invaded them, only to run away again. Iphicrates then advancing from his retreat, fuddenly attacked them with great flaughter, and took a confiderable number prifoners.

47. IPHICRATES having a two day's march to make through a fandy country, deftitute of water, ordered the army after fupper to fill the water cafks. and as foon as the fun was down, he begun his march, which he continued all night. The next morning he encamped, and ordered the troops to refresh themfelves. And having refted all day, and in the evening taken their fuppers, when the night came on, they packed up their baggage, and renewed their march. Thus inftead

of a two day's march, he had only one day, and that a day of rest, to encounter the heat of the climate, and the scarcity of water."

48 IPHICRATES, having acquired at Epidaurum great spoils, in his retreat to his ships was pursued by the Lacedæmonian governor of the country, who had posted himself on an eminence, to intercept him. Before his baggage Iphicrates drew up his heavy-armed troops, intermixing here and there with them some of his light-armed and other less effective* forces, to increase their numbers, concealing himself at a small distance with the rest of his army. Those advancing against the Lacedæmonian, he quitted his heights to engage them, of which Iphicrates, with the other part of his troops, having wheeled about, took possession, and falling upon his rear entirely defeated him.

49 IPHICRATES having about Phlyuntes some narrow defiles to pass, while the enemy hung upon his rear, ordered his troops to clear the pass with all expedition. while he, with a body of his best troops falling back into the rear to cover them, attacked the enemy, disordered and confused in the eagerness of their pursuit, and made great havock amongst them

50 IPHICRATES, having made an irruption into Thrace, encamped on an open plain, almost surrounded by a ridge of mountains, and accessible only in one pass by a bridge, that the Thracians crossed in the night, with intention to attack his camp. which, having lighted in it a number of fires, he evacuated, and skirting the mountains concealed himself in a piece of shrubby ground near the bridge, while the Thracians advanced against his camp, not doubting by the

---

* On this passage I will observe in general, that the οπλιται, or heavy-armed troops, were the first and most considerable body in the Grecian infantry engaging with broad shields and long spears The ψιλοι, or light-armed men, fought chiefly with arrows, darts, slings, &c. Those who are here stiled κυφες, were probably the baggage keepers, &c. ordered into the ranks only to swell the shew of numbers.

fires but he was still there, Iphicrates in the mean time quitted his station, passed the bridge, and effected a safe retreat.

51. IPHICRATES, when in command of a numerous army, consisting both of naval, and land forces, kept always in hand a quarter of their pay, as a security against their desertion. By this means he preserved his army compleat, and his troops rich, having always a fourth part of their pay in arrears.

52. IPHICRATES, having encamped opposite to the Lacedæmonian allies, in the night made his army change their dress: the soldiers dressed themselves in the habit of the servants, and the servants in that of the soldiers. They in the military dress walked about at pleasure with the air of freemen, leaving the care of their arms to the servants: they in the servile dress, as their service required, were employed about the arms. The enemy, seeing this, did the same. their soldiers leisurely amused themselves without the limits of the camp, while their servants were engaged in their ordinary employment within. At a signal given, the troops of Iphicrates, seising their arms, instantly advanced against the enemy's camp, from whence the servants precipitately fled, and the soldiers thus surprised unarmed, were either slain, or taken prisoners.

53. IPHICRATES, on another occasion, being encamped directly opposite to the enemy, and observing that they dined regularly at a certain hour, made his men dine early in the morning, and immediately after attacked the enemy. whom, without ever closing, they with their darts engaged all day at a distance. And in the evening after both sides had retreated, and the enemy were sate down to their repast, his own soldiers having dined heartily early in the day, he attacked the enemy while at their supper, and made no small havock amongst them.

54. THE narrowness of the roads at Phlyuntes obliging Iphicrates to march with a narrow front, and his lines extended to the rear, which was much galled by the enemy, he ordered them to march quicker, and,

with

STRATAGEMS OF WAR. 117

with a select body of troops, falling back into the rear, he vigorously attacked the enemy, fatigued with the pursuit, and in no order, cut many of them to pieces, and made the rest prisoners.

55. IPHICRATES, when lying at Corcyra he received intelligence of Crinippus having sailed from Sicily with eleven store ships, in a small island near which his course lay ordered a beacon to be lighted: and weighing anchor in the night, he fell in with him, and took every ship but one.

56. IPHICRATES, while in Thrace, having had intelligence of a conspiracy being formed by two of his generals, selected a party of his best and most confidential troops and ordered them as soon as he had charged the suspected generals with the conspiracy, immediately to seise their arms, and those of the corps they commanded. which was accordingly done. The conspiracy afterwards being clearly proved, Iphicrates ordered the generals to execution, stripped the soldiers, and turned them naked out of the camp

57 Two thousand mercenaries having revolted to the Lacedæmonians, Iphicrates dispatched after them private letters to the generals of the revolters, reminding them of the time appointed, and assuring them they might then depend on assistance from Athens well knowing, that those letters would be intercepted by the * GUARDS OF THE ROADS. This was accordingly the case, and the Lacedæmonians, upon the intercepted letters being carried to them, dispatched a body of troops to apprehend the revolters. who, in this untoward situation, real traitours to the Athenians, and suspected of treachery to the Lacedæmonians, had nothing left but to endeavour to make their escape from both

58. WHEN Iphicrates commanded at Chios, to convict a party of

---

* The Φυλακις των οδων were centinels stationed on the publick roads, to make enquiries of all passengers respecting their business, &c. and to transmit information to the neighbouring towns of any particular occurrences, that might affect either private persons, or the state.

the

the Chians whom Iphicrates fuspected of favouring the interests of Lacedæmon, he ordered some captains of vessels secretly to weigh anchor in the night, and the next morning to return into harbour, habited in the Lacedæmonian dress. Those, who were in the Lacedæmonian interest, as soon as they saw them, run with great joy to welcome them to the harbour when Iphicrates, advancing with a body of troops from the city, surrounded, and took them, and sent them to Athens to be punished

59 IPHICRATES, once particularly pressed for money, while the soldiers mutinied, and insisted on a general meeting being called, habited some men, who were acquainted with the Persian language, in a Persian dress, and ordered them when the assembly was most crowded to be introduced, and to tell them in the barbarian manner, that a party were on their march and very near, who were charged with money for payment of their arrears: and we, added they, were dispatched before, to apprise you of it. On this intelligence, the soldiers immediately dissolved the assembly

60 IPHICRATES, having ravaged Odrysius, and brought off much booty, was pursued by the Odrysians in great force. And being weak in his cavalry, and the enemy in theirs particularly strong, he ordered his own to attack with flaming torches in their hands which so affrighted the horses of the enemy, unaccustomed to the sight of fire, that they would not stand the charge, but turned about and fled.

61 IPHICRATES once advanced against a city, a river flowing through the midst of it, which he was obliged to pass above the city, before he could commence the attack. He therefore crossed the river in the night, that the water, rendered muddy by the passage of so great a body of men, might not discover his approach to the enemy. The next morning he appeared before their gates, and begun the attack, while they were ignorant of his having crossed the river

62. IPHI-

62. IPHICRATES having taken many of the Odryſians priſoners, when galled by the enemy's ſlings and arrows, ſtripped his priſoners naked, and with their hands tied behind them placed them in the front of his army. The Odryſians, ſeeing their friends thus poſted in the place of danger, no longer continued the diſtant action with arrows and ſlings.

63. WHEN ordered againſt the Phœnicians with a fleet of a hundred ſail, Iphicrates, as ſoon as he approached the Phœnician coaſt, which was flat and muddy, found the enemy drawn up to receive him. Obſerving their poſition, he ordered the maſters of the ſhips, to form a line and wear to the ſhore, and at a ſignal given to drop their anchors, and the ſoldiers, every man immediately to take up his arms, and each by his reſpective oar to jump into the ſea. As ſoon as Iphicrates ſuppoſed the ſea ſhallow enough for his purpoſe, he gave the ſignal, the veſſels inſtantly dropped anchor, the ſoldiers quitted them in perfect order, and under cover of their ſhields advanced to the ſhore. The enemy, intimidated by the order of their march, and their reſolution, abandoned themſelves to flight: when the Grecians purſued them, and in the rout cut many of them to pieces. Many alſo they made priſoners, and poſſeſſed themſelves of conſiderable ſpoils, which were ſecured on board their ſhips, while they encamped themſelves on the ſhore.

CHAP. X.

TIMOTHEUS.

AT a time, when there was a great ſcarcity of money in the Athenian camp, Timotheus perſuaded the ſuttlers to take his drafts for currency, aſſuring them, thoſe drafts ſhould all be redeemed with ſpecie. The ſuttlers truſted to the general's honour, and ſupplied the army with pro-

provisions upon the credit of his own notes. The money was afterwards punctually paid, and Timotheus by this stratagem not only supplied the wants of his army, but established his credit among the suttlers.

2. Just as the fleet under Timotheus was ready to sail, one of the men was seized with a fit of sneezing* The master of the vessel bade him suppress it: and the sailours refused to embark. Timotheus smiled, and with great composure observed, "What a wonderful omen is this, that among such a number of men, one of them should happen to sneeze" The sailours saw the propriety of their general's observation, laughed at their own superstition, and embarked

3 Timotheus having given orders for the army immediately to charge, and several of the men being yet behind, one of his lieutenants asked, if they had not better halt, till the rest came up. "By no means, 'replied Timotheus.' all that will fight bravely are ready, and those, who will not do that, are not worth waiting for."

4 In a naval engagement between the Athenians and Lacedæmonians at Leucas, Timotheus commanded the Athenians, and Nicomachus the Lacedæmonians. The battle being fought on the festival Skira†, Timotheus in the morning ornamented his ships with myrtle, then gave the signal for attack, and obtained the victory: the soldiers exerting themselves with uncommon courage, in confidence that they fought under the immediate protection of the goddess.

5 When Timotheus invested a city, he appointed to his troops a particular district, in which he gave them liberty to live at free quarters. But in the rest of the country he made them pay for whatever they had. Nor did he suffer them to destroy either house, or cottage, or even to cut down a growing tree, but merely to supply themselves with the

* Sneezing was always considered by seamen, as an unlucky omen.

† A festival in honour of Minerva, the tutelary Deity of the Athenians.

product of the country And by this conduct he knew, if he was fuccefsful, he fhould be able to raife the greater contribution from the people, and if the war was protracted, he fhould want for his army neither provifions, nor other accommodation And what was ftill of greater confequence, he by this means fecured the efteem of his enemies.

6 Timotheus advancing to a naval engagement with the Lacedæmonians took on board him the ftores* of twenty triremes, which he lodged in the holds of the reft of the fleet, that lay quietly on their oars, while the light veffels advanced againft the enemy, whom they harraffed with various movements and manœuvres. As foon as he faw them appear fatigued, and feebly handle their oars, he with the reft of the fleet advanced to action, and frefh, and in full ftrength, obtained an eafy victory over an enemy weak and exhaufted by tedious and laborious manœuvres

7 In an incurfion into Olynthia, to avoid being harraffed by the Olynthian horfe, Timotheus marched in the form of the Plinth†, pofting his baggage and cavalry in the centre, the carriages faftened in continued lines to each other, and round them he formed his heavy-armed troops. And in this order he penetrated into Olynthia, the Olynthian cavalry being able to make no impreffion on him

8. Timotheus, having encamped at Amphipolis, received intelligence in the evening that the enemy were advancing in force againft him, and would reach him the next day. That he might not difcourage his troops, he concealed from them the ftrength of the enemy, and

---

* Πληρωματα is a term of very large extent, comprehending fometimes thofe who rowed, as well as all other perfons in the fhip, and was fometimes applied to any thing contained in it. In the inftance before us, it can only fignify thofe contents, which would be of no ufe in an action.

† See above, book 2. chap. 2. ftrat. 9.

as if advancing against an undisciplined army, he ordered the baggage and attendants on the camp to march first, directing their rout through a rugged and unfrequented road, where it was probable the enemy might have neglected to station a guard. Himself marched at the head of the phalanx, and the light infantry he posted in the rear. In this order he reached the river Strymon, where he embarked his army, and burned all the ships on the river, that were more than he could fill. And all these were the operations of a single night: by which he effected a safe retreat.

9. TIMOTHEUS, having undertaken the siege of Samos, for that enterprise engaged seven thousand mercenaries. But not being able regularly to make good to them their pay, and observing the island to be rich and well cultivated, he suffered them on a part of it, for that purpose assigned, to live at free quarters, and the product of the rest he sold, protecting those who were employed in gathering it. And having from thence raised considerable sums, he paid his troops part of their arrears, and thus securing their perseverance, he at last took the city by storm.

10. WHEN Timotheus lay before Samos, and the continued influx of strangers occasioned such consumption of provisions, as created a scarcity, he ordered no flour to be sold, nor a pint of oil, or wine, and of corn not less than a bushel, nor of any liquors less than a barrel: and prohibited all corn-mills, except on the hills. The consequence of which regulations was, that when the strangers found they could not purchase at Samos what was wanted for present use, they brought their provision with them and the whole product of the island became thus appropriated to the demands of the army.

11. TIMOTHEUS, with a fleet of forty ships, having occasion to dispatch five, with provisions for several days, on a secret expedition, was afraid of openly applying so large a share of provisions, as was re-

required, to that expedition, left the troops, whom he had not been able regularly to pay, should murmur at the apprehension of being reduced to short allowance He therefore ordered the whole fleet to get under sail, each ship taking on board three days provision, and to anchor at a certain island. There he directed every captain of a ship to land two days provision: which he secretly put on board the five ships destined for the distant expedition, and with the remaining part of his fleet returned to his former station

12 PREVIOUS to an engagement, to which Timotheus was advancing, with the Spartan general Nicolochus, he ordered the compliments of several ships to be landed, and to rest on the shore till wanted. and with twenty of his swiftest sailing vessels bore down upon the enemy, directing the captains not to advance within dart's cast of them, but to pass them, to advance, and retreat, and by every manœuvre harrass and fatigue them In this kind of flying fight as soon as Timotheus observed the enemy by heat and fatigue almost exhausted, he gave signals for a retreat And taking on board the men, that had been left during the distant engagement to rest themselves on the shore, he renewed the action with the wearied foe, took many of their ships, and disabled others

13 TIMOTHEUS, when lying before the Lacedæmonian fleet, being afraid lest ten of the enemy's ships, that the admiral had previous to the engagement dispatched to intercept his store-ships, should fall in with them, resolved to retreat and cover them. And at the same time apprehensive lest the enemy should attack him in his retreat, and, while the small vessels were endeavouring to form, come up with, and in that imperfect state bring him to an engagement, he ordered the captains of the triremes not to form again, but to make the first land they could. while he, having cleared the decks, and put the prisoners in the holds, with the rest of his fleet in the shape of a crescent, gently wore away before the enemy, his sterns foremost, and beaks directed towards them.

14. In a war with the Chalcidians, in which Timotheus commanded, assisted by Perdiccas, he mixed the Macedonian money with the Cyprian brass, and from thence struck a new coin, of the value of five drachms, one fourth of which consisted of silver, and the rest was an alloy of brass. By this means having enriched his military chest, he persuaded the suttlers and inhabitants of the country to take it as currency. which he received in payment of them again, and thus it passed between the army and their suppliers in the place of more valuable coin.

15 The Toronæans when besieged by Timotheus, threw up moles of a prodigious height against him, consisting of baskets of sand: which he contrived means, by long machines pointed with sharp steel, and fixed to the tops of his masts, to cut, and let out the sand. The address of Timotheus on this occasion induced the Toronæans to comply with the conditions he imposed on them.

16 In a naval engagement with the Lacedæmonians, in which Timotheus commanded, assisted by the Corcyræans and other allies, he posted his prime sailours in the first line, directing the rest of the fleet to lie upon their oars, and keep themselves quiet. As soon as he saw the enemy's strength weakened, and their efforts slackening from the impetuosity of the first attack, he gave the signal for the rest of the fleet to advance: which being quite fresh easily compleated the victory over an enemy already exhausted with the fatigues of the day*.

17 After Timotheus had defeated the Lacedæmonian fleet at Leucas, and destroyed several of their ships, being afraid of ten of them, which still remained undamaged and disposed for action, he drew up his fleet in the form of a crescent, posting his small ships within the circle, which projected to the enemy. and in this disposition

---

* This seems to have been a favourite stratagem with this commander which we find in three different instances he employed with success

he

he retreated, with his sterns foremost, and the beaks advanced toward the enemy, who did not venture to attack him, but suffered him, in this order to make good his retreat*.

CHAP. XI.

CHABRIAS

TO divert his men from an unnecessary carnage, Chabrias bade them remember, that the victims of their swords, though enemies, were men, flesh and blood, and of the same nature with themselves

2 CHABRIAS obtained a naval victory at Naxos, on the sixteenth day of the month Boedromion; which he considered auspicious, as being one of the days on which the Eleusinian mysteries are celebrated Themistocles also on one of those days defeated the Persians at Salamis, but the day, on which the batle of Salamis was fought, was that particularly dedicated to Bacchus †. so that Themistocles might be supposed to have the immediate protection of the God, but Chabrias on his side only the auspices of the mysteries

3 A Lacedæmonian fleet of observation, consisting of twelve sail, having escaped Chabrias, and made the land To decoy them out to sea again, he detached twelve ships, fastened two by two together, with their sails also joined. The enemy, supposing them to be only six ships, weighed anchor, and advanced against them As soon as Chabrias thought them too far from shore, to escape him, he separated the sails, set his ships at liberty, and bore down upon the enemy half of whom he captured, with their compliments of men on board.

* This stratagem too, with some variation, we find twice employed by Timotheus against the Lacedæmonians And it is observable, that the crescent is a form, which we see at this day frequently adopted.
† That was the sixth day of the mysteries.

4. CHABRIAS, being obliged to retreat before a superior force, and marching through a narrow defile, posted his best troops in the rear, and himself led the van. In this order pursuing his march, while none who were posted in the rear dared to desert his ranks, and contrary to orders pass the general, he with little loss effected his retreat.

5 The treasury of Thamus king of Ægypt being much exhausted, and he in want of money, Chabrias advised him to command the wealthier part of his subjects to contribute to his present occasions whatever gold and silver they could: engaging in proportion to their contributions to remit their respective tributes. By this method he raised a great sum, and without injury to any one and afterwards with strict punctuality discharged his engagements.

6 CHABRIAS having made an irruption into Lacedæmonia, and being obliged to pass a river, secured the booty, of which he had taken a considerable quantity, by sending it over the river, and lodging it in the country of an Athenian ally and halting with the rest of his army, which he ordered to refresh themselves, he waited a supposed event, which according to his expectation took place. For the Lacedæmonians, having been apprised of his rout, marched out to intercept him at the river, and recover their spoil and, after a long and laborious march of two hundred furlongs, came up with him; but fatigued, in no order, nor in any respect prepared for action. Chabrias on the contrary, his troops rested, and well refreshed, in good order attacked them, and gained an easy victory.

7. WHEN Chabrias commanded in Ægypt, as ally to the king, against the Persians, who had invaded his country with a numerous army, and a powerful fleet. finding that the Ægyptians had great store of ships, but wanted mariners to work them, he selected from the stoutest of the Ægyptian youths a compliment sufficient to man

two

two hundred ships. And having taken the oars out of the ships, he seated the Ægyptians in order on benches, which he directed to be raised on the shore: then gave them the oars, and intermixed with them some mariners who understood the Ægyptian, as well as Grecian, language. These instructed them to handle their oars . and in a short time the king possessed a fleet of two hundred sail, compleatly manned*.

8. CHABRIAS, whenever his army consisted of new levied troops, previous to an action used to order proclamation to be made, that whoever were indisposed, should quit their ranks. The cowards took advantage of this order, pretended illness, and laid down their arms. Those therefore he never led to action, but employed them in securing posts , where their numbers at least might render them formidable to the enemy. And as soon as he conveniently could, he shortened their pay.

9 ADVANCING against a city, which was at war with Athens, Chabrias landed a body of heavy-armed troops by night; and by break of day entered the harbour, and made a feint to disembark his troops at some distance from the city. The citizens sallied out, to dispute his landing: when the ambuscade of heavy-armed troops fell upon their rear, slew some, and re-imbarked with a considerable number of prisoners.

10 TEN of the most stout and active of his heavy-armed troops Chabrias landed from each of his ships by night in the enemy's country, with orders to ravage it. The citizens, to protect their property, sallied out of the city, and advanced against the ravagers As soon as this was observed, Chabrias advanced with his fleet directly against the city: whose approach of course drew back to the protection of it the attention of the troops, that were advancing against the invaders;

---

* This Stratagem of teaching the use of the oar by land is mentioned by Polybius as having been practised by the Romans. See L. I.

while

while he with a detached squadron, brought to shore above the city, and took on board again the troops that had been ordered to ravage the country, together with the booty they had taken.

11. When Chabrias in a naval action engaged Pollis at Naxos, he commanded his captains, if they found themselves hard pressed, privately to strike off the ornamental distinctions and names from their respective ships; and those on the enemy's ships remaining would be a sufficient mark to them, where to attack. Accordingly Pollis's captains, not being able to distinguish, for wantof their figure-heads, the enemy's ships, frequently passed the Athenians without attacking them · doubting whether they were friends or foes. While the Athenians knew the enemy, from their marks of distinction, and their own ships as perfectly, from having none; and this device secured to the Athenians the victory.

12. Chabrias, after landing three hundred men by night in Ægina, continued his voyage. But the citizens, having discovered the invaders, marched out against them, and attacked them with great superiority of force. This Chabrias observing, changed his course, and bore away to the city. from whence the enemy fearing left he should cut off their retreat precipitately quitted the field.

13. When the sea run high, Chabrias to prevent the waves from lashing over the ship fastened hides on each side, from prow to stern; which had the proposed effect, and kept the sailors dry. It also lessened the appearance of danger, which did not a little confuse the crew, and enabled them to keep the deck.

14. In long voyages to guard against storms, Chabrias carried two occasional helms, which he fixed on either side the ship near the rowing benches. When the sea was calm, he used the common helm; but in storms, when the ship rode high on the water, he dropped the other helms, to keep her steady, and give a better command in directing her.

15. Cha-

15 Chabrias having invaded Lacedæmonia, and ravaged the country, when purfued by the Spartans under the command of Agefilaus, pofted himfelf on an eminence, where he fecured his prifoners and booty, and ftrongly entrenched himfelf. The Lacedæmonians encamped at the diftance of five furlongs from him. As foon as night came on, he ordered a number of fires to be lighted, and directed his troops at two o'clock to ftrike their tents, and begin their march over the farther part of the mountain, leaving their cattle behind them. The Lacedæmonians in the mean time, feeing the fires, and hearing the lowing of the cattle, fuppofed the Athenians ftill in camp, and early in the morning advanced to attack it: which when they approached, and found empty, Agefilaus exclaimed, " Chabrias is an able general."

CHAP. XII.

PHOCION.

THE Athenians eager on a war againft Thebes, which Phocion ftrenuoufly oppofed, carried their point againft him, and nominated him general. He immediately ordered proclamation to be made for every Athenian, who could bear arms, under the age of fixty, to follow him from the affembly, and with five days fubfiftence attend him to the field. A great confufion enfued, particularly amongft thofe who were advanced in years, who, murmured, and flew about exclaiming at the harfhnefs of the orders. When Phocion addreffed them, " Why, friends, you have no room to complain of being called out on account of your age, when I, your general, at the age of eighty, go with you." The obfervation ftopped their murmurs. and on fecond confideration they took Phocion's advice, and dropped the projected war.

CHAP. XIII.

CHARES

CHARES having entertained a suspicion that the enemy had spies in his camp, placed a strong guard without the trenches, and ordered every man to accost his neighbour, and not to part till each had told the other, who he was, and to what company, and band, he belonged. By this device the spies were apprehended being unable to tell either their company, band, comrade, or the word.

2. When in Thrace, and the season very severe, Chares observed the men starved themselves, in order to save their cloaths, and, benumbed with cold, did not discover in their performance of his orders their usual alertness: he therefore ordered them to change cloaths with each other. The soldiers then no longer solicitous to spare another's cloaths, as they had done their own, wrapped themselves up warm, and became ready, and alert as usual, in executing their general's commands.

3. Chares, in his retreat from Thrace, while the Thracians hung on him, and galled his rear, having a dangerous ground to pass, and wishing to retard the enemy's pursuit, mounted his trumpets, and, detaching a party of horse to attend them, ordered them to make a circuitous march, and as soon as they had got upon the enemy's rear, to sound the charge, On hearing it, the Thracians halted. and, supposing themselves surrounded by an ambuscade, confusedly left their ranks, and fled leaving Chares without further loss or danger to make good his retreat.

CHAP. XIV.

CHARIDEMUS.

THE Ilienſians, having made themſelves maſters of a city in the territories of Charidemus, and in excurſions from thence committed acts of depredation, Charidemus ſurpriſed and took an Ilienſian ſervant loaded with booty: and by promiſe of great rewards prevailed on him to betray the city into his hands. To eſtabliſh the traitor's intereſt with the watch, he ſupplied him with ſheep and other booty, on his nocturnal expeditions, which he ſhared amongſt the watch, and thereby obtained free leave to paſs and repaſs. On a night agreed on between them, he paſſed the gates, with a party he had engaged, on the pretence of aſſiſting him in bringing back a greater ſpoil. His companions Charidemus ſeized, and threw into irons, and habiting ſome of his own troops in their dreſs, he furniſhed them with a quantity of plunder, and amongſt it a horſe. In order to admit the horſe, the centinel opened the whole gate · when the ſoldiers, together with the horſe, ruſhed in, ſlew the guard, and opening the gates to the reſt of the army made themſelves maſters of the city. Thus it might be ſaid, if we were inclined to be humourous, that Ilium was taken a ſecond time by the ſtratagem of a horſe.

CHAP. XV.

DEMETRIUS PHALEREUS.

DEMETRIUS PHALEREUS, when near being taken by the king of Thrace, hid himſelf in a load of ſtraw; and thus eſcaped into an adjoining territory.

CHAP. XVI.

PHILOCLES.

PHILOCLES, a general of Ptolemy, having besieged Caunus, bribed the superintendants of corn into a conspiracy. They accordingly had it proclaimed in the city, that they meaned that day to give out the corn to the soldiers who immediately left the walls, in order to see the corn measured out. Philocles took the opportunity of the absence of the soldiers from their posts; and, while the walls were left undefended, made his attack, and carried the town.

BOOK IV.

THE PREFATORY ADDRESS.

THIS Book of Stratagems I alfo addrefs to your facred majefties, Antoninus and Verus which I have written with more particular pleafure than the reft, as containing the exploits of your heroic anceftors, who filled the throne of Macedon

CHAP. I.

ARGÆUS

IN the reign of Argæus king of Macedon, the Taulantii under their king Galaurus made an incurfion into Macedonia. Argæus, whofe force was very fmall, directed the Macedonian young women, as the enemy advanced, to fhew themfelves from mount Erebœa. They accordingly did fo, and in a numerous body pouring down from the mount, their faces concealed under chaplets, brandifhed their thyrfufes inftead of fpears. Galaurus, intimidated by their numbers, whom inftead of women he fuppofed to be men, founded a retreat when the Taulantii, throwing away their arms, and whatever might retard their efcape, abandoned themfelves to a precipitate flight. Argæus, having thus obtained a victory without the hazard of a battle, erected a temple to Bacchus* Pfeudanor, and ordered the prieftefles of that god, who were before called Kladones† by the Macedonians, to be ever afterwards diftinguifhed by the title of Mimallones.

* Ψευδανορ fignifies a deceiver in a man's appearance.
† Κλαδοναι fignifies branch-bearers, alluding to the Thyrfus. And Μιμαλλοναι denote imitators.

CHAP. II.

PHILIPPUS.

PHILIP once broke a Tarentine of rank, who had a command in his army, because he used warm baths saying, "You seem a stranger to the Macedonian customs, which do not indulge the use of warm water even to a woman in child-bed

2 ENGAGING the Athenians at Chæronea, Philip made a sham retreat. when Stratocles, the Athenian general, ordered his men to push forwards, crying out, "We will pursue them to the heart of Macedon." Philip coolly observed, "The Athenians know not how to conquer." and ordered his phalanx to keep close and firm, and to retreat slowly, covering themselves with their shields from the attacks of the enemy As soon as he had by this manœuvre drawn them from their advantageous ground, and gained an eminence, he halted, and encouraging his troops to a vigorous attack, made such an impression on the enemy, as soon determined a brilliant victory in his favour.

3. PHILIP, while encamped against the Thebans, was informed that two of his generals, Æropus and Damasippus had taken from the stews a singing girl, and introduced her into the camp. and the fact being proved, he banished both of them the kingdom.

4. HAVING blocked up a city of Thrace, Philip sent to the besieged a flag of truce. who convened an assembly, and introduced to it the flag, anxious to know the enemy's proposals Philip in the mean time directed a vigorous attack, and carried the city, while the people were more attentive to the supposed conditions of peace, than the real attacks of war.

5. AFTER an engagement with the Illyrians, Philip proposed a truce with them, for the purpose of burying their dead. which being

agreed

agreed to, as soon as the last man was buried, his army being drawn up and waiting the signal to engage, he instantly ordered them to charge, and put the enemy, who were unprepared, to a general rout.

6. While Philip was trying his strength with Menagetes in wrestling. the soldiers around were clamorous for their pay, in which he was much in arrears to them, and had not wherewith at the present to make it good Dropping with sweat, and covered as he was with dust, he ran up to them with a laugh, "You are right, ' said he,' my dear lads, and I have been perfuming* myself with that barbarian, in order to pay my respects to you, for the credit you have been so obliging as to give me." Having thus said, he ran through the midst of them, and plunged into a fish-pond. The Macedonians laughed at the humour of the prince: who continued amusing himself in the water, till the soldiers were tired out with the neglect he paid to their remonstrances, and went away. In his hours of gaiety Philip often used to mention this device, by which he had with a stroke of buffoonry got rid of demands, that no arguments could have reasoned away

7 Philip, at Chæronea, knowing the Athenians were hot† and inexperienced, and the Macedonians inured to fatigues and exercise, contrived to prolong the action. and reserving his principal attack to the latter end of the engagement, the enemy weak and exhausted were unable to sustain the charge.

8. Having marched against the Amphissenians, Philip found himself obstructed by the Athenians and Thebans, who had made

---

* The humour expressed by Philip on this occasion lies in the custom, which with the antients prevailed, of washing and perfuming themselves, previous to going to an entertainment, where form or respect was required.

† The word οξυς which I have translated "hot," implies in this place, "active and impressive in the attack." The reader is referred to the second stratagem in this book, which alludes to the same action.

them-

themselves masters of a defile, which thus secured he was unable to force, and therefore had recourse to stratagem. He wrote a letter to Antipater in Macedonia, informing him that the Thracians were in rebellion, and that he was obliged for the present to defer his expedition against the Amphissenians, and to march into Thrace. This letter he dispatched by a way, where he knew it would be intercepted; which accordingly was the case, and Chares and Proxenus the generals, who commanded against him, after they had deliberated on the contents of the letter, quitted the post they possessed. Of their movement Philip immediately availed himself, and passing the defile without opposition, afterwards defeated the allies, and took Amphissa.

9. PHILIP was not more successful in his arms, than he was in treaties and negotiations: and indeed he piqued himself more on advantages gained by these, than by dint of arms. For in the latter he observed his soldiers shared in the glory, but in the other it was all his own.

10. PHILIP accustomed the Macedonians to constant exercise, as well in peace, as in actual service: so that he would frequently make them march three hundred furlongs, carrying with them their helmets, shields, greaves, and spears; and, besides those arms, their provisions likewise, and utensils for common use.

11. WHEN Philip advanced to Larissa, he pretended a fit of illness, in order to decoy the Aleuadians to visit him: intending to seize them, and for their liberty oblige them to give up their towns. But Bæscus apprised the Aleuadians of the stratagem, which thereby fell to the ground.

12. PHILIP desired permission in a full assembly to address the Sarnusians, which being granted, he directed the soldiers, who attended him, to carry cords under their arms. When reaching out his arm, as if to harangue them, the signal he had fixed on, his men immediately

seised

STRATAGEMS OF WAR.

seifed on all the Sarnusians present, bound them, and sent more than ten thousand prisoners into Macedonia.

13. When closely pressed by the Thracians, Philip ordered that as soon as he sounded a retreat, the rear under cover of their shields, should sustain the enemy's attack, and, by acting only on the defensive, retard their pursuit, and thus favour the retreat of the army.

14. In an irruption into Bœotia, Philip's direct march was through a narrow pass, which the Bœotians had secured, and from whence he could not dislodge them, he therefore took another rout, and laid waste the whole country before him. The Bœotians, not bearing to see their country thus desolated, quitted their post, and gave him an opportunity of passing the defile, and pursuing the march he at first projected.

15. Philip had raised the scaling-ladders against the walls of the Methonensians, and a strong body of Macedonians advanced to the attack. As soon as they had mounted the walls, he ordered the ladders to be taken away · thereby leaving the assailants no hopes of safety, but in their courage.

16. The country of the Arbelians, into which Philip had made an irruption, being rough, and craggy, and covered with wood, the Barbarians concealed themselves in the thickets where Philip, a stranger to the country, knew not how to follow them, but by tracing their steps with blood-hounds.

17. The Athenians demanding of Philip the restitution of Amphipolis, and he being at that time engaged in a war with the Illyrians, however unwilling to give it up to the Athenians, consented to make it free. with which though the Athenians appeared contented, they were not perfectly satisfied. Philip therefore, as soon as he had finished the Illyrian war, returned at the head of a powerful army to Amphipolis, and in defiance of the Athenians, who had before shewn themselves dissatisfied, made himself master of the place.

S   18. Phi-

18. Philip having besieged Phalcidon, a city of Thessaly, the Phalcidians capitulated, and his mercenaries entered the city to take possession. But an ambush being placed on the houses and towers, the mercenaries fell a sacrifice to a shower of darts and stones. While the attention of the citizens was thus directed to that part of the city, where the mercenaries entered, and the ambuscade was placed, Philip raised the scaling ladders against the walls on the opposite part of the town, and by a vigorous assault carried it; before the force, employed in the ambuscade, had time to recover their posts, and man the walls.

19. Philip, when he formed the design of reducing Thessaly to the crown of Macedon, did not directly attack the Thessalians in the field. But when the Pallenensians were engaged in war with the Pharsalians, and the Pherensians with the Larissæans, and other states in Thessaly with each other; his practice was in those struggles to give assistance to which ever power applied to him for it. And his victories on those occasions were never marked with cruelty or devastations. He neither disarmed the conquered, nor destroyed their fortifications; but his great object was to create factions, rather than heal them; to protect the weak, and crush the powerful. He endeavoured always to ingratiate himself with the bulk of the people, and cultivated the favour of oratorical demagogues. By these stratagems Philip made himself master of Thessaly, and not by arms.

20. Philip having long laid before Caræ, a well-fortified town, which he was at last unable to carry, found his best exertions necessary to effect a safe retreat, and carry off with him his machines. For this purpose he availed himself of a very dark night, and ordered the smiths' to take his machines in pieces, imitating in the noise, as much as they could, the fabrication of new ones. The Carians, hearing the sound of hammers, applied themselves to strengthen their gates, and to counter-work the effect of the enemy's supposed operations by new erections.

And

And while they were thus employed, Philip in the night ſtruck his tents, and carried off his machines

21. WHEN Philip advanced againſt the Byzantines, he found them ſtrongly ſupported by various allies. To break the confederacy, he diſpatched revolters into the enemy's quarters, to propagate a report, that he had detached forces into the different countries of the allies, and that ſome of their cities were at that inſtant in danger of being taken. And to give colour to this intelligence, he made detachments from his army, which he ordered out on ſhort marches different ways, without any intention to act offenſively. Theſe motions agreeing with the report of the revolters, the allies deſerted the Byzantines, to repair to the aſſiſtance of their reſpective countries.

21. As Philip, after having reduced to his obedience the countries of the Abderites and Maronites, was returning from his expedition with a great fleet, and powerful army, Chares placed an ambuſcade of twenty ſhips near Neapolis to annoy him. Philip, ſuſpecting ſuch attempt, manned four of his beſt-ſailing veſſels with the ſtouteſt and moſt experienced hands he could pick out. and ordered them to make what ſail they could before the fleet, and to paſs Neapolis, holding not far from the ſhore. In purſuit of thoſe four ſail, Chares puſhed out with his twenty ſhips. with which however, being light, and well-manned, he was not able to come up. And while he was chaſing them without effect, Philip ſlipt ſafely by Neapolis with the reſt of the fleet.

CHAP. III.

ALEXANDER.

ALEXANDER whoſe ambition was, to unite all mankind to him, as the common head and ſuperiour of human nature, paſſed a decree, that

that mankind should no longer be called mortals, human beings, or men, but Alexanders.

2. ALEXANDER, in his wars, directed his generals to order the Macedonians to shave their faces, that their enemies in engaging might never lay hold on their beards.

3. AT the siege of Tyre, Alexander having resolved to join the city which was then insular to the continent, by raising a mound in the surrounding waters*, himself first carried a basket of sand, which he threw into it. As soon as the Macedonians saw their king at work with his own hands, they all instantly threw aside their robes, and soon raised the ground.

4. HAVING left a part of his army before Tyre, Alexander himself marched into Arabia. His absence gave the Tyrians new spirits who advanced beyond their walls, engaged the Macedonians in the field, and frequently defeated them. Parmenio, Alexander's general, gave him notice of what had passed, who suddenly returning, and seeing the Macedonians retreating before the enemy, instead of flying to their assistance, marched directly to the town, which he surprised, evacuated by the Tyrian forces, and took it by storm. The Tyrians, finding their city taken, surrendered themselves and their arms to the discretion of the Macedonian conqueror.

5. WHEN Alexander advanced against Darius, he ordered the Macedonians, as soon as they drew near the Persians, to fall down on

---

* In my translation of this stratagem I have rather endeavoured to explain an historical fact, than content myself with a literal translation, which would have imperfectly represented the great design Alexander in this work conceived, and executed. For a more full account of which the curious reader is referred to Arrian. In Polyænus the object is merely to shew Alexander's address in promoting alacrity in his army in the prosecution of so laborious an undertaking. And even so far considered, the passage seems faulty. Μιταβαλιν χαμα τοις ‑υχιν, being a phrase, that very imperfectly describes the meaning it was intended to convey.

their

their hands and knees and, as soon as ever the trumpet sounded the charge, to rise up and vigoroufly attack the enemy. They did fo and the Perfians, confidering it as an act of reverence, abated of their impetuofity, and their minds became foftened towards the proftrate foe. Darius too was led to think, he had gained a victory without the hazard of a battle. When on found of the trumpet, the Macedonians fprung up, and made fuch an impreffion on the enemy, that their centre was broken, and the Perfians entirely defeated.

6. At Arbelæ, where the laft battle between Alexander and Darius was fought, a confiderable body of Perfians had made a circuit, and feifed the Macedonian carriage-horfes and baggage. Parmenio, obferving their movement, defired Alexander to order a detachment to protect them. By no means, replied Alexander, I have no troops to fpare againft prædatory parties : my bufinefs is with the enemy, and I muft not weaken my phalanx. If we be conquered, we fhall not want our baggage : and if we conquer, both our's and the enemy's will become our own.

7. After the conqueft of Afia, the Macedonians being inftant with Alexander, and extravagant in their demands, on prefumption of their fervices, he ordered them to take their pofts by themfelves in arms, and oppofite to them he ordered his Perfian troops to do the fame. The forces being thus feparated, " Now, 'faid he,' Macedonians, chufe your general. and I will take the Perfians. If you beat me, I will comply with all your demands. and you, if I beat you, will learn to be quiet." Struck with the greatnefs of foul, this ftratagem difcovered, the Macedonians ever after conducted themfelves with more moderation.

8. In his firft action with the Perfians, Alexander feeing the Macedonians give way, rode through the ranks, calling out to his men,

" One

"One effort more, my Macedonians, one glorious effort." Animated by their prince, they made a vigorous attack, and the enemy abandoned themselves to flight. Thus did that critical moment determine the victory.

9. ALEXANDER in his Indian expedition advanced to the Hydaspes, with intention to cross it. When Porus appeared with his army on the other side, determined to dispute his passage. Alexander then marched towards the head of the river, and attempted to cross it there. Thither also Porus marched, and drew up his army on the opposite side. He then made the same effort lower down, there too Porus opposed him. Those frequent appearances of intention to cross it, without ever making one real attempt to effect it, the Indians ridiculed; and concluding that he had no real design to pass the river, they became more negligent in attending his motions. When Alexander by a rapid march gaining the banks, effected his purpose on barges, boats, and hides stuffed with straw, before the enemy had time to come up with him: who deceived by so many feint attempts, yielded him at last an uninterrupted passage.

10. ALEXANDER finding his men, glutted with the immense wealth of which they had possessed themselves in Persia, and which they carried about with them in carriages, did not at all relish this new expedition into India, ordered first the royal carriages to be destroyed, and afterwards all the rest. The Macedonians, thus deprived of their treasures, immediately became anxious for more, and, in order to obtain it, of course ready for new enterprises.

11. THE Thracians endeavouring to make an impression on the Macedonian phalanx by a great number of chariots, which were directed against them, Alexander ordered his men to avoid them, if they could, and if not, to throw themselves on the ground, holding over them their shields:

by

by which means the carriages on fpeed paffed over, without hurting them. And by this manœuvre the numerous carriages of the enemy were rendered ufelefs.

12 When Alexander advanced againſt Thebes, he planted in ambuſh a concealed body of troops under the command of Antipater, while he himſelf marched openly againſt the enemy's ſtrongeſt works. which the Thebans with great obſtinacy defended In the midſt of the engagement Antipater ſecretly quitted his ambuſh, and wheeling round attacked the walls in an oppoſite quarter, where they were weakeſt, and ill-manned, and made himſelf maſter of the city. He immediately hoiſted the Macedonian colours • which Alexander ſeeing called out, " The town was his own." The Thebans, who had till then made a gallant reſiſtance, as ſoon as they ſaw their city in the poſſeſſion of the enemy, abandoned themſelves to flight.

13. The Macedonians having fled from the field, Alexander changed the coat of mail into a breaſt-plate. which was a protection to them, as long as they boldly faced the enemy: but if they fled, they expoſed to the foe their naked backs This had ſuch an effect • that they never afterwards fled, but, if they were overpowered, always retreated in good order

14 After Alexander had learned from the augurs, that the auguries were propitious, he ordered the victims to be carried round the army, that the ſoldiers, not depending on what was told them, might be convinced with their own eyes of the ground of their hopes in the enſuing action.

15 When Alexander entered Aſia, to render Memnon general of the enemy's forces ſuſpected by the Perſians, he ordered the party, he had detached to ravage the country, not to touch his property, nor commit any depredations on his eſtates.

16. When Alexander ſurveyed the advantageous poſition of the Perfians

fians on the opposite side of the Granicus, determined to dispute his passage over it, he changed his ground and, at the head of his phalanx, plunging into the river at a place above the enemy, he effected a passage, and after an obstinate engagement routed the Persian army

17 At the battle of Arbela, Darius had planted the ground between the two camps with crows-feet which Alexander having discovered, advanced, with his right wing aslant, skirting the armed ground and in that order directed the army to support him To oppose that manœuvre, and throw him upon the ground he seemed to avoid, the Persian weakened his lines and detached his cavalry which Alexander observing, supported by Parmenio, and flanked by the crows-feet, fell upon the weakened lines of the enemy, threw them into disorder, and begun the rout

18 Alexander, after he had passed the Tygris, while the Persians were laying the whole country waste with fire, sent a deputation to expostulate with them on their outrages, and to conjure them to regard their own preservation, and spare the country

19 Alexander, when in Hyrcania, having been informed that his character and conduct were aspersed both by the Macedonians and Greeks, assembled his friends, and told them, the situation of his affairs at home required him to send letters to Macedonia, and inform his subjects, that he should certainly return within three years: and he desired his officers at the same time to write letters to their respective friends, to the same purport, which to a man they all did As soon as the letter-carriers had got about three miles from the camp, he ordered them to be brought back, opened all the letters, and from thence learned the opinion, that every one entertained of him.

20. Alexander having closely besieged a fortified place in India, the besieged agreed to evacuate the fort on condition that they might be permitted to march out with their arms. Which being complied with,
the

the garrison marched out, and encamped on a hill, where they entrenched themselves, and posted a guard. Upon Alexander's advancing against them, the Indians urged to him the obligation of the treaty. To which the Macedonian replied, " I gave you leave to quit the fort, but not a word was mentioned in the treaty of any further movement.

21. PITTACUS, the grandson of Porus, advantageously posted himself in a narrow valley to intercept Alexander in his march. The valley was long, but not more than four furlongs wide: and terminated in a very strait defile. Adapting his march to the nature of the ground, Alexander formed his cavalry into a double phalanx, and ordered them, bearing upon their reins, to march in a close compact body. and, as soon as the enemy attacked their right wing, to receive them upon their spears, and give their horses the rein, and, when they had cleared the pass, to attack the enemy's rear. Having thus given his orders, he begun his march nearly in the shape of a gnomon. As soon as those, who were posted in the left wing, saw the rear of the right on speed; setting up a shout, and in the same manner giving reins to their horses, they attacked the Indians. who afraid of being blocked up in the valley, precipitately fled to the narrow pass, in order to make their escape, when many were cut to pieces by the Macedonians, and many more trampled to death by their own horse

22. In the battle against Porus Alexander posted part of his cavalry in the right wing, and part he left as a body of reserve at a small distance on the plain. His left wing consisted of the phalanx and his elephants. Porus ordered his elephants to be formed against him, himself taking his station on an elephant at the head of his left wing. The elephants were drawn up within fifty yards of each other, and in those interstices was posted his infantry. So that his front exhibited the appearance of a great wall, the elephants looked like so many towers, and the infantry like the parapet between them. Alexander directed his

infan-

infantry to attack the enemy in front, while himself at the head of his horse advanced against the cavalry. Against those movements Porus ably guarded But the beasts could not be kept in their ranks, and, wherever they deserted them, the Macedonians in a compact body pouring in closed with the enemy, and attacked them both in front and flank. The body of reserve in the mean time wheeling round, and attacking their rear, compleated the defeat

23 THE Thessalians having secured the post at Tempe, which Alexander saw it impracticable to force, he cut holes in the rugged rock of Ossa, which served as steps, on which he marched his army and thus over the top of Ossa opened himself a passage into Thessaly, while the Thessalians were employed in defending the pass at Tempe. At this day may be seen the rock of Ossa cut in the manner of a ladder, which now bears the name of Alexander's ladder.

24. IN Macedonia and among the Greeks, Alexander's court of justice was plain and simple, but among the barbarians, in order to strike them with the greater awe, it was most splendid and imperial. In Bactria, Hyrcania, and India when he heard causes, the apparatus and formality of his court were as follows. The pavilion was large enough to contain a hundred tables, and was supported by fifty pillars of gold: and the canopy was adorned with various gold ornaments. Stationed round the pavilion within were, first, five hundred Persians, dressed in purple and white vests: and next to those an equal number of archers in different dresses of yellow, blue, and scarlet Before those stood five hundred Macedonians, with silver shields, the tallest men that could be picked out. In the middle of the pavilion was a golden throne, on which the monarch sate to hear causes attended on either side by his guards. Round the pavilion on the outside were ranged a number of elephants, and a thousand Macedonians in the Macedonian habit. Behind those were five hundred Sufians in purple dresses · and the whole

was

was surrounded with ten thousand Persians, distinguishable for their shape, and size, and dressed in the Persian manner, with scimitars at their sides Such was the court of Alexander amongst the barbarians.

25. ALEXANDER, marching through a sandy desert, himself as well as his army were in great distress for water; when one of the scouts, having in the hollow of a rock discovered a little, brought it to him in his helmet. After he had shewed it to his army, in order to revive their spirits with the hopes of water being near at hand; without moving it to his lips, before them all he poured it out upon the ground. The Macedonians immediately set up a shout, and bade him lead on, for their king's example had taught them to conquer thirst.

26. ALEXANDER by a forced march endeavoured to gain the Tigris, before Darius . when a panic* seised his rear, and ran through the army. The king ordered the trumpets to sound the signal of safety, the first rank immediately to throw down their arms at their feet, and the next to do the same. This order being observed through the whole army, they were convinced the cause of their confusion was a panic . from

---

* These panic fears were sudden consternations that sometimes seised men without any visible cause, and were therefore imputed to the operations of dæmons, especially Pan, upon men's fancies. Instances of it occur in more stratagems of Polyænus, than this one and there is frequent mention made of it in antient history. We are informed, when Brennus, the Gallic general, had been defeated by the Greeks, the night following he and the remainder of his troops were seised with such terrors and distractions; that ignorant of what they were doing, they fell to killing and wounding one another, till they were all destroyed. Such another fright gave the Athenians great advantage against the Persians in memory of which piece of service Miltiades erected a statue to the god Pan. The reasons why these terrors were attributed to Pan are variously asserted. One is the device of Pan mentioned in the second chapter of Polyænus's first book of Stratagems.

In these terrors, whereof there was either no apparent cause, or at least none answerable to the greatness of the sudden consternation, it was an usual method to do something directly contrary to what the danger would have required, had it been really such, as it was vainly imagined. Thus Alexander, in the instance before us, ordered his men to disarm themselves.

whence as foon as they recovered themfelves, they took up their arms, and purfued their march

27 AFTER Alexander had defeated Darius at the battle of Arbelæ, Phrafaortes a relation of that monarch in great force pofted himfelf at the gates of Sufa which is a narrow pafs between high and fteep mountains. This the Macedonians in vain endeavoured to force: the barbarians eafily defended it, annoying the enemy with arrows, flings, and ftones Alexander ordered a retreat, and encamped about thirty furlongs diftant The oracle at Delphos had formerly declared, that a Lycian ftranger fhould be his guide againft the Perfians A herdfman came up to Alexander, in his ruftic drefs, faying, his name was Lycius; and informed him, there was a private road, which winded round the mountains, covered with wood, and known to no one but himfelf and well known to him, as affording excellent pafturage. Alexander remembered the oracle, and liftened to the herdfman's information He then ordered the whole army to remain in camp, and light a number of fires in fuch confpicuous places, as might be beft feen by the Perfians and gave private orders to Philotas and Hephæftion, as foon as they faw the Macedonians fhew themfelves on the mountains, to attack the enemy below Himfelf with his guards, one heavy-armed troop, and all the Scythian archers, conducted by Lycius, marched eighty furlongs through the private road, and halted in the middle of a thick wood About midnight by a circuitous march he gained a pofition a little above the enemy, who were then buried in fleep: and in the morning founded the charge from the top of the mountains. Hephæftion and Philotas immediately marched out of the camp, and advanced againft them on the plain who, thus attacked both above and below, were part of them cut to pieces, fome thrown from the precipices, and others taken prifoners.

28. ALEXANDER having been obliged in the heat of fummer to
make

make an expeditious retreat, the enemy hanging upon his rear, directed his march near a river, when obferving that his men, who were very thirfty, looked anxioufly at the water, left by ftopping to drink they fhould lofe their ranks, and alfo retard his march, he ordered proclamation to be made, " That no man fhould touch that river, for its waters were fatal " Fearing the confequences they refrained from drinking it, and without intermiffion purfued their march. Which as foon as they had performed, and the army was encamped, both Alexander and his officers drank openly of the ftream, and the foldiers, laughing at the trick their general had played them, drank freely of it too, liberated from every fear either of the enemy, or the water.

29. WHEN Alexander penetrated into Sogdiana, a country rough and rugged and traced with no roads, his march was attended with great difficulties. In the middle of it extended a high and craggy rock; its tops acceffible only to the birds. Around it was a thick and continued wood which rendered the product of the place ftill more fecure. There Ariomazes pofted himfelf, with a numerous and determined band of Sogdians. On the part of the rock, where he had fortified himfelf, were fine fprings, and plenty of provifion. Alexander riding round, and reconnoitring the place, obferved behind the rock a flope particularly well-covered with wood. There he ordered three hundred young men, expert in climbing precipices, without their arms to endeavour to make their way through the trees, affifting each other by faftening as they went up fmall cords to the boughs And as foon as they had reached the top, loofing the white belts they had on, they were directed to fix them upon poles, and extend them above the trees, that the gleaming girdles brandifhed about might be feen as well by the Macedonians below, as the Barbarians above them. The active and intrepid band, as foon as they had with difficulty reached the top, at fun-rife according to orders brandifhed their belts, when the Macedonians

cedonians set up a general shout Ariomazes apprehending the whole army were in possession of the top of the mountain, and above their heads, surrendered himself and his rock to Alexander, supposing his power and abilities divine.

30 THE Calthæans, a people of India, Alexander had entirely exterminated, having slain all that were able to bear arms, and levelled their city Sangalata with the ground. This act prejudiced him much in the opinion of the Indians, who considered him as a savage, and a free-booter. In order to remove these prejudices, from the next city, he reduced in India, he took hostages, and advancing against Pæta, a large and populous city, before his army he placed the hostages, old men, and boys, and women. As soon as the enemy saw their own countrymen, and from the condition in which they appeared concluded the humanity with which their conqueror had treated them, they opened their gates, and with his hostages readily received him: and this account of his clemency being studiously propagated induced other Indian nations voluntarily to submit to him.

31 THE country of the Coffæans Alexander found rough and uncultivated, the mountains high and almost inaccessible, the posts defended by a numerous and resolute body of men: he had therefore little hopes of making himself master of it. At that time he received information of the death of Hephæftion, who died at Babylon: in consequence of which he ordered a general mourning, and put the army in motion, in order to celebrate his funeral. The Coffæan scouts seeing that, and supposing them going to evacuate the country, reported the motions of the Macedonian army; and the Coffæans began to disband. Alexander, having received intelligence of the error, into which his movement had betrayed the enemy, detached a body of horse to secure the posts on the mountains: then wheeling round he joined the detachment of cavalry, and compleated the conquest of the country. This
cir-

circumstance, it was said, arising from Hephæstion's death, consoled Alexander for the loss of his friend

32. In the palace of the Persian monarch Alexander read a bill of fare for the king's dinner and supper, that was engraven on a column of brass: on which were also other regulations, which Cyrus had directed. It run thus.

" Of fine wheat flour four hundred artabæ (a Median artaba is an Attic bushel), of second flour three hundred artabæ, and of third flour the same: in the whole one thousand artabæ of wheat flour for supper. Of the finest barley flour two hundred artabæ, of the second four hundred, and four hundred of the third in all one thousand artabæ of barley flour. Of oatmeal two hundred artabæ. Of paste mixed for pastry of different kinds ten artabæ. Of cresses chopped small, and sifted, and formed into a kind of ptisan, ten artabæ. Of mustard-seed the third of an artaba. Male sheep four hundred. Oxen a hundred. Horses thirty. Fat geese four hundred. Three hundred turtles. Small birds of different kinds six hundred. Lambs three hundred. Goslings a hundred. Thirty head of deer. Of new milk ten marises (a maris contains ten attic choas). Of milk whey sweetened ten marises. Of garlick a talent's worth. Of strong onions half a talent's worth. Of knot grass an artaba. Of the juice of benzoin two minæ Of cumin an artaba. Of benzoin a talent worth. Of rich cider the fourth of an artaba. Of compound juices an artaba. Of cumin paste the fourth of an artaba. Of millet seed three talents worth. Of anise flowers three minæ. Of coriander seed the third of an artaba. Of melon seed two capises. Of parsnips ten artabæ. Of sweet wine five marises. Of salted gongylis five marises. Of pickled capers five marises. Of salt ten artabæ. Of Æthiopian cumin six capises (a capis is an attic chænix). Of dried anise thirty minæ Of parsley seed four capises. Oil of Sisamin ten marises, Cream five marises. Oil of cinnamon five marises. Oil of

acan-

acanthus five marifes. Oil of sweet almonds three marifes. Of dried sweet almonds three artabæ. Of wine five hundred marifes (And if he supped at Babylon or Sufa, one half was palm wine, and the other half wine expressed from grapes). Two hundred load of dry wood, and one hundred load of green. Of fluid honey a hundred square palathæ, containing the weight of about ten minæ. When he was in Media, there were added—of bastard saffron seed three artabæ, of saffron two minæ. This was the appointment for dinner and supper. He also expended in largesses five hundred artabæ of fine wheat flour. Of fine barley flour a thousand artabæ: and of other kinds of flour a thousand artabæ. Of rice five hundred artabæ. Of corn five hundred marifes. Of corn for the horses twenty thousand artabæ. Of straw ten thousand load. Of vetches five thousand load. Of oil of Sisamin two hundred marifes. Of vinegar a hundred marifes. Of cresses chopped small thirty artabæ. All, that is here enumerated, was distributed among the forces, that attended him. In dinner, and supper, and in largesses, the above was the king's daily expenditure.

WHILE the Macedonians read this appointment of the Persian monarch's table, with admiration of the happiness of a prince, who displayed such affluence, Alexander ridiculed him, as an unfortunate man, who could wantonly involve himself in so many cares, and ordered the pillar, on which these articles were engraved, to be demolished observing to his friends, that it was no advantage to a king to live in so luxurious a manner, for cowardice and dastardy were the certain consequences of luxury and dissipation. Accordingly, added he, you have experienced that those, who have been used to such revels, never knew how to face danger in the field.

CHAP.

CHAP. IV.

ANTIPATER

ANTIPATER, in the Thracian war, having advanced into the country of the Tetrachoritæ, ordered fire to be set to the horses' hay, which lay before his pavilion. And as soon as it flamed out, the trumpets sounded the charge, when the Macedonians repaired to the royal pavilion, with their spears all raised on high. The Tetrachoritæ, struck with terror at such marks of frantic desperation, made a precipitate retreat, leaving to Antipater a cheap and easy victory.

2. When Antipater attempted to cross the Sperchius, and found the Thessalian cavalry drawn up on the other side, ready to dispute his passage, he retreated to his camp and ordered the Macedonians to rest on their arms, and not to unbridle their horses. The Thessalians, left without an enemy, directed their horses with all speed to Lamia, to dine at their own houses. Antipater in the mean time by an expeditious march advanced to the river, crossed it without opposition, and afterwards took Lamia by surprise.

3. To impress the Thessalians with an opinion, that his cavalry was very numerous, Antipater advanced with a number of asses and mules, which he mounted with men, armed as troopers: but the first line of every troop he formed of his real cavalry. The enemy seeing so formidable an appearance, and supposing not only the front lines, but all the rest, to be cavalry, abandoned themselves to flight. This stratagem Agesilaus also employed against Æropus in Macedonia, and Eumenes against Antigonus in Asia.

CHAP. V.

PARMENIO

PARMENIO, after the battle at Issus, having been detached by Alexander to Damascus, to escort the baggage, fell in with a body of heavy-armed troops. Apprehensive that the Barbarians, who had the care of the baggage, might, during the action, through fear desert their charge, and run away, he dispatched three troops of horse to them, with injunctions to proclaim, that whoever of them did not hold his horses with his own hands, should be put to death. This proclamation had its effect: the Barbarians all held their horses, and took good care of the baggage.

CHAP. VI.

ANTIGONUS

ANTIGONUS made himself master of Corinth by the following stratagem. While Alexander was in possession of the fort, he died: and left Nicæa a widow, who was then not very young. Antigonus proposed a marriage between her and his son Demetrius: to which the splendour of royalty easily obtained her consent. A sacrifice was offered, and all the previous ceremonies of marriage, according to the Grecian institution, were performed. A great concourse of people were assembled on the occasion: and the guards attended Nicæa, dressed in royal robes, and wantoning in affected state to the theatre. But the bride had no sooner entered it, than Antigonus, no longer solicitous about the nuptial ceremonies, made a vigorous attack upon the fort,

and

and carried it with ease, while the guards were chiefly employed on the festivity of the royal nuptials. Thus Antigonus possessed himself of all Corinth and so terminated the proposed nuptials.

2. ANTIGONUS, in treating with an embassy, used previously to inform himself from the public records, who were the persons that composed the last embassy from the same quarter, the subject of it, and every particular relative to it. With all these circumstances he, in the course of conversation, would usually entertain the ambassadors: and by these means wormed himself into a degree of familiarity with them, and at the same time impressed them with an idea of his extraordinary memory.

3 AT the siege of Megara, Antigonus brought his elephants into the field among which the Megarensians, after having daubed their swine with pitch, and set fire to it, let them loose. The animals grunting and crying under the torture of the fire, sprung forwards as hard as they could among the elephants who confused and frighted broke their ranks, and ran different ways. Antigonus ordered the Indians ever after, in training up their elephants, to bring up swine among them: that the beasts might thus become accustomed to the sight of them, and to their noise

4 ANTIGONUS by a device once saved Antipater from being stoned by the Macedonians Through the midst of the camp run a rapid river, over which was a bridge On one side were the Macedonians, on the other Antigonus with his own horse. The soldiers were instant and clamorous for their pay, and threatened Antipater with death, if he any longer trifled with them, and did not immediately comply with their demands. Unable to make good to them their arrears, and alarmed at the danger that threatened his disappointment of them, he consulted Antigonus, who advised him to leave the camp, and undertook to favour his escape. Antigonus accordingly passed the

bridge in full armour, and rode directly through the phalanx, thereby dividing it, and turned first to one division, and then to the other, as if he was going to harangue them. The Macedonians paid every attention due to his rank and character, and followed him with great solicitude to hear what he had to offer. As soon as they formed round him, he begun a long harangue in defence of Antipater, promising, assuring, and urging every consideration to induce them to acquiesce, till he should be in a situation that might enable him to satisfy their demands. During this prolix harangue, Antipater passed the bridge with a party of horse, and escaped the soldiers' resentment.

5. ANTIGONUS, when in force superiour to the enemy, always engaged coolly; but if inferiour, attacked with all possible vigour. esteeming a glorious death preferable to an ignominious life.

6. WHILE Antigonus wintered in Cappadocia, three thousand heavy-armed Macedonians revolted from him. and having advantageously posted themselves on the mountains, they ravaged Lycaonia, and Phrygia. Antigonus thought it cruel, to put such a number of men to death, and yet was afraid, lest they should join the enemy, who were commanded by Lacetas. He therefore put in execution the following stratagem. He dismissed Leonidas, one of his generals, who immediately went over to the revolters, and offered to join them. His offer they readily embraced, and appointed him their general. The first step he took, was to prevail on them not to attach themselves to any party. which eased Antigonus of his apprehensions. He contrived afterwards to draw them from the mountains to a place, where cavalry might act, of which they were destitute. There Antigonus with a detachment of horse surprised them, and seised Holcias and two of the principals in the revolt, who threw themselves upon his mercy, and begged their lives. which he granted, on condition, that they would without tumult and confusion quit

the

the camp, and return into Macedonia They accepted the terms, and Leonidas was difpatched to conduct them to Macedonia, and deliver them at their refpective homes.

7 As Antigonus was in full march after Attalus, Alcetas, and Docimus, three able generals of the Macedonians, and in hopes of furprifing their camp in the ftreights of Pifidia. the elephants gave mouth, and apprifed the Macedonians of his approach, for he only in his army ufed thofe beafts Alcetas with the heavy-armed troops immediately endeavoured to gain the fummit of the fteep and craggy mountains. Inftead of following him, Antigonus wheeled round the mountain, with all poffible expedition directing his march to the quarter where the army was encamped whom he furprifed, and furrounded before they had time to form, and thus obtained a victory without flaughter, the enemy furrendering themfelves prifoners of war

8. ANTIGONUS fitted out a fleet of a hundred and thirty fail, the command of which he gave to Nicanor · who engaged the fleet of Polyfperchon, which was commanded by Clitus The battle was fought in the Hellefpont, when Nicanor, whofe inexperience engaged the enemy with the fwell of the tide againft him*, loft feventy fhips. The victory became decifive on the part of the enemy when juft at even Antigonus reached the fleet Undaunted at the defeat he had received, he ordered the fixty fhips that remained, to be ready to renew the action the next morning and on board each of them pofted fome of the braveft and moft refolute men of his own guards, whom he commanded to threaten

---

* When it is confidered, that fhips of war, though not wholly deftitute of fails, were chiefly rowed with oars, and efpecially in engagements, that they might be more able to tack about upon any advantage, and approach the enemy on his weakeft fide where there was a flux of the tide, it may be eafily conceived to have been a matter of great confequence to gain it.

death

death to all, who would not bear boldly down upon the enemy. And Byzantium, then in alliance with him, being situated near at hand, he ordered from thence light-armed, and heavy-armed troops, and archers, of each a thousand, whom he posted on the shore, in order to support the fleet, by annoying the enemy with javelins and arrows. This was all effected in a single night. At day break a shower of javelins and arrows was poured upon the enemy, who just turning out, and scarcely awake, were desperately wounded before they well knew the quarter from whence they were attacked. Some cut their cables, and others weighed their anchors, while nothing prevailed but noise and confusion. Antigonus at the same time ordered the sixty ships to bear down upon them: when, thus attacked from the sea quarter, and from land, the conquerors were obliged to resign their victory to the conquered.

9 AFTER the naval victory in the Hellespont, Antigonus ordered his fleet to cruize towards Phœnicia. while the sailours were adorned with chaplets, and the ships decorated with the ornaments of the enemy's fleet. And his captains he ordered to sail as near as they could to the harbours, and cities, they passed, that so the victory might be published throughout all Asia. The Phœnician ships, bound for Rosium, a port of Cilicia, and charged with great sums of money from Eumenes, were under the conduct of Sosigenes. and while he was observing the tides at Orthiomagis, the crews of the Phœnician vessels, when they saw the victorious fleet splendidly adorned, seised the treasures they carried, and leaped on board the vessels of Antigonus, who thereby became possessed both of great treasures and an addition of hands.

10 AFTER an engagement between Antigonus and Eumenes, in which the victory was undecided, Eumenes sent a herald to Antigonus, to treat with him for mutual consent to bury their slain. Antigonus having been informed his own loss exceeded that of the enemy, to

con-

conceal the fact, detained the herald, till his own slain had been all burnt. And after they were buried, he difmiffed the herald, and acceded to the propofal.

15 WHILE Antigonus lay in winter quarters at Gadamertes, a city of the Medes, Eumenes blocked him up there: having pofted a cordon of troops to the extent of a thoufand furlongs. The roads on which the troops were pofted, lay over the mountains. Below was a level plain, that boafted nothing but fulphur mines, and ftinking bogs, barren and uninhabited, as affording neither water, nor grafs, nor wood, nor plant Through this plain Antigonus determined to march, thereby efcaping the force that was pofted on the road, and paffing through the midft of the generals, whofe ftation was on either fide of the plain For this purpofe he ordered ten thoufand cafks to be got ready and filled with water, and provifion for ten days, with barley for the horfes, and what fodder they might have occafion for As foon as thefe preparations were made, he in the night began his march through the inhofpitable plain, ftrictly forbidding any fires to be lighted, left thofe, who were pofted at the feet of the mountains, fhould obferve them, and by that means difcover their march. Nor indeed would it have been difcovered at all, had his orders been exactly complied with. But on a night particularly cold, fome of the foldiers lighted fires the flames of which the enemy obferving, difcovered his movement, juft as he had cleared the plain, and falling upon his rear, did fome execution there. But that affects not the ftratagem, which was fo happily conceived, that had it been as properly executed, not a man would have been loft.

12. ANTIGONUS, having pofted himfelf on the fide of a mountain, and obferving Eumenes's ranks, drawn up on the plain, to be very weak, ordered fome troops of horfe to wheel round, and fall upon his rear. which they did, and brought off a confiderable part of his baggage.

13. ANTIGONUS engaged Eumenes at Gabiæ. The foil of the plain, on which they fought, was light and sandy: and two great armies engaging on it, raised such clouds of dust, as prevented both armies from discovering each other's movements. They fought hand to hand, when Antigonus, having learned that the baggage of the enemy was left at a little distance behind, with which were their wives, and children, mistresses, slaves, gold, and silver, and whatever of value they, who had followed the fortunes of Eumenes, had brought from the army of Alexander, detached some choice troops of horse to seise the baggage, and bring it off to his own camp. They accordingly, while the armies were closely engaged, wheeled round, and, their movement concealed by a cloud of dust, executed their orders, and brought off the baggage. After the battle was over, it appeared that Antigonus had lost five thousand men, and Eumenes only three hundred. The latter therefore retreated to their camp in high spirits on the decided success of the day. But as soon as they discovered their baggage was carried off, and every thing lost, that was dear to them, the palm of victory became shaded with mourning, and every expression of grief: with which they were so far transported, the more they reflected on their loss, that many of them sent a deputation to Antigonus, with a tendre of their service. Finding the effect that the loss of their baggage had on Eumenes's army, Antigonus followed it up with a proclamation, that he would restore without ransom to every soldier his property. Numbers upon this proclamation immediately revolted to him, not only Macedonians, but also ten thousand Persians under the command of Peucestes. For as soon as he saw the Macedonians incline to Antigonus, he followed their example. And in short such a change of sentiment and fortune did this circumstance produce, that his own guards*

---

* The royal guards, stiled Argyraspides, from their silver shields. See Book IV. Ch. III Str 24.

delivered

delivered up Eumenes a prisoner to Antigonus, who became monarch of all Asia.

14. Having heard that Python, governor of Media, had raised a foreign army to support him in a revolt, Antigonus dissembled his belief of it; observing to those who had given him the information, " I can give no credit to this report of Python, for I intended myself to furnish him with five thousand armed Macedonians and Thracians, and a thousand guards." Python informed of this, and giving full credit to the regard Antigonus had expressed for him, immediately waited on him to receive the intended supplies. When introducing Python to the Macedonians, he signified to them his crime, and ordered him to execution.

15. The Argyraspides, that had delivered up to him Eumenes as his prisoner, Antigonus liberally rewarded. But to guard against a similar act of perfidy in them to himself, he ordered a thousand of them to serve under Sibyrtius governor of Arabia. Others he disposed of in garrisons, in remote and uncultivated countries. And thus he very soon got rid of them all.

16. When Antigonus besieged Rhodes, he committed the conduct of the siege to his son Demetrius, proclaiming safety to the Rhodians, both as to their persons and property. And also to all merchants about Syria, Phœnicia, Cilicia, Pamphylia, and even to those of Rhodes who had concerns on the sea, he gave leave to trade securely on any sea, provided they never touched at Rhodes. That, thus deprived of all foreign assistance and supplies, the city might be the more easily reduced; the auxiliaries Ptolemy had sent them not being able to hold out long against Demetrius.

17. Antigonus, having taken into pay some Gallic mercenaries under the command of Biderius, at the rate of a gold Macedonic, gave up to them, as hostages in security of payment, some men and boys of rank and family. The enemy, against whom the Gauls were engaged

by Antigonus, brought him to an action: after which the mercenaries demanded their pay. But when Antigonus directed payment to be made to all, that bore arms, according to his agreement, the Gauls demanded pay for all that attended the army, whether they bore arms, or not, even women and children: alledging, that the agreement was to every Gaul a gold Macedonic. The sum to be paid, if only every soldier received pay, wou'd amount to thirty talents; but, if paid to all indiscriminately, to a hundred. On Antigonus's refusal to comply with their unreasonable demands, they retired to their camp, vowing vengeance against the hostages. Fearing they might proceed to acts of cruelty, he sent a deputation to them; informing them, that rather than they should be diffatisfied, he would comply with their demands: and directed them to send some they could confide in, to receive the money. Overjoyed at the compliance of Antigonus, and the prospect of so great riches, some Gallic chiefs were dispatched to settle the business, and receive the money: whom, as soon as they arrived at the Macedonian camp, Antigonus seised, and informed the Gauls, they should never be given up till he had first received his own hostages. The Gauls found it in vain to contend, therefore gave up the Macedonians, and in return received their own chiefs, and thirty talents.

18. ANTIGONUS, determined to crush Apollodorus tyrant of the Cafiandrenfians, invested Cafiandria: but, after a ten month's blockade, was obliged to raife the fiege. He then applied to the famous pirate Aminias, whom he found means to prevail on, to second his designs. Aminias accordingly proceeded to cultivate the good opinion of Apollodorus, undertook to reconcile Antigonus to him, and to compromise the dispute between them : as also to supply him with provisions and wine. The tyrant, satisfied with the friendly professions of Aminias, and presuming on the absence of Antigonus, became less strict in his discipline and duty on the walls. Aminias in the mean time directed ladders to

be

STRATAGEMS OF WAR.

be privately conftructed, as high as the walls and at an advanced poft, not far from them, called Bolus, he concealed two thoufand men, and with them ten Ætolian pirates under the command of Melotas Thefe at day-break, obferving the walls thinly guarded, crept fecretly to the parapet between the towers, and, as foon as they had fixed the ladders, gave the fignal Amınıas with the two thoufand men immediately advanced, mounted the ladders, and made themfelves mafters of the place Antigonus, on notice of his fuccefs, returned to Caffandria, and difpoffeffed the tyrant.

19 ANTIGONUS, being encamped oppofite to the enemy who were commanded by Eumenes, and with an inferiour force, while frequent embaffies paffed between the two camps, directed that, as foon as the next embaffy arrived, a foldier fhould abruptly introduce himfelf, panting, and covered with duft, and inform him, the allies were at hand Antigonus, hearing this, jumped up in an affected tranfport of joy, and difmiffed the ambaffadors. The next day he extended the front of his army twice its former length, and advanced beyond the trenches The enemy apprifed by their ambaffadors of the arrival of the allies, and obferving the phalanx fo much extended, which they fuppofed had a proportionable depth, did not dare to hazard an engagement, but made a precipitate retreat

20. ANTIGONUS, in order to make himfelf mafter of Athens on as eafy terms as poffible, concluded a peace with the Athenians in the autumn. *After which they fowed their corn, and referved for their own ufe only as much of their old ftock as would ferve them till their next crop was reaped. But as foon as the corn was near ripe, Antigonus made an irruption into Attica. When, having nearly finifhed the ftock they had in their granaries, and finding themfelves prevented from reaping the crop then on the ground, they opened their gates to Antigonus, and complied with all his demands.

X 2 CHAP

CHAP. VII.

DEMETRIUS

DEMETRIUS, though much diſtreſſed for money, by new levies doubled his army. And when ſome of his friends in ſurpriſe aſked him, how he expected to pay them, difficult as he found it to ſupport a ſmaller force: the more powerful, replied he, we are, the weaker we ſhall find our enemies, and the more eaſily make ourſelves maſters of their country. From thence tributes, and free gifts will come in, that will ſoon fill our coffers.

2. AFTER Demetrius had determined on his European expedition, wiſhing to conceal from his men the place of their deſtination, unleſs any croſs accidents during their voyage ſhould make it neceſſary to diſcloſe it, he delivered to every maſter of a veſſel a tablet ſealed up, with inſtructions, ſo long as the fleet kept together, not to break the ſeal: but in caſe of a ſeparation, they were directed to open the tablet, and there they would find the place they were to endeavour to make.

3. IN purſuance of a plan Demetrius had formed to ſurpriſe Sicyon, he retired to Cerchreæ, and there gave himſelf up to luxury and pleaſures. This threw the Sicyonians off from their guard, who apprehended no danger from a quarter, where nothing ſeemed to prevail but effeminacy and diſſipation. Informed of the impreſſion his conduct had made on them, he iſſued his orders for the mercenaries under Diodorus on a certain night to attack the gates, that face Pallene, and the fleet at the ſame time to ſhew themſelves in the haven, while he advanced up to the walls with the main body of his army. The city, thus vigorouſly attacked in various quarters at once, yielded to the ſudden ſtorm, and opened her gates.

4. DEME-

STRATAGEMS OF WAR.

4 DEMETRIUS, having failed on an expedition to Caria, left Diodorus captain of his guards in charge of Ephefus, which he engaged to betray to Lyfimachus for fifty talents Of this compact Demetrius gained intelligence when attended by a few fmall veffels he fteered directly to Ephefus, ordering the reft of the fleet to difembark at the place of deftination When he approached Ephefus, in one of the fmall veffels with Nicanor he entered the Ephefian haven: and concealed himfelf in the body of the fhip: while Nicanor fent for Diodorus to come on board him, as if to receive fome orders from him concerning the difbanding of a part of his forces Diodorus, fuppofing Nicanor to be alone, in a little wherry immediately attended him But as foon as ever he reached the fhip, Demetrius fpringing from the place of his concealment, leaped into the boat, and overfet it, with the men on board, that were all taken up except Diodorus, who was left to perifh in the water. Thus was Ephefus fecured in his poffeffion, the execution of the plot being timely prevented.

5 AFTER Demetrius had taken Ægina and Salamis in Attica, he fent to the Piræenfians for arms for a thoufand men, jointly with him, to attack the tyrant Lachares. They readily entered into his views, and fent the arms with which he armed his troops, and then attacked thofe who had furnifhed him with them.

6 DEMETRIUS made himfelf mafter of the Piræum by the following ftratagem Without employing his whole fleet againft it, he fitted out fome galleys, with inftructions to conceal themfelves at Sunium. From thofe he felected twenty, and ordered them not to fteer directly to Athens, but to fhape their courfe with all fpeed, as if bound for Salamis. Demetrius Phalereus, the Athenian general, was in the intereft of Cafiander: and from the tower obferved thofe fhips, which he fuppofed to be the enemy, and to be fteering to Corinth But in the evening according to their private inftructions, changing their courfe, they

CHAP. VII.

DEMETRIUS

DEMETRIUS, though much diſtreſſed for money, by new levies doubled his army. And when ſome of his friends in ſurpriſe aſked him, how he expected to pay them, difficult as he found it to ſupport a ſmaller force; the more powerful, replied he, we are, the weaker we ſhall find our enemies, and the more eaſily make ourſelves maſters of their country. From thence tributes, and free gifts will come in, that will ſoon fill our coffers.

2. AFTER Demetrius had determined on his European expedition, wiſhing to conceal from his men the place of their deſtination, unleſs any croſs accidents during their voyage ſhould make it neceſſary to diſcloſe it, he delivered to every maſter of a veſſel a tablet ſealed up, with inſtructions, ſo long as the fleet kept together, not to break the ſeal: but in caſe of a ſeparation, they were directed to open the tablet, and there they would find the place they were to endeavour to make.

3. IN purſuance of a plan Demetrius had formed to ſurpriſe Sicyon, he retired to Cerchreæ, and there gave himſelf up to luxury and pleaſures. This threw the Sicyonians off from their guard, who apprehended no danger from a quarter, where nothing ſeemed to prevail but effeminacy and diſſipation. Informed of the impreſſion his conduct had made on them, he iſſued his orders for the mercenaries under Diodorus on a certain night to attack the gates, that face Pallene, and the fleet at the ſame time to ſhew themſelves in the haven, while he advanced up to the walls with the main body of his army. The city, thus vigorouſly attacked in various quarters at once, yielded to the ſudden ſtorm, and opened her gates.

4. DEME-

STRATAGEMS OF WAR.

4. DEMETRIUS, having failed on an expedition to Caria, left Diodorus captain of his guards in charge of Ephesus. which he engaged to betray to Lysimachus for fifty talents Of this compact Demetrius gained intelligence when attended by a few small vessels he steered directly to Ephesus, ordering the rest of the fleet to disembark at the place of destination When he approached Ephesus, in one of the small vessels with Nicanor he entered the Ephesian haven: and concealed himself in the body of the ship: while Nicanor sent for Diodorus to come on board him, as if to receive some orders from him concerning the disbanding of a part of his forces Diodorus, supposing Nicanor to be alone, in a little wherry immediately attended him. But as soon as ever he reached the ship, Demetrius springing from the place of his concealment, leaped into the boat, and overset it, with the men on board, that were all taken up except Diodorus, who was left to perish in the water. Thus was Ephesus secured in his possession, the execution of the plot being timely prevented.

5 AFTER Demetrius had taken Ægina and Salamis in Attica, he sent to the Piræensians for arms for a thousand men, jointly with him, to attack the tyrant Lachares They readily entered into his views, and sent the arms with which he armed his troops, and then attacked those who had furnished him with them.

6 DEMETRIUS made himself master of the Piræum by the following stratagem Without employing his whole fleet against it, he fitted out some galleys, with instructions to conceal themselves at Sunium. From those he selected twenty, and ordered them not to steer directly to Athens, but to shape their course with all speed, as if bound for Salamis. Demetrius Phalereus, the Athenian general, was in the interest of Cassander. and from the tower observed those ships, which he supposed to be the enemy, and to be steering to Corinth. But in the evening according to their private instructions, changing their course,

they

they sailed directly to the Piræum, and made themselves masters of it. As soon as this was known, the whole fleet got under sail, and the forces on board took possession of the forts, as the fleet had done of the harbour. Liberty was then ordered to be proclaimed to the Athenians enamoured of which they gladly received Demetrius as their friend and benefactor.

7. WITH a hundred and eighty ships Demetrius sailed against Salamis in Cyprus, which was possessed and defended by Menelaus, a general of Ptolemy, who lay by with sixty ships, in constant expectation of being joined by Ptolemy himself with a hundred and forty sail more. Not thinking himself able to engage two hundred ships at once, Demetrius directed his course round a neck of land above Salamis, where he concealed himself, and debarking his land forces, planted an ambuscade. Ptolemy soon after appeared, and, having fixed upon an open, level, and convenient part of the shore for landing, disembarked his troops. The army of Demetrius immediately attacked them on the first confusion of landing, and, almost as soon as they engaged, secured the victory. While Demetrius, unexpectedly bearing down upon his fleet, obliged Ptolemy to consult his safety by flight; in which Menelaus, who had sailed from Salamis to his assistance, was forced to attend him.

8. CORINTH being betrayed to Demetrius, he entered it in the night at the Coryphæan gate. But apprehensive lest an ambuscade should be formed against him by some party in the city, he advanced first against the Lechæan gate; where the army having set up a general shout, and drawn the attention of the Corinthians to that quarter, he wheeled round, and entered the Coryphæan gate, which was thrown open by the conspirators. And while the Corinthians were engaged in the defence of a different quarter, Demetrius without danger made himself master of the city.

9. WHEN

STRATAGEMS OF WAR.

9 WHEN Demetrius and the Lacedæmonians were encamped against each other, Lycæum a mountain of Arcadia extending itself between the two camps the Macedonians expressed some uneasiness at their situation, unacquainted as they were with the mountain. The north wind blowing full against the enemy, Demetrius resolved to take advantage of it. and setting fire to the gate of his camp advanced to the attack The sparks and smoak, carried by a sharp wind amongst the Lacedæmonians, so incommoded them, that the Macedonians pushing forwards obtained a compleat and easy victory

10 THE Spartans taking advantage of a narrow pass, through which Demetrius in his retreat was obliged to march, fell upon his rear and severely galled him In the narrowest part of the defile he heaped a number of carriages together, and set fire to them. which so effectually obstructed the enemy's pursuit, till the carriages were all consumed, that Demetrius, in the mean time pursuing his march with what expedition he could, made good his retreat.

11. DEMETRIUS dispatched a herald to the Bœotians, with a proclamation of war. The letter, which announced it, was delivered at Orchomenis to the Bœotian chiefs. and the next day Demetrius encamped at Chæronea The proclamation of war, so closely followed by the approach of the enemy, awed the Bœotians to terms of submission

12 HAVING the Lycus to pass, a very rapid river, not fordable by the infantry, and only by such of the horse as were most able and strong, Demetrius drew up his cavalry in three lines across the river. by which the force of the waves was broken, and the foot by that means enabled to cross it.

CHAP.

CHAP. VIII.

EUMENES

EUMENES, closely pursued by the Galatians, and at the same time so indisposed in health, as to be carried on a litter, when he found it impracticable to escape their pursuit, and was near being overtaken, directed those that carried his litter, to stop at a hill which he saw near the road, and there to place it. The Barbarians, who had closely pursued him, not supposing he would have halted, unless in dependance of a body of troops in reserve he might have posted there in ambush, gave up the pursuit.

2. INTIMATION had been given Eumenes, that the Argyraspides were meditating innovations; the principals in which cabal were Antigenes and Teutamates, who behaved with rudeness to him, and seldom attended his pavilion. Having convened the generals, he told them a dream, which had twice occurred, and in which it was threatened, that on paying a proper regard to it their common safety depended. The dream was this, " Alexander the king sate in his pavilion in the midst of the camp, holding his sceptre in his hand, and distributing justice. when he commanded his generals to transact no public business of any kind except in the royal pavilion, which he ordered to be called the pavilion of Alexander." The Macedonians, who adored the memory of Alexander, out of the royal treasures erected a magnificent pavilion, in which was raised a golden throne, ornamented with the insignia of royalty, and on it was placed a crown of gold with the royal diadem. Beside the throne were arms, and in the midst of them a sceptre : before it a golden table, with frankincense on it and perfumes. There were also silver benches for the generals, that might attend in council

on public affairs Next to Alexander's pavilion Eumenes pitched his own and the other generals theirs in order. Eumenes, after all was compleated, received the generals not in his own, but Alexander's pavilion. and among the reft Antigenes and Teutamates attended, in fact upon Eumenes, in appearance, to do honour to Alexander.

3. EUMENES, when in Perfia he was apprehenfive of his army by bribes and largeffes being won over to the interefts of Peuceftes, and that there was a defign of placing him on the throne, produced a letter in Syriac characters, as if written by Orontes a fatrap of Armenia, to this purport Olympias, with a fon of Alexander, hath left Epire, and advanced into Macedonia, of which fhe has by force poffeffed herfelf, having flain Caffander, who had ufurped the throne. The Macedonians, hearing this, thought no more of Peuceftes, but with infinite joy proclaimed the mother and fon of Alexander his heirs to the throne

4 ANTIGONUS having heard, that Eumenes when in Perfia had fent his troops into winter quarters, immediately advanced againft him : who, being informed by Peuceftes of his march, directed his officers, with their children, in the night to take fire with them to the higheft and moft expofed places, and there ride about at the diftance of feventy furlongs. Then leaving a fpace of about twenty furlongs, he ordered them to fet a great quantity of wood on fire; making the outward fires very large, another range of fires lefs, and a third ftill fmaller, in imitation of a real camp. Antigonus's army from this appearance fufpecting that Eumenes had embodied his forces, ventured not to attack him, but filed off another way, on purpofe to avoid the fuppofed fuperiority of the enemy

5 WHEN Eumenes found he could not by any arguments divert his foldiers from their intention of plundering the enemy's baggage, he contrived to furnifh the adverfary with private intelligence of their defign.

in confequence of which he placed a ftronger guard upon it; which the foldiers of Eumenes obferving, dropped their intention.

CHAP. IX.

SELEUCUS

IN an engagement between Seleucus and Antigonus, the evening put an end to the undecided action, and both armies retreated to their refpective camps, determined to renew the conflict the next day. The foldiers of Antigonus in the mean time put off their arms, and entertained themfelves in their tents. But Seleucus ordered his men to fup, and fleep in their arms, and lie down in order of battle; that they might be ready for action, whenever the charge was founded. At break of day the army of Seleucus rofe, and ready armed, and formed, immediately advanced againft Antigonus; whofe troops unarmed, and unformed, afforded an eafy victory to the enemy.

2 SELEUCUS and Demetrius were encamped againft each other: the former in high fpirits, but the latter diffident of fuccefs. Demetrius therefore determined to fall upon the enemy in the night; placing his hopes of victory on a vigorous attack. The army readily embraced his plan, and were fanguine in their expectations of furprifing Seleucus. At the time appointed they rofe, and armed: when two Ætolian youths, of Demetrius's army, applied to the advanced guard of Seleucus's camp, and demanded to be immediately introduced to the king. As foon as they had informed him of the preparations making in the enemy's camp for action, Seleucus, fearing left he fhould be attacked before he was in a pofture of defence, ordered the trumpets immediately to found the charge. The whole camp was inftantly in an alarm, each queftioning the other about the fuddennefs of the order, and haftily lighting

his

his faggot. Demetrius, when he faw the troops ftanding round the fires, and heard the trumpets found the charge, fuppofed them ready for battle, and therefore declined the intended attack.

3. SELEUCUS, learning that the foldiers of Demetrius were much difpirited, felected a body of picked men from his guards, which with eight elephants he pofted in his front, in a narrow pafs, flanking the enemy, and, advancing before them, threw off his helmet, and called aloud " How long will ye be fo mad, as to follow the fortunes of a freebooter, who is almoft famifhed, when your merits will find their reward with a king, who reigns in affluence and you will partake with him of a kingdom, not depending on hope, but in actual poffeffion." Influenced by this harangue, many threw afide their fwords and fpears, and, clapping their hands, revolted to Seleucus.

4. WHEN the charge of the tower of Sardis, with the royal treafures, was by Lyfimachus committed to Theodotus, which, fuch was the ftrength of its fortification, Seleucus defpaired of carrying by ftorm he ordered proclamation to be made, that he would give an hundred talents to any one who would kill Theodotus. As the lure of fuch a fum might be fuppofed of weight to influence fome or other of the foldiers, Theodotus became fufpicious and afraid of them, and for that reafon feldom expofed himfelf in public The army on the other hand refented his fufpicions of them In this unpleafant fituation, one party alarmed by fufpicion, and the other warmed by refentment, Theodotus determined to be beforehand with his troops, and therefore in the night himfelf opened the gates, introduced Seleucus, and delivered up to him the treafures.

5. DEMETRIUS had encamped under mount Taurus, when Seleucus, apprehenfive left he fhould fecretly make his efcape into Syria, detached Lyfias with a body of Macedonians to fecure the pafs of the Amanidian mountains, through which he muft be obliged to march,

and there to kindle a number of fires. By this judicious movement Demetrius saw his intended rout cut off, and his escape precluded.

6 SELEUCUS, after an unsuccessful engagement with the Barbarians, fled towards Cilicia and to conceal himself, in those circumstances, even from his own troops, attended only by a few friends, he passed for the armour-bearer of Amaction, general of the royal forces, and assumed his habit. But as soon as a number of horse and foot, the shattered remains of his army, had shewn themselves, he re-assumed his royal robe, discovered himself to his army, and again put himself at their head.

CHAP. X.

PERDICCAS

IN a war between the Illyrians and Macedonians, many of the Macedonians having been taken prisoners, and others acquitted themselves very indifferently on dependance of being ransomed in case they were taken, Perdiccas directed the deputation, that was sent to treat for the ransom of the prisoners, on their return to declare, that the Illyrians would receive no ransom, but had determined to put the prisoners to death. All hopes of ransom being thus precluded, the Macedonians in future fought with more resolution, finding that their only hopes of safety were placed in victory.

2 PERDICCAS, in his war with the Chalcidensians, when his coffers were very low, struck a coin of brass mixed with tin, with which he paid his army. The money, bearing the royal impression, the sutlers took as currency; and, as it bore no value beyond the king's dominions, he took it of them again in payment for corn and the product of the country.

CHAP. XI.

CASSANDER.

CASSANDER, knowing Nicanor, governor of Munichia, to be ill-affected to him, artfully over-reached, and got rid of him. He pretended that he was under a necessity of passing over to Attica when just as he was going to embark, an express, according to his own instructions, arrived with pretended letters from his friends in Macedonia to this effect that the Macedonians invited him to assume the throne, universally dissatisfied as they were with the government of Polysperchon. On reading those letters, Cassander appeared in high spirits, and embracing Nicanor, who attended him, he congratulated him as a friend on the participation of his own greatness: "And, now, 'says he,' other business requires our attention, the settling of an empire's concerns demands our common cares." Thus saying, he took him aside to a neighbouring house, as if to confer in private with him on business of importance when he was immediately seised by a party of guards, who had been previously posted there for that purpose Cassander then convened an assembly of the people, and gave leave to any one, who had any thing to offer against Nicanor, to urge it And while accusations from different quarters were preferring against him, he secured Munichia And Nicanor, who was convicted of many acts of injustice, was sentenced to death.

2 At the same time that Cassander had besieged Salamis, he also engaged the Athenians by sea, and defeated them. All the Salaminians, he had taken in the action with the Athenians, he liberated and sent to Salamis without ransom which had that effect on the people, that,

in consequence of such an act of favour and humanity, they voluntarily surrendered themselves to Cassander.

3. WHILE Cassander besieged Pydna, a town in Macedonia, in which Olympias was shut up, Polysperchon dispatched a sloop with orders to land close by the town in the night of which he by letter apprised Olympias, and desired her to embark on board it. The courier was intercepted, and carried before Cassander, to whom he confessed his errand. As soon as he had read the letter, he closed it and again affixed on it Polyspherchon's seal, directing the courier to deliver the letter, but not to inform her that he had seen it. The letter was accordingly delivered. and Cassander took care to intercept the sloop. Olympias, agreeably to the purport of the letter, came out of the city in the night, in expectation of finding the vessel at the place appointed. when piqued at her disappointment, and thinking herself deceived by Polysperchon, she surrendered both herself and the city to Cassander.

4. WHEN Cassander returned from Illyrium, at the distance of a day's march from Epidamnum, he planted in ambush a body of horse and foot, and after that set on fire the villages on the most exposed situations in the extremity of the territories of Illyris and Atintanis. Supposing Cassander had entirely evacuated the country, the Illyrians ventured out of the city, and went abroad to different parts, as their different business required their attention. The ambuscade, then sallying out, took prisoners not less than a thousand men, and, the gates of the city being thrown open, Cassander made himself master of Epidamnum.

CHAP.

CHAP. XII.

LYSIMACHUS.

LYSIMACHUS apprehenfive left the Autariatæ, who had been plundered of their baggage in an engagement with Demetrius, barbarians as they were, and ftripped of their property, fhould meditate a mutiny or revolt, fummoned them without the trenches, on pretence of receiving a donation of corn. and on a fignal given, ordered every man to be cut to pieces Their number amounted to fix hundred.

2 AFTER Lyfimachus had taken Amphipolis by the treachery of Andragathus, he loaded him with prefents, and promifed him ftill greater, if he would attend him into Afia. But as foon as they arrived at the ftraits of Thrace, he not only ftripped him of all he poffeffed, but, after expofing him to the torture, put him to death.

3. LYSIMACHUS, conducted Arifton, fon of Autoleon to his father's kingdom in Pæonia under pretence that the royal youth might be acknowledged by his fubjects, and treated with due refpect But as foon as he had bathed in the royal bath in the river Arifbus, and they had fet before him an elegant repaft, according to the cuftom of his country, Lyfimachus ordered his guards to arm upon which, Arifton, inftantly mounting his horfe, efcaped to Sardis, and left Lyfimachus in poffeffion of Pæonia.

---

* A man, civilized to every great and good purpofe of humanity, feels with indignation the diftinction of barbarifm applied to every nation but his own by fuch a monfter of cruelty and treachery, as Lyfimachus.

CHAP. XIII

CRATERUS.

THE Tyrians having with advantage attacked the Macedonians, while employed on their works, Craterus ordered a retreat. But after the Tyrians, who had continued eagerly to pursue them, had considerably fatigued themselves, he gave the signal to face about, and charge. The colour of the action was immediately changed they who had pursued, now began to fly, and the fugitives became the pursuers

CHAP. XIV.

POLYSPERCHON.

POLYSPERCHON, to spirit up his men against the Peloponnesians, who were in possession of a pass between the mountains, put on an Arcadian cap, and double vest, and taking a staff in his hand, "Such, 'says he,' are the men, against whom we are now engaged." Then, throwing his Arcadian dress aside, and taking up his own arms, "and such, 'added he,' my fellow soldiers, are the men, who engage them, men, who in great and various battles have won glorious victories." This short harangue so animated his troops, that they unanimously requested him to lead them instantly to the charge

CHAP. XV.

ANTIOCHUS, son of Seleucus.

DINON, a general of Ptolemy, with a strong garrison so ably defended Damascus against Antiochus, that he despaired of carrying it by a regular siege, and had therefore recourse to stratagem. He directed his army, and the whole country round, to celebrate a Persian festival with the utmost profusion of luxury and ordered all persons of consequence, to contribute their shares to supply it. While Antiochus, and his army were thus engaged, Dinon hearing of the voluptuous celebrity remitted a little of his attention to his charge. Of this Antiochus was no sooner apprised, than he ordered his troops to take four days provision of raw flour, and marching them through a desart, by rough and unfrequented ways, arrived before Damascus, when the citizens supposed he was revelling in his camp, and by a vigorous attack surprised, and took it

CHAP. XVI.

ANTIOCHUS, son of Antiochus

WHEN Antiochus besieged Cypsela a city in Thrace, he had in his army many Thracians of good rank and family, who were commanded by Tius and Dromichætes To those he gave gold chains, and arms studded with silver, ornamented with which they marched out to battle The Cypsehans, seeing their friends and acquaintance so richly equipped, concluded they had taken the best side . threw down their arms, and revolted to Antiochus, instead of enemies becoming allies.

CHAP. XVII.

ANTIOCHUS HIERAX.

ANTIOCHUS, having revolted from his brother Seleucus, made his escape into Mesopotamia and in his march over the Armenian mountains was joined by Arsabes. The two generals of Seleucus, Achæus and Andromachus, in great force pursued him, and an obstinate battle was fought in which Antiochus was wounded, and fled to the upper parts of the mountain, leaving the main body of the army to encamp on the sides of it. He then directed a report of his death to be propagated, and ordered the army in the night to advance to the heights of the mountain. The next day the army of Antiochus sent ambassadors, Philetærus the Cretan and Dionysius of Lysimachia, to demand the body of Antiochus in order to bury it, and on condition of receiving it, to engage to surrender themselves prisoners of war. Andromachus agreed to the conditions, informed them the body of Antiochus was not then found, and proposed to send an escort for the prisoners and arms. A detachment of four thousand men was accordingly dispatched, not prepared for action, but as a deputation to receive the prisoners. As soon as they advanced to the sides of the mountains, those who were posted on the heights vigorously attacked, and made great havock among them. While Antiochus, appearing in his royal robes, presented himself to them, both alive, and victorious.

CHAP. XVIII.

PHILIP, son of Demetrius.

WHEN Philip besieged Prinassus, a Rhodian city, in Peræa*: he found the walls so exceedingly strong, that he saw no other way to succeed against it, than by undermining them. But when the pioneers begun to dig, they found nothing but a hard rock, which so blunted their tools, that they could make no advance in the undertaking. To conceal from the enemy the difficulties he had to encounter, he contrived a kind of awning to cover the workmen. notwithstanding all which, they plainly perceived the little progress he was able to make. He therefore directed the soldiers to bring in the night a quantity of earth from eight or ten furlongs distance, and lay it at the mouth of their mine. The garrison from the walls seeing the quantity of earth, thrown up at the mouth of the mine, every day so greatly increasing, concluded the walls must be undermined: and thus intimidated surrendered the city to Philip. He then discovered to them the stratagem he had practised, and left them to lament their credulity.

2. PHILIP son of Demetrius, when engaged in a war with Attalus and the Rhodians, finding himself inferiour to the enemy, considered how to effect a secure retreat by sea. He sent an Ægyptian revolter, to give intelligence to the enemy, that he was making preparations for a naval engagement, intending next day to have his fleet ready for action. And in the night he kindled a number of fires, to induce them to think the army remained in camp. Attalus, according to this

---

* Peræa was a country on that part of the continent, which lies directly opposite to Rhodes.

intelligence,

intelligence, made preparations also on his side to receive him. And to strengthen his fleet he drew off the guards that were posted at the place of Philip's intended embarkation; which gave him an opportunity of embarking his army, and he thereby effected his escape.

CHAP XIX.

PTOLEMY.

WHEN Perdiccas had marched down to the river Memphis, with intention to cross it, Ptolemy tied his baggage to a number of goats, swine, and oxen, and left the herdsmen with some of his horse to drive them. The baggage thus dragged along the ground by those animals raised a prodigious dust, and exhibited in appearance the march of a numerous army. With the rest of his cavalry Ptolemy pursued the enemy, and came up with them as they were crossing the river, part having already passed it: who, from the dust, suspecting a numerous army in their rear, some fled, others perished in the river, and a great number were taken prisoners.

CHAP. XX.

ATTALUS.

ATTALUS, previous to an engagement with the Gauls, to whom he was very inferiour in force, to animate his men against the superiority of the enemy, offered a sacrifice; Sudinus a Chaldæan priest performing the ceremony. Upon his hand, in the black juice of the oak apple, the king inscribed, "The king's victory," in inverted letters, not from the left to the right, but from the right to the left. And when he embowelled

bowelled the victim, he placed his hand under a warm and spungy part, which took from it the impreffion. The prieft then turning over the reft of the parts, the gall, the lungs, and the ftomach, and obferving the omens to be drawn from them, turned to the part which contained the infcription of the king's victory which exulting with joy he fhewed to all the foldiers This they eagerly read, and affuming confidence, as if Heaven had affured them of victory, unanimoufly requefted to be immediately led againft the barbarians whom they charged with extraordinary vigour, and obtained the victory they had been taught to expect *

CHAP XXI.

PERSEUS, son of Philip

PERSEUS in his wars with the Romans, who made ufe of elephants in their army, which they procured partly from Lybia, and partly from Antiochus king of Syria, to accuftom his horfes to the formidable appearance of thofe animals, directed fome elephants to be made in wood, in fize and colour as nearly as poffible refembling the real ones. And to imitate the terrible noife the beaft fometimes made, he ordered a trumpeter to enter his body, and directing his trumpet through his mouth to found the loudeft, harfheft notes he was able. And by this means the Macedonian horfes were trained to bear the noife and fight of the elephants without emotion.

* A fimilar ftratagem Frontinus has afcribed to Alexander and this, which Polyænus hath afcribed to Attalus, Frontinus has given to Eumenes.

BOOK

BOOK V.

THE PREFATORY ADDRESS.

THIS Fifth Book of Stratagems I offer to your moſt ſacred majeſties, Antoninus and Verus. Nor do I myſelf aſſume ſo much praiſe in compoſing this work, as I attribute to you in the diligent attention you have been pleaſed to employ upon it, conſidering the high dignity with which you are inveſted, and the critical time, when you are ſo particularly engaged both in concerns of peace and war. But indeed generals cannot form themſelves to victory by ſurer means, than by ſtudying the arts by which antient generals obtained it. To princes engaged in war treatiſes on warlike operations cannot be uſeleſs. Eloquence is learned by ſtudying the works of celebrated orators: and, by obſerving the conduct of illuſtrious generals, chieftains are taught, in various ſimilar inſtances that may occur, to form their own. And ſo far theſe ſtratagems I truſt may be of ſervice, as they will place before your eyes the beſt models of imitation in the field of military fame.

CHAP. I.

PHALARIS.

THE people of Agrigentum having determined to build a temple to Jupiter the governor within the caſtle, both becauſe the ground there was the firmeſt and hardeſt, and therefore the moſt proper for the foundation, and alſo becauſe the ſite was the moſt elevated, and as

ſuch

such properest for the temple of the Deity Phalaris undertook to superintend the work, and at a fixed sum engaged to finish it, employing the ablest workmen, and supplying the best materials. The people from his occupation, which was that of a publican*, supposing him a proper person for conducting the work, accordingly contracted with him for it, and paid into his hands the money. With this he hires a number of strangers, farms the prisoners, and buys a quantity of stones, timber, and iron. As soon as he had laid the foundation, he pretends his materials had been stolen, and directs proclamation to be made, that whoever would discover those, who had stolen the stones and iron from the castle, should receive a sum of money in reward. The people expressed great indignation at the theft, and gave him the leave which he requested, in future to prevent such larcenies, to fortify the castle, and throw a trench round it. He then struck off the prisoners' irons, and armed them with battle-axes, hatchets, and stones, and, while the citizens were intent on celebrating the feast of Ceres, suddenly fell upon them, slew many of the men, made himself master of the persons of the women and children, and possessed himself of the sovereignty of Agrigentum.

2 PHALARIS, having formed a design to disarm the Agrigentines, pretended to entertain them with some very magnificent games without the city. As soon as a great concourse of the citizens had gone out of the city to attend them, the gates were shut, and the guards according to his orders searched every house, and carried off whatever arms they found.

3 THE Agrigentines being engaged in a war with the Sicanians, when Phalaris, who lay before their city, found he could not reduce it,

---

* The Τελωται, or publicans, were those that received the fines due for the celebration of publick worship. They were at Athens ten in number, and chosen out of the πεντακοσιομεδιμνοι

he

he entered with them into a treaty of peace. And having in his camp a great ſtore of corn, he agreed to leave it to them, on condition of receiving from them an equal quantity after their harveſt With thoſe terms the Sicanians readily complied, and received the ſtores. Phalaris then contrived to bribe the intendants of the granaries, in ſome places ſecretly to unroof them, through which the rain was introduced, and rotted the corn. As ſoon as the harveſt was over, Phalaris according to compact received his quantity of new corn; and the old turning out rotten, the Sicanians were reduced by diſtreſs, after having given up to him their ſubſiſtence, to ſurrender their liberties too.

4. PHALARIS diſpatched an embaſſy to Teutus, the chief of Veſſa, which was eſteemed one of the moſt flouriſhing and powerful cities in Sicania, to ſolicit his daughter in marriage. Teutus accordingly gave his conſent; when Phalaris ſent a number of ſoldiers in chariots, without beards, and in women's dreſſes, as ſervants charged with preſents to the bride. But as ſoon as they were introduced into the houſe, they drew their ſwords, and ſecured all within: and Phalaris, immediately after arriving, made himſelf maſter of Veſſa.

CHAP. II.

DIONYSIUS.

THE mercenaries having attacked the houſe of Dionyſius, tyrant of Sicily, and forced their way into it with a determination to murder him, he came out to them in a mean dreſs, and with duſt on his head: and told the ſoldiers, he gave himſelf up to them, to treat him as they pleaſed. His appearance ſo altered, and humiliated, changed their reſolutions, and they left him ſafe, and uninjured. Theſe very men

Dionyfius not long after furrounded with his troops in Leontium, and cut every one of them to pieces.

2. DIONYSIUS, fon of Hermocrates, was in the fervice of the Syracufans, and acted as fecretary to their generals. of whofe conduct in the courfe of an unfuccefsful war with the Carthaginians the Syracufans complained, and Dionyfius ventured fo far as to accufe them of treachery. Some in confequence of his accufation were executed, and others banifhed. when pretending that he was in danger from the cabals of their partifans, and their refentment for the active part he had taken againft thofe who had been already convicted, the Carthaginian war ftill continuing, he obtained of the people a guard for his perfon. By means of that he poffeffed himfelf of the fovereignty of Syracufe, and became the greateft tyrant the Syracufans ever knew and, dying at an advanced age, he left the fovereignty to his fon.

3. DIONYSIUS always with particular caution adverted to confpiracies, and having been informed that a foreigner then in the city had given out that he was poffeffed of an infallible fecret for difcovering confpiracies and treafon, he ordered him to be fent for. As foon as he came to the caftle, he defired all prefent might withdraw: for he would not make the fecret common, but was ready to difcover it to Dionyfius alone. When the company were accordingly withdrawn, "Only, 'faid he,' profefs as I have done, that you are poffeffed of the fecret I pretend to difcover, and no one will venture to enter into any confpiracies againft you." Dionyfius, pleafed with the device, liberally rewarded the man; and told his guards, the man had difcovered to him the moft aftonifhing means of detecting confpirators: which fo intimidated them, that they never in future ventured to form any defigns againft him.

4. DIONYSIUS, having engaged in a foreign expedition, committed the charge of the caftle and the treafury to Andron: of both which, in the abfence of Dionyfius, Hermocrates advifed him to poffefs himfelf.

Dio-

Dionyfius, who within a few days returned from his expedition, without having heard any thing of any fuch propofition, but ever fufpicious as tyranny always is, told Andron he had been informed of a propofal that had been made to him to betray his truft, the particulars of which he wifhed to hear from himfelf Andron gave credit to what he faid, and confeffed every circumftance of the fact After which Dionyfius ordered him to be executed, for not having difcovered the propofal, that had been made to him, immediately on his return · and Hermocrates, who had married his fifter, he confined in prifon, but, to oblige her, afterwards banifhed him into Peloponnefus

5 DIONYSIUS, having gained over a party in Naxos to betray the city to him, late in the evening attended with feven foldiers advanced to the walls. The confpirators from the towers propofed to him, to attack it with all his force But he, wifhing to make himfelf mafter of it without any lofs, fummoned the garrifon on the walls to furrender · threatening, in cafe of their refufal to put every man to the fword. One of his floops at the fame time by his order entered the port of Naxus, with trumpets on board, and boatfwains, who apprifed the Naxians of their fituation, informing them, they all belonged to feparate fhips, which they would foon fee in their harbour. The terrour of fo great a naval force, and the threats of Dionyfius, prevailed on the Naxians to furrender their city, without occafioning him to ftrike a blow

6. HYMILCON having blocked up the harbour of the Motyæans, Dionyfius drew his forces out of the town, and encamped on the fhore oppofite to the enemy, who ftretched along the mouth of the harbour. He bade his men take courage, and both foldiers and failors exert themfelves, in running the fhips afhore · which to the number of eighty he in one day drew out upon a flat muddy piece of land, about twenty furlongs wide, that lay under the promontory which formed a fide of the harbour ; and planted the ground with wooden piles. Hymilcon, afraid left Di-

onyſius, having thus ſecured his own ſhips, ſhould take an opportunity of attacking him in rear, and ſhutting him up in the harbour, with the firſt fair wind withdrew his fleet and left Dionyſius in poſſeſſion of the harbour, his ſhips in ſafety, and the town in peace

7 Dionysius, being in poſſeſſion of the tower, held out againſt the forces of Dion, and ſent an embaſſy to the Syracuſans with propoſals of peace who, as a preliminary to any ſuch negotiation, inſiſted on his abdication of the ſovereignty with which if he complied, they were ready to treat with him, if not, they were determined upon an unremitting war. Dionyſius again diſpatched a herald, requiring them to ſend ambaſſadors, into whoſe hands he would reſign the ſovereignty, and conclude with them a peace Ambaſſadors were accordingly ſent; and the citizens reſigned themſelves up to intemperate joy on the recovery of their liberty and became leſs attentive to their defence Dionyſius in the mean time detained the ambaſſadors, and drawing out his forces advanced againſt the walls, which he forced by a vigorous attack, recovered the city, and retained poſſeſſion of the caſtle.

8 The next day Dionyſius ſet at liberty the Syracuſan ambaſſadors, that he had detained, who were followed by women, charged with letters to Dion and Megacles from the ſiſter of the one, and the wife of the other, as well as to other Syracuſans, whoſe wives had been confined during the ſiege Theſe letters were produced before an aſſembly of the people, and read the general purport of which was, an earneſt requeſt to their huſbands and relations, not to ſuffer them to languiſh in the hands of Dionyſius The addreſs of one particular letter was, "Hipparion (which was the name of Dion's ſon) to his father" But when the ſecretary opened the letter, and read it inſtead of a letter from a ſon to his father, it appeared to be a familiar letter from Dionyſius to Dion, written in the moſt friendly terms, and by great promiſes ſoliciting him to his intereſts. This letter rendered Dion ever

afterwards

afterwards fufpected by the Syracufans, and entirely deprived him of his confequence in the ftate. the object, Dionyfius had moft in view, to accomplifh.

9 THE Carthaginians having invaded the Syracufan territories with an army of thirty thoufand men, Dionyfius, who had taken care to erect various forts and caftles in different parts, fent ambaffadors to conclude a peace with them, on condition of delivering up to them all their forts and caftles. The terms were readily accepted by the Carthaginians, who were very well fatisfied with receiving poffeffion of their forts, without the hazard of a battle, and left confiderable garrifons in each of them. The main army, materially reduced by thofe detachments, which were difperfed in different parts, Dionyfius afterwards attacked with fuccefs, and entirely routed

10 DIONYSIUS, having formed a defign to reduce Himera, entered into an alliance with the Himerenfians. He then made war upon fome of the neigbouring cities, and encamped near Himera whither, the people being in alliance with him, he was frequently fending deputations: and his army was for fome time fupplied by the Himerenfians with provifions But fo great an army ftill continuing in their vicinity, without attempting any thing of confequence, raifed in the Hymerenfians a fufpicion of fome concealed defigns. and they refufed to fupply him in the fame liberal manner they had done before. Dionyfius therefore made his neceffities a pretence of breaking with the Himerenfians, advanced with all his forces againft the city, and took it by ftorm.

11. DIONYSIUS formed a defign to abridge the old foldiers of their pay at which the young ones expreffed their indignation, as an act of extreme cruelty, to ftarve thofe in their old age, who had fpent their youth in the fervice of their country Finding the oppofition his defign was likely to meet with, he convened an affembly, and thus addreffed them. " The juniors I expect to fuftain the fhock of battle:
with

with the seniors I mean to garrison my forts: and to both I intend equal pay. For they, whose fidelity has been tried, are the proper persons to be entrusted with the charge of the fortifications. and the service is attended with less fatigue." All were pleased with the regulations, and departed in good humour But as soon as the troops were dispersed, and disposed of in different stations and garrisons, he struck off the veterans from their pay, who had now no longer the body of the army to support them.

12. DIONYSIUS, in an expedition he had undertaken, had a mind to try the fidelity of his naval captains. The object of his expedition he wished to keep secret, and therefore mentioned to none of them, giving to every captain a tablet sealed up, but an entire blank within: and ordered them, as soon as they were under sail, on a certain signal given, to open their tablets, and steer their course according to the directions, they should find within As soon as they were under sail, he himself in a swift-sailing vessel, before the signal was given, run round the fleet, and of every captain demanded his tablet. Those, who had broken their seals, he ordered to be executed for breach of orders. to the rest he gave tablets, in which the real name of the city, that was the object of the expedition, was written. And by this means the expedition being kept secret succeeded, he attacked Amphipolis, of which unprepared to receive an enemy, and ungarrisoned, he easily made himself master.

13 To discover the opinion his subjects entertained of him, and know who were his enemies, Dionysius ordered the names to be given in to him of several musick girls and prostitutes. who, instead of receiving presents from him, as they expected, were by the torture made to confess, what were the sentiments they had heard their lovers express of the tyranny. Thus having informed himself of all, who were averse to his government, some of them he executed, and banished others.

14. AFTER

STRATAGEMS OF WAR.

14. AFTER Dionyfius had difarmed the citizens, whenever he had occafion to take the field againft an enemy, he marched a hundred furlongs from the city, and then delivered every man his arms And when the war was terminated, before they entered the city, and the gates were thrown open, they were ordered to ground their arms, which were carried away, and depofited in the tower, on pretence of being taken care of, and kept in order.

15. ANOTHER ftratagem Dionyfius employed, to difcover thofe who were averfe to his government, was the following He privately fet fail for Italy, and ordered a report to be fpread, that he had been killed by his own foldiers They, who were inimical to the tyranny, joyfully ran together, congratulating each other on the happy event. Who thofe were, as foon as he had been informed by his emiffaries, he ordered them to be apprehended, and put to death

16. AT another time Dionyfius pretended illnefs, and ordered a report to be propagated, that he was at the point of death. While many were expreffing their joy on the occafion, the tyrant appeared in public with his guards, and ordered all to execution, who had been exulting at the fatal event.

17 DIONYSIUS obliged the Carthaginians to pay for their prifoners a very high ranfom but the Grecian prifoners, that were in the fervice of Carthage, he difcharged without any ranfom at all. This partiality of the tyrant rendered the Greeks fufpected by the Carthaginians, who difcharged all the Greek mercenaries from their fervice This rid Dionyfius of fo formidable an enemy as the Greeks.

18. DIONYSIUS, in the war with the Meffenians, in order to encourage a fufpicion that prevailed of his having a party among them in his intereft, when he ravaged the country, ordered his men fcrupuloufly to avoid offering any injury to the eftates of particular perfons.

This

This is a stratagem I remember to have been practised by other generals. But Dionysius carried it farther in pretended secresy, he dispatched a soldier into the city, with a talent of gold for the suspected persons. The Messenians seised the messenger, with the gold upon him, and being informed by him for whose use the present was intended, the persons so rendered suspected were ordered to be tried for treason: who notwithstanding, being men of consequence, had a powerful party in their favour, and escaped the tyrant's snare. Factions however were thus promoted: and by means of them Dionysius became master of Messena.

19. His treasury being low, Dionysius imposed a tax on the people; to which, having been frequently charged with it, they did not very chearfully submit: and he on the other hand did not think it adviseable to compel the payment of it. A few days after, he ordered the civil officers to take all the offerings from the temple of Asclepius (and there were many both of silver and gold), to carry them to the forum, and there expose them to sale. The Syracusans with great avidity purchased them at high prices, and a very considerable sum of money was raised: of which as soon as Dionysius had possessed himself, he passed an edict, that whoever had sacrilegiously bought any of the offerings at the temple of Asclepius, should on pain of death immediately replace them in the temple, and restore them to the god. The edict was accordingly obeyed: the offerings were restored to the god: and Dionysius kept the money.

20. Dionysius having taken a city, part of the inhabitants of which had fallen in the siege, and part he had banished, left a small garrison in it. But the town being a large one, and not tenable with so few as he had been able to spare, he married the captive slaves to the daughters of their masters: thereby not only strengthening the garrison,

rifon, but from the natural abhorrence of each other, that muſt ſubſiſt between them and their maſters, ſecuring to himſelf the fidelity of the people.

21. DIONYSIUS, having embarked for Tyrrhenia with a hundred veſſels, and tranſports, touched at the temple of Leucotheæ, where he received five hundred talents, and then purſued his voyage. But being informed that the ſoldiers and ſailors had ſtolen a thouſand talents of gold, and many more of ſilver, before he diſembarked, he ordered proclamation to be made, that every one ſhould carry to him half of what he had got, and keep the other half himſelf, and in failure of compliance with his orders he threatened immediate death. After he had from each thus exacted a half of the plunder they had acquired, the other half he extorted from them, and gave them inſtead of it a month's ſubſiſtence of corn.

22. MANY of the Patians embraced the Pythagorean philoſophy, and diſperſed themſelves in different parts of Italy. And when Dionyſius, tyrant of Sicily, ſent ambaſſadors to the Metapontians and other Italian ſtates, to propoſe conditions of peace, Euephenus adviſed the youths, who ſtudied under him, and their fathers, to pay no credit to the tyrant's profeſſions. Dionyſius being informed of the conduct of Euephenus, determined, if he could get the philoſopher into his power, to tranſport him from Metapontium to Rhegium. It afterward happened, that he fell into his hands · and Dionyſius directed a regular proſecution of him for the great injuries he had done him. To the accuſations urged againſt him Euephenus replied, that he had acted conſcientiouſly and juſtly "Thoſe, ' ſays he,' whom I adviſed, were my friends and acquaintance. 'but' the tyrant, againſt whom I adviſed them, I know not even by ſight" He was however adjudged to die. Undaunted at his ſentence, he addreſſed Dionyſius, and told him, "He acquieſced in the decree, but had a ſiſter in Parium unmarried, whom he wiſhed to diſpoſe of before he died

died. therefore he requested leave to revisit his country, assuring him, he would in a short time return, and meet his sentence." While every body laughed at the apparent folly of the man. Dionysius, struck with the firmness of his demeanour, asked him, who would be bail for his return. "I will find, 'replied he,' a bail, who will answer for it with his life" and immediately called Eucritus, who readily engaged, at the risk of his life, to answer for his friend's appearance. Six months were allowed Euephenus for the transaction of his business at Parium. for which place he immediately set out, while Eucritus in his absence remained a prisoner at Rhegium. The fact was extraordinary. but the conclusion of it still more so. For after the expiration of the six months, Euephenus, having settled his sister, returned to Sicily, surrendered himself up to his sentence, and desired his bail might be discharged. Dionysius in admiration of the virtue, they had both displayed, forgave Euephenus, and discharged Eucritus from confinement. And taking them both by their hands, he requested them to admit him as a third into their friendship, and to continue with him, and partake of his fortunes. They acknowledged the tyrant's kindness; but requested him, if he gave them their life, to permit them to return to their former manner of enjoying it, and the prosecution of their beloved studies. By this act of generosity Dionysius gained over many Italian states to his confidence.

CHAP. III.

AGATHOCLES.

AGATHOCLES, having broken the oath he pledged to his enemies, and slain his prisoners, told his friends with a laugh, "After supper we will cast up our oaths."

2. AFTER Agathocles had defeated the Leontines, he sent their general

neral Dinocrates to Leontium, to inform his countrymen, that it was his intention, in the prefervation of his prifoners, to rival the glory of Dionyfius, who after the battle at the river Eleporus preferved the lives of all the prifoners he had taken. The Leontines in confidence of his promife fent him magnificent prefents. Agathocles then ordered all the prifoners to meet him unarmed. When the general, as directed, bade every man, who thought as Agathocles did, hold up his hand. " My thoughts, ' faid Agathocles,' are to flay every man of you :" the number of whom was ten thoufand. The foldiers, who furrounded them, according to the tyrant's orders immediately cut them to pieces.

3. AGATHOCLES having received information, that fome of the Syracufan chiefs had it in contemplation to attempt innovations, offered a folemn facrifice to the gods for a victory he had gained over the Carthaginians. And invited to the entertainment, he made on the occafion, five hundred perfons, whom he fuppofed moft inimical to his government. The entertainment was moft fumptuous and magnificent. And after the company had all drank pretty freely, he himfelf in a fcarlet robe in the Tarentine fafhion thrown loofely round him advanced into the midft of them, and fung, and played on the harp, and danced, while mirth and revelry prevailed around When all were in the height of enjoyment, Agathocles withdrew himfelf, as being tired, and wanting to change his drefs. A number of armed men immediately rufhed in, and falling upon the company with their drawn fwords, fuffered not an individual to efcape.

4. WHEN Ophelas, the Cyrenian, with a numerous army was advancing againft Agathocles hearing the Cyrenian was notorioufly addicted to the love of boys, he fent an embaffy to him, and his fon Heraclides as a hoftage, a boy of extraordinary beauty : ordering him to hold out for a few days againft his folicitations. The Cyrenian, charmed with the beauty of the boy, conceived a violent paffion for him, and

ftrongly

strongly folicited him to comply with his defires. Thus engaged, Agathocles fuddenly attacked, and flew him, and entirely defeated his army. His fon alfo he received fafe, and without any injury having been offered to him

5 AGATHOCLES having embarked in an expedition againft Carthage, to try the refolution of his men before he failed, ordered proclamation to be made, that whoever wifhed to be excufed from the expedition, might go on fhore, and take with him whatever property he had on board. As many as took advantage of the proclamation, he ordered to execution, as traitors and cowards: and extolling thofe who ftaid on board, for their courage and attachment to him, he directed his courfe with fixty fhips to Libya And as foon as he had difembarked his troops, he fet fire to his fhipping, that his men might fight with the greater refolution, when they faw themfelves deprived of every refource which the fhips might have afforded them in their flight. By thefe ftratagems Agathocles in various battles defeated the Carthaginians; and made himfelf mafter of many cities in Libya.

6. AGATHOCLES defired the Syracufans to furnifh him with two thoufand men, intending an expedition into Phœnicia, where, he informed them, he was invited by a party in his interefts, who had engaged to put him in poffeffion of the country. The Syracufans gave credit to his affertions, and fent him the fupplies he required. which as foon as he had received, he thought no more of his Phœnician expedition; but employed his forces againft his allies, and demolifhed the fortifications of Tauromenia.

7. AGATHOCLES concluded a peace with Amilcar; who drew off his forces, and returned into Libya. When convening an affembly of the Syracufans, "This is the hour, 'faid he,' that I have ever wifhed for, when I might fee my fellow citizens in full fruition of their liberty." Having thus faid, he took off his robe and fword, and declared

clared himſelf a private man. Struck with ſuch an inſtance of patriotiſm and moderation, the Syracuſans voluntarily committed to him the government of the ſtate who in leſs than ſix days, having put many of the citizens to death, and driven more than five thouſand into exile, poſſeſſed himſelf of the ſovereignty of Syracuſe

8 AGATHOCLES having received intelligence, that Tiſarchus, Anthropinus, and Diocles had formed deſigns againſt him, ſent for them, and inveſted them with the command of a conſiderable force, with which he directed them to relieve a city, then in alliance with Syracuſe, and cloſely beſieged "To-morrow, 'ſaid he,' I will meet you at Timoleontium with horſes, arms, and baggage, and forward the expedition." They received his commands with rapture, hoping to have forces put into their hands, which they meaned to have employed againſt him The next day, when they met at Timoleontium, Agathocles gave the ſignal for ſeiſing them. on which Diocles, Tiſarchus, and Anthropinus, with their guards, to the number of two hundred, were cut to pieces; and ſix hundred others, who attempted to aſſiſt them, were ſlain.

CHAP. IV.

HIPPARINUS.

WHILE Hipparinus reſided at Leontium, hearing that Syracuſe was ungarriſoned, a conſiderable force having been ordered from it under the command of Calippus, he reſolved to march a body of troops from Leontium and attack it previouſly diſpatching ſome emiſſaries to the city, with orders to ſlay the centinels Theſe orders executed, they opened the gates, through which Hipparinus entered with his mercenaries, and made himſelf maſter of Syracuſe.

CHAP.

CHAP. V.

THEOCLES:

THEOCLES advanced with the Chalcidians from Euboea against Leontium, of which he made himself master, by the affiftance of the Sicilians, who had before been in poffeffion of it. The Plataeans alfo fent thither a colony from Megarae, which they wanted to plant at Leontium under the protection of Theocles; who had told them, he was under an oath not to difturb the Sicilians, but that he would open the gates to them in the night, and they might then ufe their difcretion in regard to them. The gates being accordingly thrown open, the Megarenfians poffeffed themfelves of the forum and the tower, and attacked the Sicilians: who, finding themfelves, unarmed and unprepared, unequal to make head againft the enemy, abandoned the city, and fled. The Megarenfians then undertook to fupply the place of the Sicilians, and became allies to the Chalcidians.

2. AFTER a refidence of about fix months with the Chalcidians, Theocles by the following ftratagem expelled the Megarenfians from the city. He pretended in the courfe of the late war to have made a vow, if ever he became mafter of Leontium, to offer facrifices to twelve gods, and celebrate them in arms. The Megarenfians, who entertained no fufpicions of any hoftile defigns, congratulated him on the occafion; and wifhed fuccefs might crown his pious acts. The Chalcidians then borrowed arms of them, that, while the ceremonies were performing, they might make the proceffion. After they had halted in the forum, Theocles ordered proclamation to be made, that the Megarenfians fhould quit the city before fun-fet. They fled to the altars, and implored Theocles not to expel them from the city, or at leaft not to expel them unarmed.

unarmed. But after consulting with the Chalcidians, it was determined unsafe, to remove from their city such a number of enemies, and put swords in their hands. They were therefore dismissed without arms; and, by the permission of the Chalcidians, for one season only wintered at Troilus.

CHAP. VI.

HIPPOCRATES.

HIPPOCRATES, having formed a design to make himself master of the city of the Ergetini, who served as stipendaries in his army, in the disposition of the booty used always to allot them the largest portion, gave them an advanced pay; complimented them on being the best troops in his army, and tried all means to allure as many of them as he could into his service. The honours, the advantages, the reputation they acquired under Hippocrates, induced them in great numbers to quit their city, and enlist in his army: whom he received with peculiar marks of favour, and assembling all his forces, marched through the country of the Læstrygonians, posting the Ergetini on the shore: and the rest of his army he encamped higher up in the country. The Ergetini being thus decoyed into the field, Hippocrates detached a body to the evacuated city, with a herald to take possession of it in his name: and the Geloians, and Camarinæans he ordered to fall upon the Ergetini, and cut them to pieces.

CHAP. VII.

DAPHNÆUS.

IN an action, where the Syracufans and Italians were engaged againft the Carthaginians, the Syracufans being pofted in the right wing, and the Italians in the left, Daphnæus, hearing a loud and confufed noife on the left, hafted thither, where he found the Italians hard preffed, and fcarcely able to maintain their ground Returning to the right wing, he told the Syracufans, they were victorious in the left and a vigorous effort on their fide would render the victory compleat. The Syracufans, on confidence of the truth of their general's affertion, impetuoufly charged the Barbarians, and defeated them.

CHAP. VIII.

LEPTINES.

THE Carthaginians, failing by Pachinus, touched there, and committed great depredations on the country around it. when Leptines in the night placed an ambufcade of horfe, with orders to feife an opportunity, and fet their temporary camp on fire. As foon as the Carthaginians faw their tents and baggage on fire, thither with all expedition they hafted, to fave what property they could, but in their attempt were intercepted by the ambufh, who purfued them to their fhips with great flaughter

2 LEPTINES, failing from Lacedæmon, touched at Tarentum. and there landed with fome of his crew The Tarentines offered no violence to any of the failors, as being Lacedæmonians, but enquired

for

for Leptines, in order to apprehend him. When throwing off his robe, taking his utenfils in his hand, and fome wood upon his fhoulder, he got on board his fhip again, and flipping his anchor, put off to fea. His failors fwam to him, whom when he had received on board, he directed his courfe to Syracufe, and joined Dionyfius.

CHAP. IX.

ANNON.

AS Annon paffed by Sicily, Dionyfius difpatched a confiderable fleet to intercept him which having come nearly up with him, Annon reefed his fails, and laid to The enemy, who watched his motions, did the fame. Annon then ordered his men as expeditioufly as poffible to fet their fails and crowding all the fail he could, got clear of the enemy, who were thrown into confufion by this fudden movement, not being very expert at naval manœuvres.

CHAP. X.

IMILCON.

IMILCON the Carthaginian, who was well acquainted with the propenfity of the Libyans to liquor, in a great number of veffels of wine infufed laudanum and having lodged them in the fuburbs, he fkirmifhed a little with the enemy, and then as if overpowered retreated into the city. The Libyans, elated at their fuppofed advantage, and at having blocked up the Carthaginians in their city, made very free with the wine they found, which threw them into a profound fleep, and left them to the difcretion of the enemy.

2. IMILCON, with the Carthaginian fleet, weighed anchor in the night from Libya on an expedition to Sicily: having furnished the masters of the ships with sealed tablets, in which he wrote the place of their destination. That so, in case they should be separated, they might know what port to make, without exposing the secret of his expedition to the information of deserters. And the windows at the heads of the ships he stopped up, that the enemy might not at a distance see his lights, and be thereby apprised of his invasion.

3 IMILCON had besieged a town in Libya, to which there were two narrow and difficult approaches and to defend them, the Libyans had posted two strong garrisons Imilcon dispatched a revolter, to give them intelligence, that he intended to raise a mound on one of those approaches, where he had determined his attack, and to sink a foss across the other, to prevent the besieged from sallying out, and attacking his rear The Libyans, observing the works begun, gave credit to the revolter; and collected their whole strength against that approach, on which he had begun to erect his works When Imilcon, having previously prepared wood for the purpose, in the night filled the foss he had cut in that approach, marched his forces over it, and, while the enemy's whole attention was directed to the other pass, by that quarter carried the town.

4. HAVING besieged Agrigentum, Imilcon encamped not far from the city. From whence seeing the enemy march out in great force, he gave private directions to his officers at a given signal, to make a hasty retreat. The Agrigentines pressed closely on them in their flight, and were drawn a considerable distance from their city. When Imilcon, with a body of troops having posted himself in ambush, set fire to some wood, which he had ordered to be placed near the walls for the purpose. The pursuers seeing a great smoak arise from the walls, and apprehending some part of their city to be on fire, quitted

the

the purfuit, and with all expedition returned to the relief of it. While thofe, who had before fled, faced about, and preffed hard upon their rear And as foon as they reached the place, where the ambufh was pofted, Imilcon with his forces vigoroufly attacked them, cut many of them to pieces, and the reft were made prifoners.

5. IMILCON lay encamped near Cronium againft the generals of Dionyfius who, being between him and the town, prevented the Carthaginian forces from entering it, though the Cronians would readily have admitted them Imilcon, therefore, informed of the difpofition of the people, cut down all the wood he could find, a great quantity of which grew near the enemy's camp, and piled it in front of them. Then taken advantage of a wind, that blew directly againft them, he fet it on fire, and while they were involved in a cloud of fmoak, flipped by them, and reached the walls when the Cronians opened their gates to him, and he entered the city, while the enemy knew nothing of his march.

CHAP. XI.

GESCON.

AMILCAR, one of the ableft generals the Carthaginians ever had, commanded their forces in Lybia · but after a feries of great fuccefles, became obnoxious to a faction, who envied him his reputation, and charging him with defigns againft the liberties of the people, procured him to be condemned, and executed. And his brother Gefcon was banifhed New generals were then appointed, under whofe conduct the Carthaginian arms met with nothing but repeated defeats . till their very exiftence became a matter of doubt. In thefe difficulties what could they do? They could not raife Amilcar from the tomb. They therefore

addreffed

addressed a penitential letter to Gescon, recalling him from exile, constituting him general of their armies, and engaging to deliver up to him his own, and his brother's enemies, to be punished at his discretion. Gescon, on his return to his country, ordered his enemies to be brought before him in chains, and commanding them to lie down upon their bellies on the ground, he thrice put his foot lightly upon their necks, and said, he had by such humiliation of them taken sufficient revenge for his brother's death. This done, he dismissed them, adding, I will not return evil for evil, but repay evil with good. This conduct procured Gescon a general esteem, and the ready obedience of all parties, both of friends, and enemies, as a character equally amiable and great. And their public affairs soon took a different turn, his courage conquering, and the sweetness of his manners engaging the vanquished to him.

CHAP. XII.

TIMOLEON

TIMOLEON, having taken the field in Sicily against the Carthaginians, just as he was advancing to battle, met a mule loaded with parsley. His army was intimidated with the omen: for it was customary with them, to deck with parsley the monuments of the dead. But Timoleon, giving a different turn to the omen, cried out, " The gods have determined to us the victory: for the reward of victory in the Isthmian games is a crown of parsley." This saying, he put a sprig of parsley upon his temples, and his generals did the same ; and the rest of the army following their example, stuck a piece of parsley on their temples, and in full confidence of victory advanced to the field.

2. TIMOLEON having closely besieged the tyrant Mamercus, who by false promises, and breach of oaths, had deceived, and murdered

numbers.

numbers: he promised to surrender himself to Timoleon, and take his trial before the Syracusans, if he would engage not to stand forward as his prosecutor. The condition was complied with, and Timoleon conducted Mamercus to Syracuse. As soon as he had introduced him into the assembly. "I will not, 'said he,' prosecute this man, for so I promised him but I order him to be immediately executed. For there is no law more just, than that he, who has deceived numbers to their ruin, should once be over-reached himself."

3 TIMOLEON, according to articles of alliance, having been ordered to the assistance of the Syracusans, climbed a very high mountain; from whence he saw the Carthaginian army drawn up, to the number of fifty thousand men, in a bleak situation, directly exposed to the wind and the enemy. Immediately convening a council, "Now, 'said he,' is the moment for victory. For there exists an oracle, that hath decreed defeat to the army, that occupies the exact station the Carthaginians have taken. And the period is now at hand, that must determine the oracle." This assurance gave spirits to the Greeks, who with a very inferiour force obtained the victory.

CHAP. XIII.

ARISTON

AS Ariston with one small vessel convoyed the transports, laden with corn, an enemy's ship appeared in view, chased, and came up with him, just as he was going to land. He laid the transports as near the shore as he could, and himself kept on the outside of them. So that if the enemy attacked the men, who landed the corn, they might be galled with darts from the transports. and if they attacked the transports,

ports, he might lay upon their sides, and hem them in between them and his own vessel.

2. ARISTON, the Corinthian admiral, after a naval engagement between the Athenians and Syracusans, in which the victory remained undetermined, both fleets keeping the sea, ordered provisions to be got ready, and stood for the shore. After his forces had disembarked, and made a hasty meal, he ordered them all on board again. And while the Athenians, supposing the enemy in acknowledgment of their defeat had borne away, and left them masters of the sea, were exulting in their victory, and had landed, one employed on one thing, and one on another, in making preparations for their dinner: the Syracusans suddenly attacked them. In the Athenian fleet all was confusion, each without his dinner, getting on board his ship with what expedition he could. While the Syracusans, who had thoroughly refreshed themselves, obtained an easy victory.

CHAP. XIV.

THRASYMEDE.

THRASYMEDE, son of Philomelus, being enamoured with the daughter of Pisistratus, as she was walking in a procession, ran up to her and saluted her. Her brother resented the liberty, and represented it as an affront: when Pisistratus coolly observed to him, "If we punish some for too great an affection to us, what must we do with those who avowedly hate us?" The passion of Thrasymede every day increasing, he engaged a party of his friends to assist him in carrying off the fair; which they effected, while she was assisting at a religious ceremony. Forcing their way through the crowd with drawn swords, they seised the maid, carried her on board a ship, and set sail for
Ægina.

Ægina. Hippias, her eldest brother, was at that time scouring the seas of pirates and supposing the vessel from the expedition with which it sailed, to be of that description, bore down upon it, and took it. When Thrasymede, and the rest, were brought before the tyrant, to answer for their outrage, instead of supplicating his pardon, they told him with firmness and resolution, to treat them as he pleased: assuring him, that from the time they resolved on the enterprise, they had resigned themselves to death, and despised it. Pisistratus was struck with the dignity of mind they discovered, and gave his daughter in marriage to Thrasymede. This act procured him the favour and friendship of all his subjects, who no longer considered him as a tyrant, but as an affectionate father, and patriotic citizen.

CHAP. XV.

MEGACLES.

MEGACLES, the Messenian, exerted himself with extraordinary vigour against Agathocles tyrant of Syracuse, spirited up many of the Sicilians against him, and set a price on his head. Irritated at his conduct, Agathocles besieged Messenæ, and sent a herald to demand Megacles: declaring, that if he was not given up to him, he would storm the city, and reduce every inhabitant to slavery. Megacles, who despised death, proposed to his fellow citizens, to appoint him their ambassador; and he would voluntarily surrender himself into the hands of the tyrant. The Messenians did so, and Megacles, being introduced into the camp of Agathocles, thus addressed him, "I come in the name of my city, an ambassador from the Messenians, and the object of my embassy is to die. But first convene your friends and give me an ambassador's hearing." An assembly being accordingly summoned, Megacles was introduced

duced. and, after pleading the privileges of his country, "If, 'said he,' the Messenians had engaged in an expedition against Syracuse, with a determination utterly to destroy it, would not you have done against the Messenians every thing, I have done against the Syracusans?" Agathocles smiled at the question: and his friends, that were present, interceded for the ambassador Agathocles accordingly sent him back unhurt, concluded the war, and entered into alliance with the Messenians.

CHAP. XVI.

PAMMENES.

WHEN Pammenes marched his army through Phocis to Thebes, he found the enemy in possession of a fort called Philobœotus, to which there were two narrow approaches. one was defended by a strong post which the enemy had secured, the other was more open. Through the latter Pammenes, having contracted the extent of his lines and deepened his phalanx, ordered his army to file to the right as if with intention of forcing his way. The enemy collected all their force to oppose him, even evacuating the post they had taken, to defend the other pass. This was what Pammenes wished, who immediately detached a body of troops to secure the deserted post. and through the approach, it commanded, he marched his army without loss.

2 PAMMENES being strong in cavalry, but in infantry very inferiour to the enemy, who particularly in heavy-armed troops out numbered him, posted the few heavy-armed troops he had, and some of his light infantry, against the strongest quarter of the enemy's army· and ordered them after a faint skirmish to fly, and thereby draw the heavy-armed troops of the enemy from the main body of the army. This succeeding as he wished, he advanced at the head of a body of cavalry
from

STRATAGEMS OF WAR.

from the other wing, fell furiously upon their rear, and the troops, that had before fled, facing about, he inclosed the enemy, and either took them prisoners, or cut them to pieces.

3. PAMMENES formed a design to make himself master of the harbour of the Sicyonians, which was then under the protection of Thebes. And, at the same time he advanced against the city by land, he manned a merchant-man with soldiers which anchored at the mouth of the harbour. Towards the evening some of them, without arms, went on shore, as merchants, to make purchases, and see the market. After the evening was somewhat advanced, and the ship had entered the harbour, Pammenes with a great and confused noise attacked the city. All run to the quarter, where the attack was made. Even they, who lived on the beach, left it, and fled to the assistance of their friends in the city. The armed troops in the mean time went on shore, and made themselves masters of the harbour without opposition.

4. PAMMENES ordered his men to observe the orders of the trumpet, in a manner contrary to their proper signification. As soon as they heard the retreat sounded, they were instructed to charge; and when the trumpet sounded the charge, they were directed to retreat. And of both those devices he availed himself with success.

5. PAMMENES, with a small force, being surprised by the enemy, who were very superior in number, dispatched a spy into their camp, who informed himself of the WORD, and returned, and discovered it to Pammenes. At midnight he attacked the camp, and, while the enemy in the dark could not distinguish each other, nor know their friends from their foes, who had possessed themselves of the WORD, obtained a complete victory.

CHAP

CHAP. XVII.

HERACLIDES.

DEMETRIUS, having engaged in an expedition into Lydia, in his absence committed the charge of Athens to Heraclides. The Athenian generals fought to avail themselves of this opportunity; and for that purpofe endeavoured to gain Hierocles, general of the mercenaries to open the gates of the citadel in the night, and admit the Athenian troops, who would murder Heraclides, and make themfelves mafters of the place. This confpiracy, in which the generals Hipparchus and Mnefidamus were principals, was formed at Iliffus, during the celebration of the leffer myfteries * Hierocles, however, faithful to Heraclides and his truft, informed him of the dark defign. who concerted meafures with him for admitting them, opening only a part of the gates In the night four hundred and twenty men were accordingly admitted, under the conduct of Mnefidamus, Polycles, Callifthenes, Theopompus, Satyrus, Onetorides, Sthenocrates, and Python. Heraclides, having previoufly introduced into the citadel two thoufand men, difpatched without noife or confufion the confpirators and their forces as faft as they entered

2 HERACLIDES, the Tarentine architect, engaged with Philip, father of Perfeus, with his own hand to deftroy the Rhodian fleet. When, leaving the royal palace, he expofed to the people marks of the king's cruel ufage of him, and fled to the altars. The people expreffed great compaffion for him: and by favour of them he got into a boat, and efcaped to Rhodes. " To you, ' faid he to the Rhodians,' I fly

---

* The 'effer myfteries were celebrated at a place called Agræ near the river Iliffus.

for refuge from the cruel treatment I have experienced at the hands of Philip, only for preventing an unjuft war he meditated againft you And in proof of the truth of what I fay, here is his letter, addreffed to the Cretans in which he exprefsly declares his intention of making war upon the Rhodians." The letter feemed to place his veracity beyond a doubt: the Rhodians therefore received him courteoufly, and thought he might be ferviceable to them againft Philip. When, taking the advantage of a rough and boifterous night, he fet fire to all their docks. Thirteen of them were entirely demolifhed, and all the fhipping that was in them As foon as he faw the fire take effect, he got into a boat, and, flipping off, paffed over into Macedonia, where he afterwards held the firft place in Philip's friendfhip.

CHAP. XVIII.

AGATHOSTRATUS.

THE Rhodians being engaged in a war with Ptolemy, whofe fleet then lay at Ephefus, Chremonides, Ptolemy's admiral, embarked, and put to fea, intending to give the Rhodians battle. Agathoftratus failed with the Rhodian fleet as far as Melia and having fhewn himfelf to the enemy, as if declining an action, returned into port. The enemy gave a general cheer, at feeing the Rhodians retreat, and returned alfo into port. When Agathoftratus with all expedition putting to fea again, in a clofe compact line bore down upon them, juft as they were landing at the temple of Venus, and, vigouroufly attacking them thus unprepared for action, obtained a compleat victory.

CHAP. XIX.

LYCUS

LYCUS a general of Lyfimachus, when Anœtus general of Demetrius was left in charge of Ephefus, and harboured there a number of pirates, who committed great depredations on the neighbouring countries, found means to bribe Andron the chief-pirate, to betray Ephefus to him. And the confpiracy was thus conducted: the pirate introduced into the city a body of Lycus's troops, without arms, in their coats and cloaks, and bound as prifoners. As foon as they advanced to the citadel, he ordered them to draw their fwords, which they had concealed under their arms: and having flain the centinels and guard, they gave the fignal agreed on to Lycus, who, forcing his way to them with the reft of his army, took Anætus prifoner, and made himfelf mafter of Ephefus. But after paying the pirates, according to his agreement, he expelled them from the city, juftly concluding, he could not depend on their fidelity to him, who had been fo very perfidious to their former friends.

CHAP. XX.

MENECRATES.

MENECRATES having attacked Salamis in Cyprus, when his men twice driven from the walls had fled to the fhips, renewed the attack a third time, and gave orders to the mafters of the veffels to weigh anchor, and bear away to an adjacent promontory, and behind it to anchor and lie concealed. The foldiers, having prepared their engines and ladders

ders, again attacked the walls, and were again beaten off but when they could see nothing of their ships, finding no hopes of safety left them, but in victory, they returned to the charge, and, acquiring courage from despair, drove the besieged from the walls, and made themselves masters of the place

CHAP. XXI.

ATHENODORUS

ATHENODORUS having been defeated by Phocion at Ataines, and obliged to retreat, administered an oath to all his officers and soldiers, to fight as long as they were able to stand then led them to the same spot, and renewed the action When the conquered, under the restriction of the oath, became victorious, and the victors fled.

CHAP. XXII.

DIOTIMUS.

DIOTIMUS with ten ships was convoying some transports, when he was intercepted by the Lacedæmonians with a fleet of twenty ships at Chios. Keeping close in with his transports, he maintained a running fight, and, separately attacking the enemy's ships, as they came up with him, defeated a fleet of double his force without any loss, by his address and excellent manœuvres.

2 WHEN Diotimus with ten ships advanced against the Lacedæmonian fleet consisting of the same number, conscious as they were of the Athenians' superiour seamanship, he could not bring them to an action He afterwards joined his ships, two by two, together, hoist-

ing only the sails of one, and thus put to sea. The Lacedæmonians, by the appearance of the sails discerning only five ships, and supposing that the whole strength of the enemy, immediately bore down upon them. As soon as they had advanced too near to escape him, Diotimus loosed his ships, and received their fleet with an equal force. And, so superiour were the Athenians to the enemy in naval science, that he sunk six of the enemy, and took the other four.

3. DIOTIMUS, the Athenian admiral, being ordered upon an expedition, that required dispatch, privately told the captains in the fleet, that he meaned only to take with him those vessels that were the best sailers, and could keep up with him. This was given out by him, not intending to leave any behind, but in order to make them exert themselves, and by their alacrity and speed give vigour to the expedition.

4. INTENDING an invasion of an enemy's country, Diotimus landed in the night a small party from each ship, of which he formed an ambuscade. Early in the morning he lay to that part of the shore, near which he had planted the ambuscade, ordered the soldiers on deck, to prepare for action, and made a feint as if with intention to put some boats, with armed men in them, on shore. The enemy advanced to the place, to dispute their landing. When at a signal given, the troops sallying out from their ambush, fell upon their rear, slew many of them, and put the rest to flight. Diotimus then landed his army without further opposition.

CHAP.

CHAP. XXIII.

TYNNICHUS.

WHEN Theodosia a city of Pontus was besieged by the neighbouring tyrants, and in danger of being taken, Tynnichus with a ship of burthen, and one man of war, relieved it. Taking with him as many soldiers as he could, three trumpets, and some canoes*; in the night he arrived near the town: and in a separate canoe posted each trumpeter, ordering them to advance at proper distances from each other, and sound the charge not separately, but together, and at regular intervals, so that it might appear to be the sound not of a single trumpet, but of several. The besiegers apprehending the arrival of a superiour fleet, quitted their station, and thought themselves fortunate in effecting an escape leaving Tynnichus, master of the port, to throw into the town a reinforcement.

CHAP. XXIV.

CLITARCHUS.

CLITARCHUS upon the advance of an enemy, lest he should be blocked up in the town, marched out his forces; then ordered the gates to be locked, and the keys thrown over the walls: which he took, and shewed to his soldiers; who, finding all hopes of a retreat thus cut off, fought bravely, and their courage was crowned with success.

* Σκαφος properly signifies a small boat made by scooping or hollowing one single piece of timber. And the term, though not restricted to boats of that construction, always denotes those of the smallest size.

CHAP. XXV.

TIMARCHUS.

TIMARCHUS, the Ætolian, having landed his forces in a very populous part of Asia, left his men should be deterred from prosecuting the enterprise by the great numbers the enemy might bring into the field, to preclude all hopes of effecting a safe retreat, set fire to his ships. His army, seeing no alternative, but death, or victory, exerted themselves for the latter, and obtained it.

CHAP. XXVI.

EUDOCIMUS.

SOME disputes happening in the camp, which Eudocimus in vain endeavoured to compose, and the parties being on the point of deciding their differences by arms, he ordered couriers*, as having just arrived, to signify the approach of the enemy, and that they had even begun to destroy the palisades. The news of the enemy's approach immediately

---

* The σκοποι, or scouts, were dispersed in different parts without the camp, to watch the roads, as well as to observe the enemy's motions in their camp, and to give intelligence of every particular they could discover, respecting their designs, their varied position, or their sudden movements, their accession, or diminution of force, their dependencies, or disappointments, in short to convey every article of information of every kind, that might concern them. The ἡμεροσκοποι, which I have here translated couriers, were somewhat different from the εκ-του and their office was to convey from the scouts to the generals, between whom they were continually passing and repassing, what observations those had made The ὁρμοκηρυκες were not always employed but only when the urgency of affairs required the continued attention of the σκοπω

composed

composed the internal commotions, and in the common cause every one flew to his post.

CHAP. XXVII.

PAUSISTRATUS.

PAUSISTRATUS, the Rhodian admiral, finding a great loss of arms, ordered his men on board, each in his arms And as soon as they were all embarked, he commanded every man to disarm, and certain officers, whom he appointed for the purpose, to take care that no arms were carried on shore

CHAP. XXVIII.

THEOGNIS.

THEOGNIS, to put an end to factions that were forming in the army about their stations in companies and bands, dispatched in the night a body of horse and officers, with orders to post themselves in a conspicuous place at some little distance, where they might be seen by the army, and taken for the enemy. Upon whose appearance Theognis in affected hurry and confusion ordered the army immediately to form, and the men to fall into their ranks, as if the enemy were actually in sight and advancing against them the apprehension of which left them no time for contention, but each readily posted himself in his old station Theognis then told them, the supposed enemy were their friends and fellow soldiers. But, added he, in future let us have no more disputes about stations. but each of you maintain the post, ye have now taken.

2. APPREHENSIVE that spies had introduced themselves into the camp, Theognis posted guards on the outside of the trenches, and then ordered every man to take his station by his own arms. The spies in consequence of this order became very distinguishable being either moving off, or having no arms by which to post themselves.

CHAP. XXIX.

DIOCLES

DIOCLES, the Athenian general, when pursuing his march in an enemy's country he could not make his men keep their ranks, or carry their arms, was continually changing the WORD. The men from thence concluding the enemy were not far off, took their arms, and preserved their ranks.

CHAP. XXX.

CHILIUS

CHILIUS the Arcadian, when he resided at Lacedæmon, learning that the Spartans entertained a design of fortifying the isthmus, and withdrawing themselves from the general alliance of the Athenians and the other Greeks that were situated without the peninsula, observed to them; if the Athenians and other Greeks should ever be on terms of friendship with the Persians, the Barbarians would find a thousand ways into Peloponnesus. The Lacedæmonians felt the force of his observation, thought no more of the isthmus, but joined the general alliance of Greece.

CHAP. XXXI.

CYPZELUS.

CYPZELUS, after having delegated the most eminent of the Bacchiades to consult the oracle at Delphos concerning some publick affairs, that concerned the Corinthians, proscribed their return to Corinth And having thus rid himself of the most powerful family in the state, he easily possessed himself of the sovereignty.

CHAP. XXXII.

TELESINICUS

TELESINICUS the Corinthian engaged the Athenians before the harbour of Syracuse. When, the battle having continued great part of the day, and both parties being much fatigued, Telesinicus dispatched a sloop to the city, directing them to bring provisions down to the beach. Which done, at a sudden signal, the battle yet undecided, the Corinthian fleet retreated into port. On their quitting the sea, the Athenian fleet also stood to land, and the men went on shore, and were differently employed in preparing their dinner. Telesinicus in the mean time, his men having taken a short and hasty repast, put to sea again, and, covering his decks with dartsmen and archers, on a sudden attacked the Athenians, who from their different engagements run to their respective ships with tumult and confusion: and bearing down upon their sterns, before they had time to get about, he obtained an easy and compleat victory.

2 TELESINICUS, observing that the enemy dined when he did, and regulated their motions by his own, directed some of his best sailing vessels to take their refreshment early in the morning and at the usual time, he gave the signal for the rest of the fleet to dine. The enemy did the same: when those ships that had already dined, attacked them unprepared and in disorder; and the rest of the fleet, after a short repast, coming up, by a compleat victory soon put an end to the engagement.

CHAP. XXXIII.

POMPISCUS

IT was a general rule with Pompiscus the Arcadian, whenever he encamped, to fortify against the roads leading to his camp both with palisades and trenches: and also to make new roads behind them. That any scouts, or spies, who should endeavour in the night to enter the camp, might fall into the trench; and, the road being turned, not be able to find their way back.

2 POMPISCUS, perceiving the enemy from the vicinity of their station observed his signals and orders, privately instructed his men to act directly contrary to them.

3. POMPISCUS, having so formed his camp, as almost to inclose a city he had invested, in a single quarter purposely left it open. That approach he ordered should be safe and free to all, who might have occasion to use it: and directed his marauding parties to molest none who should be found there, whether going to the city, or coming from it. The citizens, finding themselves unmolested in that quarter, went into the country as their concerns called them, and passed backwards and

forwards

forwards without apprehenfion. When informed by his fcouts, that great numbers of the inhabitants were abroad, he fuddenly attacked, and made them prifoners.

4 FINDING he could not carry a town by ftorm, Pompifcus bribed a deferter to convey intelligence to the enemy, that the Arcadians had recalled him, and that he had it in orders to raife the fiege. Rejoiced at the news, and feeing the army foon after ftrike their tents, and retreat, they gave full credit to the information of the deferter, and came in crowds out of the city to feife whatever they might find worth carrying off in the enemy's camp. Pompifcus, fuddenly returning, fell upon them, and made himfelf mafter both of them, and the town.

5 IN order to capture the enemy's fcouts, Pompifcus always had few roads to his camp, and thofe very open and expofed and his marauding parties he ordered to pafs and repafs through bye-ways. The fcouts, not venturing through the publick roads, ufed to take the byeways, and thus foon fell into the foragers' hands.

6 POMPISCUS employed as fcouts perfons, who were ftrangers to each other, that they might be the lefs likely to form cabals, and give in falfe reports. He alfo ordered them to have no communication whatever with any perfons in the camp, that no one, who might know them, fhould have it in his power to apprife the enemy of their errands.*

CHAP. XXXIV.

NICON.

NICON, the Samian captain, in order to pafs the enemy's fleet undifcovered, painted his fhip in the fame manner with theirs; and

* From this ftratagem we learn one particular ufe of the δρομοκηρυκι, of which fee Chap. XXVI of this book.

chufing

chufing out some of the ableft and moft expert hands he had on board, he put them to the oars, and then wore down to them, his crew, as soon as they came near enough, faluting by figns those of the adverfe fleet who were at firft furprifed, nor, till she had dropped into the rear, and from thence had ftruck into a different courfe, and got out of their reach, knew that she was an enemy.

CHAP. XXXV.

NEARCHUS.

NEARCHUS the Cretan made himfelf mafter of Telmiffus, then in the hands of Antipatridas, by the following ftratagem. He failed into the harbour. When Antipatridas, who was an old acquaintance of his, came out from the fort to him, and afked him if he was on particular bufinefs, and whether he was in want of any thing The Cretan told him, he had fome mufick girls on board, and fome flaves that were in irons, whom he should be glad to leave on shore with him. Which Antipatridas readily granted. The women were accordingly conducted into the fort, and the flaves carrying their inftruments and baggage attended them In the flutes were concealed fmall fwords, and targets in the bafkets which, as foon as they had entered the caftle, thofe, who had attended them thither, immediately laid hold on, poffeffed themfelves of the fort, and made Nearchus mafter of Telmiffus.

CHAP. XXXVI.

DOROTHEUS.

DOROTHEUS the Leucadian in a single ship, being pursued by two, steered towards a harbour and slipping by the mouth of it, suddenly tacked about, and briskly bearing down on the vessel which was first in the pursuit, and which supposing it his intention to enter the harbour had crowded all her sail in that direction, before she had time to alter her course and stand to him, sunk her on the first attack. And the other ship, seeing the fate of her companion, immediately sheered off.

CHAP. XXXVII.

SOSISTRATUS

SOSISTRATUS prevailed on the Syracusans to pass a general decree for the banishment of all those, with their families, who had connection with Agathocles, or were in any degree instrumental in raising him to the sovereignty. They were accordingly conducted out of the city by a body of a thousand men, consisting partly of horse, who fell upon them and slew most of them. Those that escaped Sosistratus afterwards proscribed, and confiscated the property of the exiles; which he employed in hiring with it a body of Greeks and Barbarians, and, liberating those who had been condemned to the quarries, he took them also into his service. those became his guards, and by their assistance he obtained the sovereignty of Syracuse.

CHAP. XXXVIII.

DIOGNETUS

DIOGNETUS the Athenian, having advanced against a city, in the night planted an ambuscade, and the next day with a naval force openly attacked it. The enemy on his approach immediately marched out of the city, to dispute his landing: when the ambuscade, defenceless and open as it was left, easily took possession of it. The enemy confused and dubious whether to dispute the landing of the invaders, or attempt the recovery of the city, Diognetus took the advantage of their perplexity, landed his troops, and defeated the force that advanced against him.

CHAP. XXXIX.

ARCHEBIUS.

ARCHEBIUS of Heraclea, when the enemy were perpetually harassing the country with prædatory incursions on the coasts, fastened together some fishing boats, and secured them with ropes run through their keels: then with a body of troops posted himself, near at hand, in ambush. A trumpeter, who was stationed on a tree, in order to observe the enemy, as soon as he discovered them steering towards the coast with a tender and two transports, gave notice to the ambuscade, who after they had landed, and part were engaged in plundering the country, and part in loosing the boats, suddenly sallied out, attacked, and cut them to pieces. And the tender and transports, which fell into his hands, Archebius conducted into the harbour.

CHAP.

CHAP. XL.

ARISTOCRATES.

ARISTOCRATES, having captured a Lacedæmonian ſhip, manned it with his own crew, and a conſiderable military force, and ſteered to a city in alliance with the Lacedæmonians. Thoſe, who had the charge of the harbour, readily admitted him as a friend and ally. when the men were no ſooner landed, than they fell upon the inhabitants and guards, who were leiſurely walking upon the beach, ſlew ten, who endeavoured to make ſome reſiſtance; and carried off twenty-five priſoners, for whom Ariſtocrates afterwards received a conſiderable ranſom.

CHAP. XLI.

ARISTOMACHUS.

ARISTOMACHUS having taken ſome ſhips of the Cardians, placed his own rowers at their oars, ornamented them with the colours and ſtandards of his own ſhips, which he towed after him as in triumph, and, the muſick playing, in the evening entered the harbour. The Cardians flocked out of the city, to ſee their victorious fleet when Ariſtomachus's troops landed, and made a dreadful havock amongſt them.

CHAP. XLII.

CHARIMENES.

WHEN Charimenes the Milesian fled to Phaselis, and was closely pursued by some sloops, dispatched after him by Pericles the Lycian; he put to shore, and, changing his dress, travelled on foot through the dominions of Pericles.

CHAP. XLIII.

CALLIADES.

CALLIADES master of a vessel, being overtaken by a ship of war before he could make port, so managed his rudder, as to receive upon it the oars of the enemy's first bench, and thereby break the force of their attacks upon his stern: by which he for some time kept them off, and under cover of the night found means to escape.

CHAP. XLIV.

MEMNON.

MEMNON, having determined on a war with Leucon tyrant of the Bosphorus, in order to acquaint himself with his force, and the population of the country, dispatched Archibiades in a vessel to Byzantium, as his ambassador to Leucon, to treat with him of an alliance. And with him he sent an eminent musician, an Olynthian, Aristonicus by name, the most celebrated artist of his day. that whatever towns he touched

touched at in his paffage, Ariftonicus might publickly entertain them with his mufical abilities, and, the inhabitants of courfe crowding to the theatres to hear him, the ambaffador might be enabled from the number of men he faw there to form fome eftimate of the population of the refpective places.

2. MEMNON, when encamped on a plain before the enemy, to decoy them from an advantageous poft they had taken, retreated to a greater diftance from them, and drew up only a part of his army, to induce the enemy to fufpect fome difafter in his camp And to fupport fuch fufpicion, he at the fame time difpatched a revolter over to them, to inform them a mutiny had taken place in his army, and that not venturing to truft his troops, he had for fear of an attack from the enemy retreated to a greater diftance. His retreat, and the diminifhed appearance of his army, confpired to confirm the information of the revolter they ventured therefore to quit their poft, and offered him battle When the army of Memnon, inftead of being divided by mutinies, in one firm body marched out, attacked the enemy, and obtained a compleat victory.

3 CHARES having befieged Ariftonymus in Methymna,' Memnon fent an embaffy to him, defiring him to defift from any further hoftilities againft Ariftonymus, who was his father's friend and ally, and whom he fhould, if he perfifted in the fiege, the next night with a powerful force relieve. Chares ridiculed an embaffy of that import fuppofing it impoffible by the next night to tranfport fo far an army of the magnitude he pretended But Memnon, as foon as he had difpatched the embaffy, marched his forces five furlongs, and embarked twelve hundred men with orders as foon as ever they were landed at the fort, to kindle a fire, and attack the enemy. Such an unexpected attack in the dark, and a fire at the fame time blazing, induced Chares

to make a precipitate retreat, supposing Memnon had with all the force pretended possessed himself of the citadel.

4 MEMNON with a body of five thousand troops advanced against Magnesia, and, at the distance of forty furlongs from the city which was defended by Parmenio and Attalus with a force of ten thousand men, pitched his camp, and fortified it. This done, he led his forces out: but, on the enemy's advance, sounded a retreat, and marched back his army into the camp. The enemy retreated in the same manner. Memnon again drew up his army, and as soon as the enemy advanced against him, he again retreated. The enemy also according to his movements regulated their own, advancing to the field when he marched out, and retreating when he retreated. At last, after the enemy had retreated from the field, put off their arms, and were at dinner, Memnon immediately returned and attacked them. Rising hastily from their meal, some without arms, others hastily snatching them up, and all in great confusion, before they had time to form their phalanx, he had secured a victory: many being cut to pieces, and many taken prisoners, and those, who escaped, fled for refuge to the city

5 WHEN Memnon advanced against Cyzicum, he put a Macedonian cap upon his head, and made all his army do the same. The Cyzicenian generals, observing from the walls their appearance, supposed it to be Chalcus the Macedonian, their friend and ally, marching with a body of troops to their assistance, and had opened their gates ready to receive him. They however discovered their error just soon enough to correct it, and shut their gates against him: when Memnon contented himself with ravaging their country

CHAP.

CHAP. XLV.

PHILOMEDUS.

WHEN the Phocenfians were attacked by the united forces of Thebes and Theffalis, Philomedus engaged, if they would commit the conduct of the war to him, to terminate it fuccefsfully. His engagement was embraced, and he was enabled to levy a body of mercenaries, which inftead of employing againft the common enemy, he bribed them to his own interefts, and by their affiftance poffeffed himfelf of the fovereignty.

CHAP. XLVI.

DEMOCLES.

DEMOCLES with others having been charged with an embaffy by Dionyfius the tyrant, he was accufed by the reft of the ambaffadors, as having neglected the tyrant's interefts: on hearing which, when Dionyfius expreffed his refentment, " Our quarrels, ' faid he,' originated merely in this, after fupper they would fing the Pæans of Stefichorus and Pindar, and I your's :" at the fame time repeating fome of his verfes. Dionyfius was fo pleafed with his tafte, that he thought no more of his offences.

CHAP. XLVII.

PANÆTIUS

PANÆTIUS in a war between the Leontines and Megarenfians, concerning the bounds of their refpective territories, was appointed general. And the firft use he made of his authority was to fpirit up the fervants of the camp, and the infantry, againft the purveyors and cavalry, as having every advantage in war, while themfelves ftruggled under every hardfhip, that attended it. He then ordered all to difarm themfelves, and pile their arms at the gate of the camp, to have an account taken of them, and the condition of them examined: and the horfes he directed the fervants to take, and feed. Having fix hundred heavy-armed troops, fit for an attack and devoted to his interefts, to the commanding officer of thefe he gave inftructions to take account of the arms. and then withdrew to the trees, where the fervants and horfes were ftationed, as if to indulge a little in the fhade, and there he perfuaded the fervants, to attack their mafters. Accordingly mounting their horfes, they feifed the arms, which were in charge of the heavy-armed troops, that were apprifed of his defigns and attached to his interefts: then falling upon their mafters naked and unarmed, they cut them to pieces, and with all expedition marched directly to the city, of which they took poffeffion, and invefted Panætius with the fovereignty.

BOOK VI.

THE PREFATORY ADDRESS.

To your moſt ſacred majeſties, Antoninus and Verus, this Sixth Book of Stratagems I alſo addreſs, moſt ardently hoping hereafter to employ myſelf in handing down to poſterity thoſe excellent ſtratagems you have yourſelves practiſed, whoſe wars have been an uniform ſeries of ſucceſſes. For ſuperiour as you are to antient generals in power and fortune, far more do you excel them in experience and abilities, by which you have ſo ſucceſsfully terminated foreign wars with many barbarous nations, and in concert with your father formed plans of permanent regulation for the conquered Mauruſians, the ſubjugated Britons, and the humbled Getæ. The Perſians and Parthians now call down the thunder of your war upon them. Go then, and, under the favour of the immortal gods, diſplay your wiſdom in forming plans, and your fortitude in the execution of them. I ſhall be happy to employ myſelf in a full and accurate relation of thoſe exploits, which poſterity will receive with admiration. In the mean time thoſe atchievements of antient heroes, ere yet I employ myſelf on your's, to thoſe I have already offered to you I prepare to add.

CHAP. I.

JASON.

JASON having formed a defign to attack a city in Theffaly, without communicating his defign to his army, ordered them to be reviewed, and to receive their pay. As foon as they came to the ground, in arms, and all in good fpirits, meffengers fuddenly arrived with intelligence, that the enemy had invaded their territories, and were juft fo far diftant, as the city he had it in contemplation to attack. The army, equipped for battle, urged him to make no delay, but immediately to lead them againft the enemy. He availed himfelf of their requeft, marched againft the city, furprifed, and took it. the victors and conquered being equally ftrangers to his intentions.

2. JASON the Theffalian, when his men were very importunate with him for their pay, and he had it not in his power to difcharge the arrears, run haftily into his mother's apartments, as if to efcape the violence of the foldiers. two or three of them at the fame time rufhing in with him. His mother, who was exceedingly rich, compofed all differences, and paid the arrears.

3. AFTER a war, which he had concluded with fuccefs, wanting money to pay his troops, Jafon told his mother, that in the courfe of the war he had received manifeft affiftance from Caftor and Pollux; and had vowed in cafe he fucceeded to celebrate a magnificent facrifice in honour of them. to which he had invited his generals, commanders, captains, and all who had any rank in the army. On credit of this, fhe fent him cups, ewers, waiters, and the whole fervice of table plate that fhe had, in gold and filver. of which he was no fooner in poffeffion, than he fold it all, and paid his mercenaries.

4. Jason having taken a city, that was very rich, and replete with elegant and valuable commodities, dispatched a messenger to his mother, desiring her to send all the domestics she had about her, that were versed in works of elegance and embroidery, to chuse for her such articles as they thought most magnificent, and best worthy of her acceptance. She accordingly ordered upon this errand all, in whose taste she had most reliance whom Jason retained in custody, till at a great expence she purchased their ransom.

5. Jason, with one of his brothers, went to his mother, who was amusing herself with her domestics in the room, where the needlework and embroidery were executed and pretending to have business of importance, on which to consult her, desired the domestics might withdraw. The guards accordingly conducted them from the apartment: when after a long conversation, Jason laughed, and told her, if she expected her domestics again, she must send, and ransom them.

6 Jason had a brother, whose name was Merion, a man exceedingly affluent, but very tenacious, and not at all disposed to supply his necessitous demands Having a son born, he invited the Thessalian chiefs to an entertainment on the occasion, when a name was to be given to the child, and particularly his brother, whom he wished to take a principal part in the ceremony And while Merion was thus engaged, Jason pretended to go out a hunting, but instead of that went to Pagasæ, the villa where his brother resided And surrounding the house with a troop of armed men, he bound the stewards, and brought away twenty talents of silver. He then returned in great spirits to the entertainment: at which he desired his brother to preside, and also begged him to give a name to the child. Merion, at that instant receiving intelligence that his house had been plundered, gave him the name of Porthaon, or the plunderer.

7. Jason accompanied by his brother Polidore, went to pos-

session of a city, and to sell the confiscated property in it. At bathing time he advised his brother, in order to give circulation to the blood, to rub his body well, and use as he did the strigil freely. This as he endeavoured to do, Jason observed to him, the ring he wore on his finger, incommoded him, and advised him to pull it off, and lay it aside till he was dressed. Polidore accordingly gave it to some one, that happened to stand near, to hold for him; who according to Jason's instructions carried it directly to Polidore's wife, and asked her for ten talents of gold, producing, in proof of the reality of his commission for that purpose, her husband's ring. To her it appeared so, and she immediately gave the messenger the money; which as soon as he brought to Jason, he gave up the strigil, and told his brother it was time to dress.

CHAP. II.

ALEXANDER the Pheræan.

WHILE Leosthenes lay before Panormum, Alexander not daring to hazard a general action with the whole Athenian fleet, sent in the night to the garrison at Acasium, directing them, in case the enemy detached any ships from their station, to let him know it, by lighting a torch on their tower; if they detached a second ship, they were to light another on the Magnesian tower; and if a third, they were to light a third fire on the tower of Pagasæ. Leosthenes, according to his wishes, dispatched a ship to Samos, another to Thasos, and a third to the Hellespont. The besieged informed Alexander of it by the signals agreed on; who immediately attacked the Athenian fleet thus weakened, and defeated them.

2. ALEXANDER, after the battle of Peparethus, dispatched some

vessels

vessels immediately to the Piræum, in hopes of surprising the Athenians, off from their guard, and in full security, in consequence of their recent victory, with orders to seise all the money they found on the tables. The Athenians, supposing them friends, never attempted to prevent their landing which as soon as they had effected, they sounded the charge, and with drawn swords immediately secured possession of the money tables. And while the Athenians fled into the city, to give information to the generals of what had passed at the Piræum, having possessed themselves of the money, they retreated to their ships.

CHAP. III.

ATHENOCLES

ATHENOCLES, closely besieged, against the battering ram and other offensive machines contrived to run along the sides of the fortress bars of lead, which broke the violence of the stroke, and spoiled the enemy's machines. Against this device the besiegers advanced another machine, which dislodged the mass of lead in such a direction, that in its fall it hurt no one who was under it. then, under cover of the testudo, they again advanced to the attack, and shook the walls. The besieged notwithstanding continued vigorously to exert themselves; and through brazen pipes poured melted lead from the walls, which disjointed the testudo. till the enemy contrived, from the works they had erected, in great measure to counteract the effect of the lead by discharging upon it a quantity of vinegar, by which that, as well as other combustibles which were thrown from the walls, were soon extinguished. For nothing is more effectual to the extinction of fire, than vinegar*. nor can any thing be better secured against it, than by being
rubbed

---

* Geoffrey de Vinesauf, who accompanied King Richard I. to the crusade, says of the Greek fire, which indeed is much spoken of in all the histories of the Holy wars as being frequently employed with success by the Saracens against the Christians, that with a pernicious stench and livid flame it consumed even flint and iron, and would continue to burn a
con-

rubbed over with that liquid, which the fire no sooner touches, than it is quenched. They also hung round it sponges filled with water And some, against the melted lead, covered their machines with sand and dirt.

CHAP. IV.

PHILOPÆMEN.

PHILOPÆMEN thought it not the part of good generalship, always to lead the phalanx. but used to ride through the ranks, and be sometimes in the van, sometimes in the centre, and at other times in the rear: by which means he saw every thing, and was always at hand to correct whatever in any part of the army he saw amiss.

2. PHILOPÆMEN having been defeated by the Lacedæmonians, and pursued to the Eurotas, as soon as he had passed the river, ordered the cavalry to unbridle their horses, and give them water. Close by was a thick covert: where the Lacedæmonians, from the confidence he discovered, supposing an ambuscade was planted, ventured not to cross the river, but gave up the pursuit

3. INSTEAD of the use of the target and short spear, Philopæmen introduced into the Achaian army the use of the long spear and shield; as also the helmet, coat of mail, and greaves: and, instead of skirmishing with javelins, as light armed troops, he made them stand close and firm to the battle. All elegancies in dress he likewise discouraged, and the luxuries of the table, observing, that military men ought to be above every thing, that was not absolutely necessary By these arts Philopæmen formed his army nor did any general of his age lead to the field braver, or more hardy troops.

---

considerable time under water but by sprinkling sand upon it, the violence of it was abated, and vinegar poured upon it effectually extinguished it. Whether this very extraordinary property of vinegar in extinguishing fire may not suggest a useful hint in accidents of that kind on board of ship, is a subject perhaps not unworthy consideration.

CHAP.

CHAP. V.

ARATUS.

ARATUS made himself master of the Acrocorinthus,* which Antigonus had garrisoned, and left in charge of Perseus the philosopher, and Archelaus general of the forces, by the following stratagem. There were at Corinth four brothers, Syrians by nation, one of whom was Diocles, who belonged to the garrison, that defended the fortress The other three had been concerned in robbing the royal treasury and had sold the gold to Æsia a money-changer at Sicyon, whom Aratus employed in money concerns. One of the brothers was frequently at this money-changer's house, and a constant guest at his entertainments. The discourse one day turning upon the Acrocorinthus, he observed that in the precipices, on which it was built, he had discovered a cleft, through which a hollow way obliquely run, extending to the very walls. The money-changer told this to Aratus, who studied by every means to cultivate Erginus's acquaintance, to whom he engaged to pay seven talents, whenever he should be master of the Acrocorinthus. Erginus accepted the proposal, and with his brothers undertook to put him in possession of it. Preparations were accordingly made for the attack Aratus posted his army near, and ordered them to rest on their arms From thence taking with him four hundred picked men, in the night he entered the cleft, and pursued his way till he reached the walls, to which he applied the ladders, and instantly scaled them. As soon as the as-

---

* The importance of this fort at that time was such, that Polybius ascribes to this exploit of Aratus in gaining it the restoration of liberty to the Corinthians as it engaged them to become a part of the Achæan government, and to unite in the general confederacy to resist the intrigues and artful policy of Antigonus. See Pol. Book III. Chap. III.

sault

fault was known within the fortress, a desperate action commenced: the moon sometimes giving a momentary light, then, in passing under a cloud, again withdrawing it, and leaving the combatants to engage in the dark. Aratus's troops in the issue prevailed, and, as soon as the day broke, opened the gates to the rest of the army. Aratus took Archelaus prisoner, but afterwards enlarged him, and gave him leave to pass over to whatever place he pleased. Theophrastus, who refused to leave the place, was slain: and Perseus the philosopher, seeing the fort taken, escaped to Cenchriæ, and from thence made his way to Antigonus.

CHAP. VI.

PYRRHUS

PYRRHUS, after having been defeated by the Romans, and lost his elephants, sent an embassy to Antigonus, to solicit his assistance; which being refused, he directed the ambassadors to declare every where the contrary, that Antigonus had engaged to assist him with a powerful force. And thus were the Tarentines, all the Sicilians, and some of the Italian states, who would otherwise have deserted him, held together by the hope of Antigonus joining the confederacy.

2. PYRRHUS, having engaged in an expedition into Peloponnesus, received with great benignity all the Spartan embassies sent by the Arcadians to treat of peace, and promised them to send his sons into Sparta, to be instructed in the institutes of Lycurgus. While the ambassadors in consequence of these professions, were magnifying the friendly and pacific disposition of Pyrrhus, he arrived at the head of a powerful army in Sparta. And when the Spartans charged him with acting so contrary to his professions, he with a smile replied, it is not your practice, when you have determined on a war, to apprise your enemy

of

of it. Therefore complain not of unfair treatment, if against the Spartans I have practised a Spartan stratagem.

3. PYRRHUS, before he engaged in a war, always endeavoured to bring the enemy to terms, by representing to them the ill consequences that must follow, by endeavouring to convince them of their own interest, by exposing to them the miseries that must attend the war, by urging every just and reasonable motive against it.

CHAP. VII.

APOLLODORUS.

APOLLODORUS, the son of Cassander, having been charged with designs against the liberty of the people, appeared in black, his wife and daughters habited in the same manner, and thus attended, surrendered himself to his judges, to dispose of him as they pleased. who, seeing him so humiliated, were touched with compassion, and acquitted him Not long after Apollodorus pursued his schemes with more success, and possessed himself of the sovereignty. The first act of his tyranny was exerted against the judges, that had acquitted him, whom he punished with great cruelty, as not having been indebted for his life to their humanity, but to his own address.

2. APOLLODORUS, when a private citizen at Cassandria, so artfully guarded both his words and actions, that he was esteemed the greatest patriot, that lived. He signed the decree for the removal of the tyrant Lachares from Cassandria, because he was the friend and ally of King Antiochus, and suspected of an intention to betray the liberties of the people to him. And when Theodotus proposed a guard for his person, he was himself the first that opposed it The Euridicæa, a feast in commemoration of the restoration of liberty to the Cassandrensians,

drenſians, was alſo of his inſtitution. And the ſoldiers, who refuſed to defend the fortreſs againſt the people, he procured to be made free of the city, and to have ſettlements allotted them in Pallene that they might continue there, the guardians of the public liberty. And at all public meetings he was continually inveighing againſt deſpotiſm, as of all things that could happen to a people moſt to be dreaded. By theſe artifices he ſo effectually deceived the people, that at the very time when he had formed a conſpiracy for poſſeſſing himſelf of the ſovereignty, he was ſuppoſed to be the moſt determined foe to it. He had gained to his intereſts a banditti of ſlaves and mechanics, whom he privately ſummoned to a meeting, where he killed a youth, whoſe name was Callimeles, and had his entrails ſerved up, of which they all partook, and drank his blood mixed with wine uniting themſelves in a horrid confederacy by theſe ſavage myſteries. By the aſſiſtance of theſe aſſociates, he poſſeſſed himſelf of the ſovereignty; and became the moſt cruel and bloody tyrant, with which not only Greece, but even Barbary was ever curſed.

CHAP. VIII.

ÆGYPTUS

ÆGYPTUS, having been diſpatched by Mauſolus to Miletum, to aſſiſt a party there, who had engaged to betray the city to him, on his arrival found the conſpiracy was detected, and that he was in danger of being apprehended. He however made his eſcape to the ſhip: but ſeeing a party on the watch to prevent the veſſel from putting to ſea, he ſent a pilot on ſhore to enquire for Ægyptus, who deſired every one he ſaw, to ſeek him out, and ſend him down to the ſhip, which was ready to ſail. The party, that had been diſpatched to prevent the veſſel from ſailing, on hearing that Ægyptus was not on board, left the

the beach, and run different ways about the city in queft of Ægyptus. As foon as the pilot returned to the fhip; he flipped his cable, and got off to fea.

CHAP. IX.

LEUCON.

LEUCON, when his treafury was very low, iffued a proclamation for a new coinage. and directed every one to carry in his money; and to receive the fame in value ftruck in a new die. A new die was accordingly ftruck, and every piece of money bore a value double to that it poffeffed before One half he kept for himfelf, and every individual received the fame current value he gave in.

2. LEUCON having had intimation of a confpiracy being formed againft his government by a ftrong party of the citizens, and among them fome of his own friends, affembled the merchants, and borrowed of them whatever fums they could advance. upon pretence that, on payment of a ftipulated fum, the confpirators would be difcovered to him. Having readily fupplied him with what he wanted, he took them to his palace, told them, that there really was a confpiracy formed againft him, and that he depended on them for his guards. for if his government was not fecure, the money they had lent him was loft. The merchants accordingly armed. and fome attended as guards of his perfon, and fome were pofted to defend the palace By the affiftance of thefe, and his particular friends, all who had been concerned in the confpiracy were apprehended and flain· and, his government thus fecured, he repaid the money.

3. IN a war againft the Heracleotæ, Leucon, having obferved that fome of the captains difcovered a difpofition to revolt, ordered them to

be apprehended, and told them, some disagreeable insinuations had been thrown against them, but that for his part he had no doubt of their fidelity however, in case the chance of war should determine the victory in favour of his enemies, that no suspicion on that account might corroborate the charge against them, he directed them for the present to retire from their employments, which he disposed of to others. And their particular friends, as if through regard for them, he promoted to magistracies and civil employs in villages As soon as the war was terminated, he observed that it was proper to make some enquiry into the charges, that had been obliquely urged against them, lest the doubt, he might have seemed to express of their fidelity, should be esteemed the effect of caprice No sooner had they appeared in court, attended by their friends, than, surrounding the place with an armed force, he ordered every man of them to be put to death.

4. THE Heracleotæ, having made war on Leucon, advanced against him with a great fleet, and in the face of him landed, and committed various depredations Observing his troops not to act with spirit against the enemy, with difficulty brought to the charge, and easily routed, he drew up his army to oppose the invaders, altering the arrangement of it, and posting his heavy-armed troops in the first line, and in their rear the Scythians with express orders to these, if the heavy-armed troops gave way, to transfix them with their javelins. The severity of these orders gave resolution to the army and put an end to the ravages of the enemy.

CHAP.

CHAP. X.

ALEXANDER, General of the Guards

ALEXANDER, who commanded the guards, that garrisoned the town and forts of Æolis, hired out of Ionia the most celebrated wrestlers, Theander and Philoxenus musicians, Callipedes and Nicostratus actors, and exhibited games to the people. The eminence of the several performers drew together a number of people from all the neighbouring cities. When the theatre was quite crowded, Alexander surrounded it with his own troops, and the Barbarians that were in his pay, and seised all the spectators with their wives and children. He meaned by this act no more than to raise a contribution on them, which he did in the ransom he demanded: then gave up his command to Thibron; and left the country.

CHAP. XI.

ARISTIDES ELEATES.

DIONYSIUS having besieged Caulonia, Aristides Eleates sailed with twelve ships to relieve it against whom Dionysius advanced with fifteen sail. Before so inferiour a force Aristides retreated: and, as the night came on, ordered torches to be lighted. These he removed by degrees, lighting others in their stead, which he floated upon large corks: and tacking about, steered for Caulonia, while Dionysius, amused with the lighted corks, so directed his course as to keep them in view, expecting to bring the enemy to an action in the morning.

CHAP. XII.

ALEXANDER, son of LYSIMACHUS.

ALEXANDER, the son of Lyfimachus and Macrides, formed a defign to make himfelf mafter of Coalium, a fortrefs in Phrygia. With that view he fecretly pofted his army in a hollow way near the place: and difguifing himfelf in a mean Phrygian habit, with a cap on his head, and attended by two youths with bundles of wood on their fhoulders, and a fword concealed under their arms, he paffed the gates unfufpected by the guard, and entered the city. Then laying afide his difguife, he publickly fhewed himfelf to the citizens, taking them by the hand, and affuring them, that he was come to protect, and fave the ftate. The gates on this affurance in full fecurity thrown open, the forces he had concealed, according to their inftructions rufhed in, and took poffeffion of Cotilium.

CHAP. XIII.

THE AMPHICTYONES.

THE Amphictyones, at the fiege of Cyrrha, having difcovered an aqueduct, that fupplied the city with water, by the advice of Eurylochus, poifoned the water with hellebore, a great quantity of which they procured from Anticyra. The Cyrrhæans, who made conftant ufe of it, were attacked with violent cholics, and difabled from duty. Under fuch circumftances the Amphictyones eafily defeated them, and made themfelves mafters of the place.

CHAP. XIV.

THE SAMNITES.

THE Samnites entered into a treaty of peace with their enemies, sanctioned by mutual oaths, on condition that they should be permitted to take from the whole circuit of the Samnite walls one single row of stones. The Samnites were exceedingly well satisfied with the terms; till they saw the enemy pick out the lowest row, which in effect demolished their walls, and left their city defenceless.

CHAP. XV.

THE CAMPANIANS.

THE Campanians made a truce with their enemies, on condition of their delivering up to them half their arms: in consequence of which, they cut their arms in two, kept one half, and returned the other half to the owners of them.

CHAP. XIV.

THE CARTHAGINIANS.

THE Carthaginians, being blocked up by Dionysius in a spot where they had no supply of water, dispatched an embassy to him with proposals of peace to which he consented on condition of their evacuating Sicily, and reimbursing him for the expences of the last war. The Carthaginian deputies agreed to accept the terms: but as their

power

power did not extend so far, as to enable them to conclude the treaty without the authority of the admiral, they desired leave to shift their camp to the place where the admiral lay, when the treaty, cleared all obstacles, might be ratified. Dionysius, contrary to the advice of Leptines, consented to their request As soon as they had changed their ground, they sent back the ambassadors of Dionysius, and refused to conclude the treaty.

2. WHEN the Carthaginians had invaded Sicily, in order to be supplied from Libya with provisions and naval stores in the most expeditious manner, they made two hour-glasses exactly of the same description, and drew round each of them an equal number of circles On one of those circles was engraved, "A want of ships of war," on another, "A want of store-ships," on another, "A want of gold," on another, "Of machines," on another again, "Of corn," on another, "Of cattle," "Of arms," "Of infantry," and "Of cavalry" The circles in this manner all filled up, one of these hour-glasses the forces kept with them in Sicily, and sent the other to Carthage directing the Carthaginians, when they saw the second torch raised, to send the particulars described in the second circle, when the third, those in the third circle, and so on By this means they received a ready supply of whatever they wanted

3 THE Carthaginians for an expedition against Sicily fitted out a fleet, consisting of ships of war and transports of which Dionysius having received intelligence with a numerous fleet opposed them. As soon as the Carthaginians discovered the enemy, they drew up their store-ships well-manned in a circle, with a space between ship and ship sufficient for the easy passage of a ship of war and in the middle of the circle they posted their triremes And thus formed, while the store-ships prevented the enemy from breaking in upon them in line of
battle,

battle, the triremes briskly pushing between them attacked them singly, funk many of them, and so crippled the reft, that they could no longer maintain the engagement

4 In their war with Hiero, the Carthaginians failed by night to Meffene, and anchored not far from Agrigentum. In the harbour the enemy had a number of ships of war, as well as store-ships and at the mouth of it were stationed guard ships. The Carthaginian admiral ordered the captain of one of the swifteft sailing triremes, to pafs the mouth of the haven, and, in cafe the enemy purfued him, to ftand out to fea, and draw them as far as he could after him. Accordingly as soon as he was difcovered by the guard ships, fuppofing him to have been fent to look into the harbour, they flipped their anchors, and gave him chafe with all the fail they could make. The Carthaginians, when they saw the guard ships out at fea, and at a sufficient diftance for their purpofe, with the reft of their force failed immediately into the harbour; burned the ships of war, which were riding at anchor; cut out several of the ftore-ships, and carried them off.

5 The Carthaginians, finding the Romans had a much greater force in Sicily than themfelves, fought to divide it. And for that purpofe fome of the citizens concerted a pretended confpiracy, and propofed to Cn Cornelius the Roman general, to betray Lipara to him, an ifland contiguous to Sicily. Cornelius liftened to their propofals, and ordered one half of his fleet with a military force on board, to fail to Lipara. The Carthaginians then put to fea, and under eafy fail advancing towards the Roman fleet, difpatched an embafly to the Roman general, fuppliantly defiring a peace. The ambaffadors, being admitted to Cornelius, requefted him to go on board the fhip of the Carthaginian admiral, who was at that time exceedingly ill, in order to conclude the treaty in perfon with them in the cleareft and moft unequivocal terms. The Roman confented: and the Libyans no fooner

faw

saw the enemy's general in their power, than they attacked them in full force, and obtained an easy victory.

CHAP. XVII.

THE AMBRACIOTÆ.

AT the siege of Ambracia the Romans, having lost great numbers, resolved on an attempt to surprise the place by undermining the walls: and had made some progress before the Ambraciotæ discovered their operations But the quantity of earth thrown up betraying to the besieged their design, they with equal exertions by countermining endeavoured to defeat it. At the extremity of the enemy's works they sunk a deep foss, in which they so disposed thin plates of brass, that the noise made by the Romans whenever they fell into it was heard by the centinel, and armed with a long spear, which they call Sarissa,* the besieged entered the foss and engaged them. But these subterraneous conflicts in a narrow dark passage producing no great advantage, the Ambraciotæ had recourse to another stratagem They constructed a vessel with a mouth as wide as the entrance into the foss, and perforating the bottom introduced into it an iron pipe, which they filled with small feathers, and set them on fire, stopping up the mouth of the pipe with saw-dust: which was supplied with fire from another brass vessel fitted to it for the purpose. The enemy's works thus filled with a constant succession of smoak and unbearable stench, they were forced to abandon their subterraneous enterprise.

* The Sarissa was a peculiar kind of spear from fourteen to sixteen cubits in length; which was particularly used by the Macedonians, and introduced first into the Achaian army by Philopœmen. See Chap IV Strat. III of this book

CHAP. XVIII.

THE PHOCENSIANS

THE Phocenſians, hemmed in at Parnaſſus, took the advantage of a moonlight night, and pouring down upon the enemy, their arms gleaming, and themſelves actuated by deſperation, with ſuch a panic ſtruck the Theſſalians, that ſome ſuppoſing them a ſupernatural appearance, others an acceſſion of force in aid of the Phocenſians, made ſo poor a reſiſtance, that they ſuffered an entire defeat: and four thouſand Theſſalians were left dead on the ſpot.

2. As ſoon as it was known in the city, that the Theſſalians had invaded Phocis, they ſunk a deep trench before the moſt acceſſible part of the walls, into which they threw pieces of broken pots and vaſes, and over them raiſed a ſtratum of earth: which, when the enemy's cavalry advanced upon it, gave way, and moſt of the horſemen, as well as horſes, were killed.

CHAP. XIX.

THE PLATÆANS.

THE Platæans, who had ſome Theban priſoners in their power, when the Thebans invaded Platæis, ſent an ambaſſador to them, declaring, if they did not immediately evacuate the country, they would put every priſoner to death. The Thebans perſiſted in their ravages, and the Platæans put their menaces in execution.

2. THE Platæans, when beſieged by the Lacedæmonians, ſallied out in the night and attacked the Spartan camp. The Lacedæmonians raiſed

ed the hostile torch,* soliciting the Thebans to their assistance. The Platæans from the city on the other hand raised the friendly torch; that the Thebans in suspense between the opposite lights, might decline marching to their assistance, till they were with more certainty informed, that they wanted it.

3 WHEN the Platæans were closely besieged by the Lacedæmonians and Thebans, and were at a loss how to convey to Athens an account of their situation, a body of two hundred men offered themselves on that service; determined, if they were discovered by the enemy, to fall in the attempt, or cut their way through them. For this enterprise a dark and stormy night was chosen; when the rest of the citizens mounted the ramparts and attacked the enemy's works. To the quarter, where the attack was directed, the attention of the besiegers was of course attracted; while the two hundred mounted the walls in an opposite quarter, and unobserved were let down by ladders on the other side. Then, not taking the direct road to Athens, by which, if the enemy should have had any information of their attempt, they would be sure to have pursued them, they took the road to Thebes. And so it accordingly happened: the Lacedæmonians pursued them by Cithæron, while the Platæans, turning a little out of the straight Theban road, reached Thebes, and from thence escaped safe to Athens.

* The signals, by which notices were communicated to confederate powers, were by smoak in the day, and in the night by torches. And those by torches were of two kinds, the hostile, and the friendly torch: which were raised from some place of eminence, generally from a fort or tower, in order to be the more conspicuous, and their intent was to signify the approach of friends or foes. The marks of distinction between the one and the other were, that the friendly torch was held fixed and steady, the hostile torch was tossed and brandished about in the air.

CHAP.

CHAP. XX.

THE CORCYRÆANS.

THE Athenians had marched out against the Corcyræan fugitives, who had posted themselves on mount Istones. Finding it in vain to make any opposition, they delivered up their arms, and surrendered themselves to the discretion of the Athenians: who accepted their submission, and granted them a truce, on condition that any attempt to escape should be considered as a breach of it. The Corcyræans, apprehensive lest the Athenians should treat them with too great humanity, privately advised them to make their escape to the Argives, and furnished them with a vessel for the purpose, in order to induce them to infringe the truce, that was granted them. After that attempt the Athenians delivered them up to the Corcyræans, as truce-breakers: who put every man of them to death.

CHAP. XXI.

THE ÆGESTIANS.

THE Ægestians, with an assurance of large subsidies, solicited the assistance of the Athenians: who dispatched ambassadors to them, to see what prospect there was of the subsidies being paid. The Ægestians in the mean time borrowed from the neighbouring cities gold and silver, in whatever shape and quantity they could obtain it, and with it magnificently decorated the temples of their gods, and their private houses. The ambassadors, observing such a profusion of wealth, reported it at Athens, and assistance was immediately sent them.

CHAP. XXII.

THE LOCRIANS

THE Italian Locrians entered into a treaty with the Sicilians, which they confirmed by an oath. Under their cloaks they carried upon their shoulders heads of garlick, and under their feet they put earth into their shoes: then swore, that they would preserve inviolate to them the fidelity of their state, as long as they trod the earth they walked on, or carried their heads on their shoulders. The next day, throwing away their garlick, and the earth from their shoes, they made a general massacre of the Sicilians, thrown off their guard, and secure in the obligation of the oath the Locrians had taken.

CHAP. XXIII.

THE CORINTHIANS.

THE Corinthians, having promised assistance to the Syracusans against the Athenians, and received information, that the latter with twenty-six sail had anchored near Naupactum, and served as a fleet of observation, equipped eighteen sail, with orders to sail to Panermus, and shew themselves to the Athenian fleet. And while that squadron amused the enemy, a number of Corinthian transports, with men and military stores sailed from Peloponnesus to the assistance of the Syracusans, and arrived safe at Syracuse.

CHAP. XXIV.

THE LAMPSACENIANS.

THE Lampsacenians and Parians, having a dispute about the boundaries of their respective territories, agreed at an early hour in the morning each to dispatch a certain number of persons from one city to the other, and that wherever the two parties met, that spot should be the common boundary of both their territories. The fishermen, who were employed on the road the Parians were to travel, which was by the sea, the Lampsacenians engaged to offer a sacrifice that morning to Neptune, to broil fish, and make libations of wine; and to request the Parians, as they passed by, in honour of the god to partake with them of the sacrifice. The Parians complied, and one mouthful of fish, and one glass of wine, induced them to take a second, and so on, till so much time was lost, that the Lampsacenians arrived first at Hermæum which is seventy furlongs from Parium, and from Lampsacum two hundred. Such was the extent of territory, which the Lampsacenians by this device gained from the Parians, Hermæum being admitted as the boundary between the two states.

CHAP. XXV.

THE CHALCEDONIANS

A TRUCE of five days was agreed on between the Chalcedonians and Byzantines, who were at war, while a congress of each state was constituted to treat of conditions of peace. Three days were spent in fruitless negotiations, when the Chalcedonians on the fourth pretended business of importance obliged them to return home. This being allowed them, the night was spent in equipping their ships, and the next day they attacked the Bizantines, who thought of nothing less than the re-commencement of hostilities, the term of the truce being then unexpired.

[*Here follows a Chasm, deficient in twenty-five Stratagems, attributed to nineteen Generals, which no Manuscript hath yet been discovered to supply*]

CHAP. XLV.

SOLYSON.

SOLYSON, the son of Callitele, a man in great esteem among the Samians, was appointed general, in a war against the Ætolians. Amidst the preparations for war, the festival in honour of Juno, which should have been celebrated in the temple of that goddess, a little distant from the city, was neglected. When Solyson observed, that it was not the duty of a general to neglect the honour of the gods, that to forfeit their assistance, was to lose his best ally, and having it, he should meet his enemies with superiour confidence. The Samians applauded the piety and true fortitude he discovered, immediately prepared for the celebration of the festival, and assembled at the temple of Juno. Solyson in the night entered the city, introduced into it the sailors from the ships, and possessed himself of the sovereignty of Samos.

CHAP. XLVI.

ALEXANDER.

ALEXANDER the Theffalian, previous to a naval engagement, ftationed on the decks a number of expert markfmen, who were furnifhed with a quantity of ftones and darts, and ordered to annoy the enemy with a volley of them, whenever they came within their reach. which fell like a fhower upon the failors, and fo difabled many of them, as to render them incapable of their duty

CHAP. XLVII.

THRASYBULUS.

WHEN Halyattes had blockaded Miletum, and expected to make himfelf mafter of the city by ftarving the people out, he difpatched a herald to conclude a truce with Thrafybulus, tyrant of the Milefians, till he fhould have built the temple of Affefian Minerva. Thrafybulus immediately ordered the citizens to bring into the market all the corn they had, and to engage each other in great entertainments. The herald reported to Halyattes the appearance of plenty he had obferved, who, from his reprefentation fuppofing the Milefians amply provided with provifions, raifed the fiege.

CHAP. XLVIII.

MENTOR.

MENTOR, having got Hermæus into his power, wrote letters in his name to all the cities, that were under his authority; ordering them to receive as their governor the person, whom he had charged with the delivery of the respective letters which he sealed with Hermæus's seal. Knowing his seal, in obedience to the mandate of the letters, the people surrendered their several cities into the hands of Mentor's officers.

CHAP. XLIX.

ANAXAGORAS.

ANAXAGORAS, Codrus, and Diodorus, sons of Echeonax, slew Hegesias, tyrant of Ephesus. When Philoxenus, governor of Ionia under Alexander, demanded them to be given up by the Ephesians But the people not complying with his requisition, he entered the town with a body of troops, apprehended the three brothers, threw them into chains, and imprisoned them in the tower of Sardis. After a long and severe imprisonment, with a file, that had been conveyed to them by a friend, they liberated themselves from their chains; and, habited in servile dresses, escaped as servants out of the prison in the night then cutting their cloaths into long pieces, they used them instead of ropes, and let themselves down by them from the walls Diodorus unfortunately fell down from the top of the walls, and laming himself, was obliged to lie where he fell till he was taken up by the Lydians, and sent to Alexander to be punished according to his pleasure. But Alexander dying at Babylon,

lon, he was sent to Perdiccas at Ephesus, to take his trial there. In the mean time Anexagoras and Codrus, who had got clear off, arrived at Athens. and, hearing of Alexander's death, returned to Ephesus, and set their brother at liberty

CHAP. L.

PINDAR.

WHILE Crœsus lay before Ephesus, the tower, which was called the traitress, fell down, and the capture of the place became inevitable. When Pindar, who possessed the sovereignty, recommended to the Ephesians, to run a rope round the walls and gates, fastening it to the pillars of the temple of Diana, and to consecrate the whole city to the goddess Crœsus in honour of the deity spared the city, as placed under her immediate protection. presented the Ephesians with their liberty, and made an alliance with them.

CHAP. LI.

THERON.

THERON, who kept privately in pay a body of the Agrigentines, ready on all occasions to obey his orders, being in want of money to make good to them their arrears, seised on a sum that had been raised for the erection of a temple to Minerva: and by this device he got it into his possession. He observed to them the work had gone on slowly, and proposed to have the building contracted for at a certain sum, and a time stipulated for the completion of the work. The citizens thought the proposal a very good one: agreed to let out the work, and lodged the money raifed for the purpofe in the hands of Gorgus, Theron's fon. As foon as the money had paffed into Theron's hands, inftead of employing architects, ftone-cutters, and other artificers, he converted the people's money againft themfelves, paid his men, formed them into a body of guards and by their affiftance poffeffed himfelf of the fovereignty of Agrigentum.

CHAP. LII.

SISYPHUS.

SISYPHUS, having fufpected Autolycus of frequently ftealing his oxen, fhod them with lead, infcribing characters on the fhoes to this effect: "Autolycus is a thief" Autolycus, according to his ufual practice ftole them away in the night Sifyphus the next morning traced them to the paftures of Autolycus, and fhewed the neighbouring farmers the footfteps of the oxen, which declared Autolycus's theft.

CHAP. LIII.

AGNON.

AGNON conceived a defign of planting an Attic colony at that part of the river Strymon, which is called the NINE-WAYS. But againft the attempt there exifted this oracle

    Athenians, why of late attempt to raife
    The ftructure proud, and colonize NINE-WAYS?
    Vain the attempt, unauthorifed by Heaven,
    Dire the decree, that rigid Fate hath given

Againft

Against the deed till from the silent tomb
At Troy the stubble of old Rhesus come
To join its parent soil. Then, then proceed.
And Fate shall give the act a glorious meed.

In consequence of this declaration of the god, Agnon dispatched some men to Troy, in the night to open the monument of Rhesus, and to bring away his bones which they bundled up in a purple robe, and brought to the Strymon. But the Barbarians, who possessed the country, would not permit him to cross the river. Agnon not in a condition to effect a passage over it by force, concluded a truce with them for three days, who retired to their own residence, leaving him, for the time stipulated between them, quiet in his post. In the night he passed the Strymon with his army, carrying with him the bones of Rhesus, which he buried at the river side, and there he intrenched himself with a fosse and palisades, resting in the day, and working at the fortifications every night. In three nights his works were compleated. when the Barbarians returned, and, finding in what manner he had during their absence employed himself, charged him with an infringement of the truce. "Of that, 'replied Agnon,' I am perfectly clear. the truce was for three days inaction, which I religiously observed. the works, you see, I erected in the intermediate nights." Such was the origin of the city, which Agnon built on the NINE-WAYS, and called it Amphipolis.

CHAP. LIV.

AMPHIRETUS.

AMPHIRETUS the Acanthian was taken by pirates, and carried into Lemnos. where he was kept in clofe confinement, the pirates expecting a very confiderable fum for his ranfom He took little fuftenance, but drank vermilion mixed with falt water, which gave a tinge to his ftools, that made his captors believe he was feifed with the bloody flux: and being afraid left his death fhould rob them of the expected ranfom, they releafed him from his confinement; hoping that exercife might reftore him to his health. But no fooner did he find himfelf at liberty, than he made his efcape in the night, and getting into a fifhing-boat, arrived fafe at Acanthum.

STRATAGEMS OF WAR.

BOOK VII.

PROOEMIUM.

THIS Seventh Book of Stratagems I addrefs to your moft facred majefties, Antoninus and Verus: in which you will obferve, that the minds even of Barbarians are competent to military ftratagems, deceptions, and devices. And you will confequently fee reafon, not to hold them in too great contempt yourfelves, and to give the fame caution in charge to your generals. On the contrary, there is nothing againft which they can be required more ftrictly to guard, than devices, wiles, and deception. in which the Barbarians excel much more, than in military prowefs Nor will any thing more effectually fecure them againft their devices, than a fettled diftruft of their promifes and profeffions. To that uniting Roman valour, we fhall be ftill more fuperiour to them, if we further add a knowledge of thofe ftratagems they have been ufed to employ.

CHAP. I.

DIOCLES.

DIOCLES the Median in this manner poffeffed himfelf of the fovereignty of the Medes. They were a vagrant people, and had no fettled habitations. had no cities, no laws, knew no principles of equity, but plundered each other of whatever the one wanted, and the other poffeffed Diocles gave laws to his neighbours, and endeavoured to inculcate on their minds the principles of juftice. They were delighted

with

with his regulations, and paid implicit obedience to his decrees. His name soon became famous among the Medes, and to determine their differences, numbers continually reforted to him, as a moft juft and upright judge. As foon as his eminence and reputation had conciliated to him univerfal efteem, he obtained guards to fecure him from the injuries, to which his determinations might expofe him. By the affiftance of thefe in the night he filled his little habitation with ftones, which he fhewed the Medes in the day, and pretended to have been thrown at him, to the great danger of his life, by thofe againft whom he had determined caufes. The people were enraged at the treatment, with which he had fo undefervedly met, and for the fecurity of his perfon allotted him a refidence on an impregnable eminence, appointed him a guard, and directed his table to be fupplied from the facred revenues. This guard he continued every day increafing; and in the end, inftead of judge, became a king.

CHAP. II.

ALYATTES.

THE Cimmerians, a people of uncommon fize, having made war on Alyattes, he took the field againft them, and directed his men to carry with them to battle a number of large fierce dogs; who, being fet on by their mafters, fell upon the Barbarians, as they would on a parcel of wild beafts, tore many of them, fo as to difable them from action, and put others to flight.

2. To weaken the Colophonians in their cavalry, in which they were very powerful, Alyattes entered into an alliance with them. And when they ferved under him, in the diftribution of prefents he always particularly diftinguifhed the horfe. At laft when he lay at Sardis, he

kept

kept a sumptuous table for them, and appointed them double pay. The cavalry, who were encamped without the city, no sooner heard of their pay being doubled, than delivering their horses to the care of the horse-keepers, they instantly resorted to the city, in great eagerness to receive their doubled pay. Alyattes on a sudden ordered the gates to be shut, and with a body of armed troops surrounded and cut them to pieces, then mounted his own men on the Colophonian horses.

CHAP. III.

PSAMMETICHUS.

TEMANTHES king of Ægypt, who was slain by Psammetichus, consulted the oracle concerning his success in his future views on the kingdom which directed him to beware of the cocks. Psammetichus, who was very intimate with Pigres the Carian, as soon as he was informed by him that the Carians were the first who wore plumes of feathers on their helmets, immediately conceived the meaning of the oracle, took into his service a great number of Carians, and advanced against Memphis. When encamping at the temple of Isis, about five furlongs from the city, an engagement was fought, in which Temanthes was defeated. From these Carians a part of Memphis is called Caromemphis.

CHAP. IV.

AMASIS.

AMASIS in an engagement with the Arabians placed behind the Ægyptians the statues of the gods they in most honour and veneration;

neration, that they might be induced with the greater alacrity to face danger supposing themselves under the immediate eye of their gods, who would not betray them, or leave them in the hands of their enemies.

CHAP. V.

MIDAS

MIDAS, pretending that he was going to perform a solemn sacrifice to the great gods, led out the Phrygians in the night as in procession, with flutes, and timbrels, and cymbals each of them at the same time privately carrying swords. The citizens all left their houses to see the procession: when the musical performers drew their swords, slew the spectators as they came out into the streets, took possession of their houses, and invested Midas with sovereignty.

CHAP. VI.

CYRUS.

IN three several engagements with the Medes Cyrus was each time defeated. A fourth battle with them he determined to hazard at Pasargadæ, where the Persians had left their wives and children. There he was again defeated but the Persians flying to the city, and there seeing their wives and children, they were struck with the reflection of what they must suffer from a victorious enemy, rallied, and attacked the Medes, who in their eager pursuit had lost all order, and obtained so decisive a victory, that the Medes never after ventured to face Cyrus in the field.

2. AGREE-

STRATAGEMS OF WAR.

2. AGREEABLE to a treaty, into which Cyrus had entered with Crœsus, he struck his tents, and from Sardis led off his forces. But as soon as the night came on he returned, attacked the city unprepared for a siege, and took it by storm

3. AFTER Cyrus had made himself master of Sardis, and Crœsus still held out in the fort, in expectation of assistance from Greece, he ordered the Sardian prisoners, the friends and relations of the besieged, to be bound, and exposed before them. a herald at the same time proclaiming, if the besieged surrendered to Cyrus the fort, they should receive their friends and relations safe and without ransom; but if they persisted in holding it against him, he would hang every man before their eyes To save their friends therefore, they chose rather to give up the fort than wait the issue of the precarious hopes with which Crœsus had flattered himself of assistance from the states of Greece.

4. AFTER the defeat of Crœsus, and his captivity, the Lydians having again revolted, Cyrus, who was himself intent on an expedition against Babylon, dispatched Mazares the Mede into Lydia, with orders, as soon as he had reduced the country into subjection, to take from them their arms and horses, oblige them to wear women's dresses, and to suffer them to entertain themselves neither in hurling the javelin, in horsemanship, nor in any martial exercises: but to oblige them all to spin, and sing, and pursue only female amusements. And by these means their minds became so dastardised and effeminate, that the Lydians, once a very warlike people, became of all the Barbarians the most pusillanimous

5. CYRUS, at the siege of Babylon, after he had compleated the channel, through which he intended to turn the Euphrates, that then run through the city, marched his army to a considerable distance: which induced the Babylonians to conclude, that he had given up all hopes of carrying the place, and they therefore became more remiss in their de-

fence of it. But suddenly diverting the courfe of the river, he fecretly marched his army through the old channel, and, while the Babylonians thought themfelves in perfect fecurity, made himfelf mafter of the place

6 When Cyrus, in an engagement with Crœfus, obferved that the great dependance of the Lydian was in his cavalry, to render them ufelefs, he oppofed in front againft them a number of camels · the nature of which animals is fuch, that horfes can bear neither the fight nor fmell of them. The horfes accordingly became ungovernable, turned about, and fled, throwing down the Lydians in their flight, and breaking their ranks · fo that victory declared for Cyrus, before he engaged.

7. To induce the Perfians to throw off the Median yoke, Cyrus made ufe of this device. He pointed out to them a barren, briery fpot; and bade them clear and cultivate it. a work, which with great labour and fatigue they effected. The next day he ordered them to bathe and clean themfelves, and attend him when he received them with a fumptuous entertainment After the day had been thus luxurioufly fpent, he afked them, which of the two days they liked beft. To which they replied; this day was as much preferable to the former, as happinefs is to mifery. Happinefs then, faid Cyrus, it is in your own power to obtain. Emancipate yourfelves from the fervitude of the Medes. The Perfians, ftruck with the greatnefs of the propofal, revolt, and create Cyrus their king. Under whofe aufpices, they not only crufhed the power of the Medes; but acquired to themfelves the empire of all Afia.

8. When Cyrus laid fiege to Babylon, the Babylonians, who had within themfelves great plenty of provifions of all kinds, derided the enterprife. But he foon difcovered the quarter where to attack them: and turned the river Euphrates, whofe natural courfe was through the town, into a neighbouring lake. Their fupplies of water thus cut off, they had no alternative; but to fubmit to Cyrus, or to die with thirft.

9. Cyrus,

STRATAGEMS OF WAR.

9 CYRUS, after having been defeated by the Medes, retreated to Pasargadæ, when finding the Persians in great numbers revolted to the enemy, he informed his army that the next day he should receive from fœderal powers that were hostile to the Medes a re-inforcement of a hundred thousand men: take therefore, said he, my lads, every man his faggot, to welcome your allies. This assurance of assistance the Persian deserters communicated to the Medes. And as soon as night came on, Cyrus ordered every man to light his faggot. The Medes, seeing a great number of fires burning, concluded that the auxiliaries were arrived, and, instead of pursuing the conquered foe, thought it expedient, in their turn to retreat.

10 AT the siege of Sardis Cyrus constructed machines of wood, that were as high as the walls and placed statues on them, in Persian dresses, with their beards on, quivers on their shoulders, and bows in their hands. And these he advanced in the night so close to the walls, that they seemed to be above the fort. Early in the morning in a different quarter Cyrus begun his attack against which the whole force that was in the town was immediately directed. When the statues on the opposite quarter being accidentally discovered, a general cry ensued and universal fear possessed the besieged, as if the fort was in the hands of the enemy. Throwing open their gates, each made his escape in the best manner he could; and Cyrus became master of Sardis at discretion.

CHAP. VII.

HARPAGUS.

HARPAGUS, to convey a letter privately to Cyrus, paunched a hare, and in the belly sewed up the letter: the bearer, equipped with hunter's nets, delivered the hare safe, passing the guards of the roads without suspicion.

CHAP. VIII.

CROESUS.

CROESUS, finding himself disappointed of the auxiliaries which the Greeks had promised him, chose out some of the ablest and stoutest Lydians; and armed them in the Græcian manner. Unaccustomed to the arms of Greece, Cyrus's men were at a loss how either to attack, or to guard against them. The clang of the spears upon the shields struck them with terrour: and the splendour of the brazen shields so terrified the horses, that they could not be brought to the charge. By this stratagem Cyrus was defeated, and made a truce with Crœsus for three months.

2. CROESUS, having been defeated by Cyrus in Cappadocia, in order to make good his retreat, ordered his men to carry with them as much wood as they conveniently could. This they deposited in a narrow defile, through which Crœsus led his forces, and pursued his march all night with what expedition he could: leaving some of his light horse, as soon as day appeared, to set the wood on fire. By this means Crœsus effected his retreat; Cyrus being by the fire greatly impeded in his pursuit.

CHAP. IX.

CAMBYSES.

WHEN Cambyses invested Pelusium, as being the entrance into Ægypt, the Ægyptians with great resolution defended it: advancing formidable

formidable machines againſt the beſiegers, and from their catapults throwing darts, ſtones, and fire. Againſt the deſtructive ſhowers thus diſcharged upon him Cambyſes ranged before his front line, dogs, ſheep, cats, Ibiſes,* and whatever animals the Ægyptians hold ſacred. The fear of hurting the animals, which they regard with veneration, inſtantly checked their operations: Cambyſes took Peluſium, and thus opened himſelf a paſſage into Ægypt.

CHAP. X.

OEBARES.

AFTER the extinction of the Magi, who had uſurped the government of Perſia, Darius and ſeven other Perſian peers became competitors for the empire: between whom it was amicably agreed thus to ſettle their pretenſions. They engaged at a particular hour, to meet on horſeback at a place fixed on for the purpoſe without the city, and that he, whoſe horſe neighed firſt, ſhould be king. OEbares, Darius's groom, as ſoon as he was appriſed of the determination, the day before the conteſt brought his horſe to the place appointed, and there introduced to him a mare then took the horſe back to the ſtable The next morning each mounted his horſe, and met at the ground according to agreement: when Darius's horſe, recollecting the place, and his enjoyment there, inſtantly neighed for his mare. The reſt of the peers immediately diſmounted, made their obedience to Darius, and ſaluted him king of Perſia.

* The Ibis is a kind of ſtork, which feeds upon ſerpents.

CHAP. XI.

DARIUS.

DARIUS having taken the field against the Scythians, when both armies were ready to engage, a hare rose from her seat, and run close by the Scythian phalanx while several of the Scythians pursued it. Darius observed on the occasion, that this was not the time to engage, when the Scythians felt their superiority so forcibly, that they could pursue a hare in front of the Persian army and accordingly ordered his trumpets to sound a retreat.

2. WHEN Darius and the seven Persian chiefs agreed to fall upon the Magi in the night, in order to know each other in the dark, he proposed to them to wear the button, that fastens the tiara behind, on their forehead, that feeling the button, they might know their friends.

3 DARIUS was the first, that imposed taxes on the people. And to remove the odium of such a measure from himself, he directed the peers in their respective provinces to raise them. They according to their orders levied very high duties. which Darius took, but reserving to himself only half, he remitted the other half to the people.

4. DARIUS undertook an expedition into Scythia · but finding himself unable to gain any advantages there, and his provision likewise running short, he began to think of a retreat. To make it with the least loss, by concealing his design from the enemy, he directed his tents to be left standing, just as they had been for some time before. And in them were many wounded soldiers, asses, mules, and dogs, and a great number of fires were lighted: which those that were left behind had orders constantly in the night to kindle. The Scythians seeing the fires, and the tents standing, and hearing the confused noise of the animals,

sup-

supposed the Persians quietly encamped, when they had effectually secured their retreat. As soon as Darius's movement was known in the Scythian camp, they pursued him as briskly as they could but he was too far out of their reach, to be overtaken.

5. WHEN Darius laid siege to Chalcedon, the Chalcedonians neglected to make those exertions, which the force of so formidable an enemy required, relying upon the strength of their walls, and their great store of provisions. Nor did Darius on the other hand make any attack upon the walls, but contented himself with ravaging at large the country round · pretending that he waited for an accession of force, before he attempted any thing directly against the city But while the whole attention of the Chalcedonians was employed upon their walls, which continuing safe, they apprehended they had nothing to fear; the Persians from a mountain called Aphasium, distant about ten furlongs from the city, opened a mine : which they continued as far as the forum. As soon as they reached that spot, which they conjectured they had, from the roots of olive trees, which grew there, they waited the approach of the night. when they entered the forum, and without the loss of a man became masters of the city, while the Chalcedonians were wholly intent on the defence of their walls

6. DARIUS, in an expedition against the Saccæ, found himself in danger of being inclosed by three armies. Advancing therefore with all expedition against that, which was nearest to him, he engaged and defeated it. And habiting his men in the dresses and arms of the Saccians, he marched against another army of the Saccæ, advancing slowly and securely as it were to meet their friends. But the Persians, according to their orders, no sooner came within spear's length of them, than, instead of friendly salutations, they fell upon them, and cut them to pieces. Thus victorious over two divisions of the enemy, he advanced

against

against the third, who, having learned the fate of the other two, submitted to him without hazarding a battle

7. The Ægyptians, on account of the cruelties exercised by Ornander their governor, having revolted, to reduce them to obedience, Darius himself marched through the desart of Arabia, and arrived at Memphis: just at the time, when the Ægyptians were commemorating the loss of Apis. He immediately ordered proclamation to be made, that he would himself give a hundred talents of gold to the man, that should produce Apis. Struck with the so great piety of their prince, they took a decisive part against the revolters, and entirely devoted themselves to the interests of Darius

8. Darius having invaded the Saccæ, their three kings, Sacephares, Homarges, and Thamyris, had retired in consultation upon the measures proper to be taken in the present emergency of their affairs. When a certain stable-keeper, Rifaces by name, was introduced to them, and proposed himself to destroy the Persian force if they would pledge themselves to him by oath, to give to his children and family all the horses and treasures, that from the destruction of the enemy should fall into their hands. This being satisfactorily settled, he drew out his knife, cut off his nose, and ears, maiming himself also in other parts of the body; and thus disfigured deserted to Darius. who gave credit to his complaints of the cruel treatment he had received from the Saccian king. But, added he, by the eternal fire, and the sacred water, I swear, that by the Persians I will have my revenge. And it is in your power, by the means I will explain to you, to give the glorious revenge I ask. Tomorrow night the Saccæ mean to shift their camp I know the spot where they intend to post themselves; and can conduct you to it by a nearer way, than they will take, where as in a net you shall inclose them. I am a horse-keeper, and know every step of the country for many miles around. But it will

be

be necessary to take with us water and provision for seven days: for this purpose order preparations to be made: no time is to be lost. Having accordingly conducted the army, in a march of seven days, into the most barren and sandy part of Media, when both their water and provisions began to run short, the Chiliarch Rhanosbates, suspecting the treachery of their conductor, took him aside, and expostulated with him. What could induce you, said he, to deceive so powerful a monarch, and so numerous an army? You have brought us to a place destitute of every necessary of life. Neither beast, nor bird inhabits it: nor do we know whither to proceed, or how to return. Rifaces, clapping his hands, answered him with an effusion of laughter, I have gained a noble victory. I have saved my country from impending danger, and by famine and thirst consigned the Persian army to destruction. The Chiliarch enraged immediately struck off his head. Darius fixed his sceptre in the ground, tying round it his tiara and the royal diadem, and climbing an eminence, implored Apollo in this moment of distress to preserve his army, and give them water. The god heard his prayers, and a plentiful shower ensued, which they received on hides, and in vases, and subsisted on it, till they reached the Bactrum: when in the preservation, they had experienced, they acknowledged the favour of the god. But though the device of the horse-keeper in this instance failed; Zopirus afterwards copied it with success against the Babylonians.

CHAP. XII.

ZOPIRUS.

DARIUS having long laid before Babylon, without being able to carry it; Zopirus, one of his peers, miserably mangled his face, and fled to the enemy as a deserter: pretending to have been thus cruelly treated by Darius. The Babylonians credited the veracity of his complaints;

plaints, which in his appearance they saw so plainly written took him into their protection, and their confidence in him by degrees increasing, they at last gave him the direction of the city. Invested with this power, he soon found means in the night to throw open the gates, and put Darius in possession of Babylon: who expressed himself on the occasion in a manner worthy a great and generous prince. I would not, said he, for twenty Babylons see Zopirus so disfigured as he is.

CHAP. XIII.

ARTAXERXES*

KING Artaxerxes ordered Orontes to send to him Teribazus, a grandee of Cyprus. Orontes, who was afraid of Teribazus, dared not to employ force against him; but took him by the following device. Under a particular room in his house there was a dungeon: over the mouth of which he directed a triclinium to be placed, but not fastened down, and to be covered with embroidered tapestry. Hither he invited Teribazus, pretending to have some private business to communicate to him: when throwing himself on the triclinium, that was prepared for him, it sunk down with him into the dungeon. Thus was he taken, and sent in chains to the king.

CHAP. XIV.

ORONTES.

ORONTES, having revolted from the king, carried on a flying war with his generals: and being driven to mount Tmolus, he there strongly

---

* This stratagem appears to me more properly to belong to Orontes, than Artaxerxes. Especially as we find the stratagems of Artaxerxes recorded afterwards, Ch. XVI.

intrenched

intrenched himfelf As foon as the enemy came up with him, and encamped againft him, he funk a very deep fofle, and in all the avenues leading to his camp ordered the guard to be doubled. With a choice body of horfe he then fallied out in the night. and, taking the way to Sardis, fell in with a large fupply of provifions, that were deftined for the enemy's camp, which he feifed, and alfo carried off from the Sardians a confiderable booty Of thefe tranfactions he fent intelligence to the camp, and ordered them the next day to draw out, and advance againft the enemy. who with great confidence marched out, and attacked them But no fooner were they engaged, than Orontes with his cavalry falling upon their rear gained a compleat victory with little lofs · the enemy leaving many dead on the field, and many were taken prifoners.

2. ORONTES, with ten thoufand heavy-armed Greeks, engaged Autophradates, who advanced againft him with the fame number, and was particularly ftrong in his cavalry. Orontes bade his men look round, and fee the extenfivenefs of the plain obferving to them, that if they loofened their ranks, it would be impoffible for them to fuftain the charge of the enemy's horfe Accordingly preferving their lines compact and clofe, they received the cavalry upon their fpears, who finding they could make no impreffion on them retreated. when Orontes ordered the Greeks, if the horfe made a fecond attack upon them, to advance three paces forward, to meet them. They did fo and the cavalry fuppofing they meaned to charge them, quitted the field, and abandoned themfelves to flight.

3 HAVING loft a great number of his allies, which Autophradates had cut off by an ambufcade, Orontes propagated a report that a body of mercenaries were on their march to join him, and took care that fuch intelligence, with every mark of confirmation he could give it, fhould be communicated to Autophradates. In the night he armed the

ftouteft

ftouteft of the Barbarians in Græcian armour, and, as foon as it was day, pofted them in his army among the reft of the Greeks, with interpreters who were acquainted with both languages, and repeated in the Barbarian language the fame commands that were given to the Greeks: and in this order he advanced to battle. Autophradates, feeing fuch a number armed in Græcian armour, concluded he had received the re-inforcement, of which he had been informed: and afraid to hazard a battle at fo great a difadvantage, broke up his camp, and retreated.

CHAP. XV.

XERXES.

XERXES, having undertaken an expedition againft Greece, engaged a number of nations in the enterprife, by propagating a report, that he had gained over fome of the principal Greeks, to betray the country to him. Suppofing therefore they were marching not to fubdue a country, but to take poffeffion, they were eafily prevailed on to join the confederacy. And many of the Barbarian ftates voluntarily offered themfelves as allies

2 SOME Greek fpies having been apprehended in the camp, Xerxes, inftead of punifhing them, ordered them to be conducted through every par tof it, and fhewn all his forces. He then bade them go back, and tell the Greeks what they had feen, and who it was that fhewed it them.

3. WHILE Xerxes lay at anchor near Abydos, waiting to intercept the Græcian fleets, a fleet of ftore-fhips fell into his hands, laden with provifions which the Barbarians propofed to fink, with all the men that were on board. Xerxes however would not confent to it, but brought them to, and afked whither they were bound. For

Greece,

Greece, anſwered they. And ſo are we, replied Xerxes: the ſtore-ſhips therefore are ours: and be gone As ſoon as they reached Greece, they ſpread univerſal terror there with the intelligence of Xerxes's invaſion.

4. To conceal the great numbers, that the Barbarians loſt at Thermopylæ, Xerxes ordered the relations of thoſe that were miſſing, to go out in the night, and privately bury them.

5 XERXES not able to bring his numerous army to act at Thermopylæ, on account of the ſtraitneſs of the paſs, loſt a number of Perſians before it; till one Ephialtes, a Trachinian, diſcovered to him a private way acroſs the mountains, through which he detached a hundred thouſand men. Theſe taking a circuit round fell upon the Grecian rear, and cut to pieces Leonidas himſelf, and every man of the little troop he commanded.

CHAP. XVI.

ARTAXERXES.

ARTAXERXES diſpatched Tithrauſtus to ſeiſe Tiſaphernes; and charged him with two letters, one to Tiſaphernes himſelf, inveſting him with the command of the expedition againſt the Greeks; and another to Ariæus, directing him to aſſiſt Tithrauſtus in apprehending him As ſoon as Ariæus, who then reſided at Colaſæ, a city of Phrygia, had read the letter, he ſent to Tiſaphernes, deſiring a conference with him on buſineſs of importance, and particularly on ſome matters of concern relative to Greece. Entertaining no ſuſpicion of any deſigns being formed againſt him, he left his forces at Sardis, and attended by a body of three hundred Arcadians and Mileſians inſtantly repaired to Ariæus: where after his journey he laid aſide his ſcimitar, and went into the bath. Ariæus with his ſervants ruſhed ſuddenly

upon

upon him, and feifed him, then put him into a covered carriage, and delivered him up to Tithrauftus who conveyed him to Celænæ, there ftruck off his head, and carried it to the king. Artaxerxes fent it to his mother Parafatis, who had long wifhed to fee the death of Cyrus revenged on Tifaphernes Nor did the mothers and wives of all the Greeks, who had followed Cyrus, exprefs lefs fatisfaction at the punifhment of a man, that had with fo great treachery circumvented their fons and hufbands.

2. ARTAXERXES by every means endeavoured to promote wars amongft the Greeks, and was always ready to affift the conquered party for by throwing in affiftance to the weaker power, he placed them on a nearer equality, and thereby the more effectually exhaufted the victor's ftrength

CHAP. XVII.

OCHUS.

AFTER the death of Artaxerxes, Ochus his fon, fenfible that he fhould not immediately have that influence over his fubjects, which his father had, prevailed on the eunuchs, his chamberlain, and the captain of his guard, to conceal his death for the fpace of ten months. And in the mean time he wrote circular letters in his father's name, and fealed them with the royal fignet, commanding all his fubjects to acknowledge Ochus as their king, and as fuch to pay him obedience. The mandate was univerfally complied with when Ochus acknowledged his father's death, and ordered a general mourning for him according to the cuftom of Perfia.

CHAP. XVIII.

TISAPHERNES

TISAPHERNES affected a particular friendship with Clearchus, admitted him to his female parties, and pretended to treat him with singular respect. The same regard he also professed for the other Græcian generals, and sent them an invitation, which was accepted by Proxenus the Bœotian, Menon the Thessalian, Agis the Arcadian, and Socrates the Achaian, who, attended by twenty captains of companies, and two hundred soldiers, were introduced to him. The generals Tisaphernes sent in chains to the king, and massacred all the rest.

2. TISAPHERNES meditated a design of invading Miletum, and seising all the deserters, that had taken refuge there. But being at the time unprepared for such an expedition, he industriously propagated the report of his having it in contemplation: so that the Milesians removed all their property from the country into the city. And as soon as he was really prepared for the enterprise, he pretended to drop it, and disbanded his army, but with private orders for no soldier to remove to any considerable distance. As soon as the Milesians saw his army disbanded, weary of having been so long in a state of imprisonment in the city, they ventured out into the country as pleasure invited, or business called them. When instantly collecting his forces, he surprised them, dispersed up and down in their fields and vineyards, and put all he met to the sword.

CHAP. XIX.

PHARNABAZUS.

PHARNABAZUS having preferred charges of misdemeanour against Lysander, the Lacedæmonians sent him letters of recall from Asia. When Lysander importuned him, to be less severe in his representation of his conduct, Pharnabazus promised he would; and addressed a letter to the Lacedæmonians, of the purport Lysander desired. But at the same time he privately wrote another letter, giving a very different account. In sealing the letter, he contrived to slip that which he had privately written, and which was in shape exactly the same with that Lysander had desired, in the place of the other, and gave it into his hand. On his return to Lacedæmon, Lysander, as the custom was, delivered his letter to the Ephori: which as soon as they had read, they shewed him, observing at the same time that there was no room for any defence, the very letter, which he himself produced, condemning him.

CHAP. XX.

GLOS.

GLOS, while on an expedition against Cyprus, suspecting the Grecians that were in his service of having endeavoured to prejudice him with the Greeks in Ionia, to discover his enemies, ordered a vessel to sail for Ionia. The master delayed for some days the sailing of the ship, under pretence of manning and victualling it; but in reality to give every one, who might be inclined to write, time to send letters by it to

their

their respective friends. As soon as the ship had cleared the harbour, the master put to land at a particular point according to Glofs's directions where he met him, and received all the letters that had been delivered to him for Ionia. In those he discovered, who were the persons inimical to his interests; whom he forbore to punish immediately, but took the earliest opportunities that offered to get rid of them.

CHAP. XXI.

DATAMES.

DATAMES, finding himself exceedingly pressed by his men for their arrears of pay, convened his troops, and harangued them assuring them that, at a place distant only three days march, he had great treasures. Thither therefore, said he, my lads, let us march with all expedition. From the confidence with which he declared it, the army believed the fact, and immediately begun their march. When he came within one day's distance of it, he ordered them to halt, and rest themselves while, taking with him some mules and camels, he repaired to a temple, decorated with the wealth of the country. There he received thirty talents of silver, which on the camels and mules he carried to the army; having first filled with it a few vases, and taken a great number of others of the same shape and size, that he pretended to be full Upon his return to the army, he shewed the full vases to the soldiers; who delighted at the sight gave him credit for what he said of all the rest. But he told them, that before he could make a distribution to each, he must go to Amisus to have the bullion coined into money. Amisus being many days march from thence, and a place very incommodious to winter in, the troops discovered no disposition to such a march, and

troubled

troubled him the whole winter with no more importunities for their arrears

2 DATAMES had formed a design against the Sinopians: but they having a very strong fleet, and he none, nor any carpenters to build him one, he entered into a close alliance with them and promised to lay siege to Sestos, a place most hostile to them, and put it into their hands The Sinopians were delighted with the proposal, and, in prosecuting the enterprise, desired to assist him with whatever he might want. He told them he had plenty both of money and men, and that all he wanted was machines, catapults, battering rams, and testudos, which would be necessary in carrying on the siege, and with which he was altogether unprovided The Sinopians immediately furnished him with all the builders and carpenters they had whom he employed in building ships, as well as machines, and having by this means procured a naval force, instead of Sestos he attacked Sinope.

3 DATAMES crossed the Euphrates, having made war on the grand monarch, and penetrated into his territories, who marched against him in great force but his army being ill supplied with provisions, he was much retarded in his march Datames in the mean time by the difficulty of procuring forage for so numerous a body of troops obliged to make a precipitate retreat before the formidable force, that was brought into the field against him, directed his march to the nearest point of the river he could gain where he linked two carriages a-breast, and to them fastened two more, and on the bottom of the circumference of the wheels nailed broad boards, to keep them from sinking in the mud He then ordered some of the stoutest men in his army to swim the river, and lead after them a number of the strongest horses that could be picked out to the horses the carriages, on which he placed his baggage, were fastened by ropes, and his men thrust them into the river, those who were

before,

before, and the horses at the same time drawing them forwards. In this manner he crossed the river without loss, and, having gained ten days march of the king, effected a safe retreat.

4. DATAMES having received intelligence, a short time before an engagement was intended to take place, that designs were formed against him by some of his own soldiers, changed armour with one of his officers who wore his armour, while he entered the battle in a borrowed suit. The conspirators, mistaking the person who wore the royal armour for the king, in their attempt upon him were discovered, and taken

5 HAVING invested Sinope, Datames received a letter from the king, peremptorily ordering him to raise the siege Unwilling to have it supposed, he obeyed orders in doing it, as soon as he had read the letter, he paid marks of respect to it, made a sacrifice on the occasion, as having received from the king a singular favour, embarked and quitted the enterprise.

6 DATAMES, closely pursued by Autophradates, reached a river, which not daring to ford in the face of the enemy, he pretended to encamp on the side of it And fixing very high and large tents in front of the enemy, he concealed the horse and baggage behind them ordering his men not to unharness a horse, or take off a bridle, and the soldiers, not to disarm themselves The enemy, when they saw Datames encamped, halted, and encamped against him took their horses from the carriages, and put them to their fodder, and begun to prepare their suppers Datames, his horses, men, and every thing in readiness for crossing the river, as soon as he saw the enemy thus disposed of, began his passage over it. which, while the adversary were collecting their scattered troops, forming their lines, getting ready their horses, and arming themselves, he safely effected.

7. IN the midst of an engagement, a tribune, having deserted from the left wing to the enemy with a body of horse, threw the foot into

confternation when Datames, running up to the difpirited troops, bade them preferve their ranks, and prepare for an attack, for the horfe had by his orders made that movement, in order to take their opportunity of fupporting the attack of the infantry. The foot believed him, and, to fnatch the victory from the cavalry, in a clofe firm body vigoroufly attacked the enemy, and defeated them · nor were they apprifed of the revolt of the horfe, till they had obtained the victory.

CHAP. XXII.

COSINGAS

THE generals of the Cæronians and Scæboans, nations of Thrace, were chofen from among the priefts of Juno And Cofingas, according to the inftitution of the country, was elected their prieft and general. whom the army however on fome difguft refufed to obey To reduce to order this refractory fpirit that pervaded the troops, Cofingas built a number of long ladders, faftening them to one another. and propagated a report, that he had refolved to climb. up to heaven, and inform Juno of the difobedience of the Thracians Stupid and ridiculous as thofe people notorioufly are, they were terrified with the idea of their general's intended journey, and the confequent wrath of heaven, implored him to drop his refolution, and engaged themfelves by an oath implicitly to obey all his future commands.

CHAP. XXIII.

MAUSOLUS.

MAUSOLUS king of Caria, having occasion for more money than he could venture to raise on his subjects, assembled his friends, and pretended his apprehensions that the grand monarch intended to strip him of his dominions He produced to them his treasures, gold, and silver, his horses, jewels, and whatever he had of value, which he said he meaned to send to the king, requesting him to permit him to enjoy his hereditary territories His friends, believing the reality of his situation according to his representation of it, the same day sent him treasures to immense amount

2 In order to make himself master of Latmus, a city strongly fortified, Mausolus pretended a desire to cultivate a strict alliance with the Latmians And with that view he restored to them the hostages, Hidrieus had taken. and composed his guard of Latmians, as men, on whose fidelity he could place most dependence In whatever they wished, he made a point to oblige them and having thus bound them to his interest, he requested them to send him three hundred men as guards for his person, pretending business, that required his presence at Pygela, and that he was apprehensive of the sinister designs of Phytus the Ephesian They immediately sent him the complement required, with which, and other forces he had in readiness, he marched to Latmus, on his route to Pygela. The citizens all came out, to see the army pass. when a body of troops, which he had by night placed in ambush, sallied out, and possessed themselves of the city, deserted by its inhabitants, and the gates left wide open. Mausolus then took a circuit round, entered with all his forces, and added it to his dominions.

CHAP. XXIV.

BORGES

BORGES by the great monarch had been appointed governor of Eion, a city situated on the river Strymon; which was closely besieged by the Greeks. Having bravely held out to the last extremity, and finding he could no longer defend the city, he determined not to sacrifice to the enemy his trust, but set fire to it, and with his wife, and children, perished in the flames.

CHAP. XXV.

DROMICHÆTES

DROMICHÆTES was king of Thrace, and Lysimachus of Macedon; when the Macedonian made war on Thrace, against whom Dromichætes employed the following stratagem. Æthis, his general, pretended to resent some insult of the Thracian prince, and deserted to Lysimachus; who trusting to his fidelity, gave himself up to his direction, till he had brought the Macedonian army into such a situation, that they had at once to contend with famine, thirst, and a powerful enemy. Dromichætes in this situation took his opportunity to attack them, defeated the Macedonians with great slaughter, and took Lysimachus prisoner. The Macedonian army is reported to have amounted to a hundred thousand men.

CHAP. XXVI.

ARIOBARZANES.

ARIOBARZANES was by Autophradates blocked up in Adramyttium by sea and land· when wanting a supply both of stores and men, which, the enemy so closely watched him, he could not get introduced, he directed Pteleuntes, who commanded the garrison in a neighbouring island, to open a correspondence with Autophradates, and pretend a readiness to betray to him his trust. Agreeably to such proposal, Autophradates ordered the fleet to sail, and take possession of the island An ample supply of stores and men were in the mean time thrown into Adramyttium· and the fleet returned to their station, without having effected any thing against the island.

CHAP. XXVII.

AUTOPHRADATES.

AUTOPHRADATES, having undertaken an expedition into Pisidia, marched his army to a defile, which he found the enemy had secured, and that, without exposing himself to great loss, he would not be able to pass it. He therefore retreated about six furlongs back And as soon as night came on, the Pisidians, who had observed his retreat, quitted also their post· when Autophradates with his light-armed troops by an expeditious march passed the defile, and, followed by the rest of his army, penetrated into Pisidia, and laid the whole country under contribution.

2. AUTOPHRADATES, observing the Ephesians, who were en-- camped

camped oppofite to him, leifurely walking about, and amufing themfelves, propofed a conference with the Ephefian chiefs, which they accordingly accepted. And while he was thus engaged with them, the generals of his cavalry and heavy-armed troops, according to the orders he had given them, fuddenly attacked the Ephefians, difperfed in ftraggling parties, and unprepared for action. part of whom were cut to pieces, and the reft made prifoners.

3. To induce the mercenaries to take the field, Autophradates procured a report to be propagated, that his pretended expedition was in reality no more than a general mufter of his troops, in order to find pretence for abridging of their pay all who fhould not make their appearance, and be ready in arms. The men therefore all armed, and attended, expreffing great alacrity for action. Autophradates immediately marched them out, convincing them, the review they had been taught to expect was againft a real enemy in the field.

CHAP. XXVIII.

ARSABES

THE Barcæans, befieged by Arfabes, fent an embaffy to him with propofals of peace which he granted them, and in confirmation of it, according to the Perfian cuftom, gave them his hand. He then raifed the fiege, recommended to them a clofe alliance with the king againft Greece, and propofed to them to furnifh him with a number of carriages which he wanted for his Græcian expedition. Agreeable to his propofal, they fent fome of their chiefs to him to concert meafures for the expedition. whom he courteoufly received, and made a magnificent entertainment for them. He alfo opened a market to all the Barcæans, where in vaft profufion things of every kind were expofed to fale.

They

They accordingly in great numbers came out to purchase: when the Persians, on a signal given, possessed themselves of the gates, rushed into the city, and plundered it, putting all to the sword, who attempted to make any resistance

2 ARSABES having revolted from the king, and become master of the greater Phrygia, took the field against his generals. When having received intelligence, that his own general of the horse was in the interest of his enemies, and had engaged, as soon as they came to action, to desert to them he went to his tent in the night, and ordered him to be examined by torture. As soon as a full confession of the fact had been made, Arsabes commanded his arms and regimentals, as well as those of all the cavalry who were privy to the conspiracy, to be instantly taken from them, and others to be accoutred in them, on whose fidelity he could depend And those he ordered, as soon as they saw the enemy make the signal for a revolt, to obey it, pass over to them, and fall into their rear The plan being thus settled, Arsabes vigorously attacked them in front, the cavalry at the same time, who had obeyed the given signal, instead of assisting, fell upon their rear, the ranks were instantly broken, and a general rout ensued

CHAP. XXIX.

MITHRIDATES

THE king ordered Mithridates to take Datames, who had revolted, either alive, or dead. With this view Mithridates pretended also to revolt, and offered to join Datames. But that cautious general desired to see some proofs of his revolt by commencement of hostilities against the king, before he trusted his professions. Mithridates accordingly begun to ravage the country, he levelled his forts with the ground, burned his villages,

villages, raised contributions, and plundered his subjects. Having taken such a decided part against the royal interest, the two generals agreed upon a conference, at which they were to meet unarmed. But Mithridates in the spot appointed for their meeting had privately concealed a number of daggers, which he had hid up and down in the ground, privately marking the places where he had concealed them. After they had amicably walked about, and spent a considerable time in conference, Datames took his leave, and they parted. When Mithridates, hastily catching up one of the daggers, which he concealed under his left arm, called back Datames, as having something farther to say, which he had forgot. He accordingly returned; and Mithridates, pointing to a mountain, told him it would be proper to secure that post, at which while Datames was very intently looking, Mithridates plunged the dagger into his breast.

2. MITHRIDATES had taken refuge in a city of Paphlagonia, where being closely pursued, he in the night stripped the houses of their furniture, vases, and whatever was valuable, and scattered them indiscriminately about the streets; he then left the city, and made the best of his way. When his pursuers the next morning entered the city, and saw vases and other things of value scattered about the streets, they immediately fell to plundering. And though their generals ordered them not to stop, but with all expedition to pursue their march; they refused to forego for any expectations a certain advantage which they had at hand. Mithridates, having thus gained considerable ground of them, effected his escape.

CHAP.

CHAP. XXX.

MEMPSIS.

MEMPSIS had been obliged to retreat before Ariboeus, who had made war on him, but at laft determined not to be blocked up in his city With this purpofe he brought out whatever was valuable his wives, his children, and his treafures he placed without the walls, and deftroyed the gates Ariboeus faw in his conduct the marks of defperation, and drew off his army not judging it advifable to engage an enemy, thus devoted to death, or determined on victory.

CHAP. XXXI.

CERSOBLEPTES.

SOME of the relations of Cerfobleptes, after having embezzled confiderable fums of money, revolted from him. He afterwards however found means to recall them to their duty· and, to detach them from each other, he gave them feparate governments of cities. After fome time had paffed, he fent orders to have them feifed on pretence of the money they had embezzled, expelled them from their cities, and confifcated their eftates.

CHAP. XXXII.

SEUTHES

SEUTHES, general of the cavalry to Cersobleptes, at a time of great distress for money, sent orders to every husbandman, to sow as much land as would require five bushels of seed. And the great quantity of corn, that was from such an increase of tillage produced, he carried down to the sea; and sold it at somewhat less than a market price: which immediately threw into the treasury a very considerable sum.

CHAP. XXXIII.

ARTABAZUS.

ARTABAZUS had besieged a city, which Timoxenus the Sicyonian agreed to betray to him. Their correspondence was carried on by a letter fixed to an arrow, which was shot at a particular place; and the answer by another arrow returned.

2. HAVING suspected Pammenes of holding a correspondence with the enemy, Artabazus sent for him on pretence of making largesses, and distributing corn to the troops. But as soon as he entered the camp; he ordered him to be seised, and delivered up to his brothers Oxythres and Dibictus.

3. ARTABAZUS the son of Pharnaces, having escaped from Plataea, came to Thessaly; where when questioned by the Thessalians concerning the battle, afraid to acknowledge the defeat the Persian army had sustained, he replied, he was on his way into Thrace, charged with secret dispatches from the king. Mardonius soon after followed him,

with the news of the victory he had obtained. Artabazus however had got out of Thessaly, before the event of the battle was known.

CHAP. XXXIV.

ARYANDES.

ARYANDES, having besieged Barcæum, in the night opened a fosse before the walls, over which he placed some beams of wood, and covered them with a little earth. Some time afterwards he proposed overtures of peace to the Barcæans, and concluded a treaty with them upon the fosse he had made: where he swore to adhere to the conditions of it, as long as the ground he stood on continued The treaty thus concluded, the Barcæans opened their gates. When the soldiers of Aryandes broke up the fosse, and the ground, on which the parties stood when they formed the treaty, no longer remaining, made themselves masters of the city.

CHAP. XXXV.

BRENNUS.

BRENNUS king of the Gauls, in order to induce them to engage in an expedition against Greece, convened an assembly of men and women, and ordered some Græcian prisoners to be produced to them, of mean persons, and infirm in body, with their heads shaven, and shabbily drest. And by them he placed some Gauls, stout handsome men, accoutred with Gallic armour. Then addressing the assembly, such as these, said he, are the men we march into the field, and such, as those you see, are the enemies, with whom we have to contend. By these means

the

the Gauls were brought to conceive such a contempt for the Greeks, that they readily offered to serve in an expedition against them.

2 When the Celtic army marched into Greece, Brennus, seeing the gold statues at Delphos, sent for some Delphian captives, and asked them by an interpreter, if those statues were solid gold. Being informed they were only brass, covered with a thin plating of gold, he told them, he would certainly execute any of them, that should propagate such a report, and ordered them therefore, whenever they were asked about it, to assert the contrary, and to say they were all gold. Then sending for some of his generals, he in their presence again asked the prisoners the same question, he had already put to them, who, as they had been directed, replied they were all real gold. This intelligence he ordered the generals to communicate to the army, that the prospect of so much wealth might spirit them up by conquest to obtain it.

CHAP. XXXVI.

MYGDONIUS

MYGDONIUS, when closely besieged, and in great distress for provisions, directed parcels of stones, and earth, to be brought into the market place, which he made up into masses with clay, and covered them over with corn, some with wheat, and others with barley. He also ordered some of the largest and fattest mules, that could be picked out, to be turned out of the city. Then dispatching a herald into the enemy's camp, he desired a deputation might be sent to treat of a ransom for the mules, and whatever other property the citizens might have lost. As soon as the deputies arrived, they were introduced into the forum, where Mygdonius attended them. And seeing there vast heaps of wheat, and barley, and hearing orders given to servants to measure

out

cut great quantities of corn in other places alfo, on their return they gave the enemy an account of the large ftores, with which the town was provided who, in confirmation of the report, confidering the fatnefs of the mules, concluded there was little profpect of reducing the town by diftrefs, and therefore raifed the fiege

CHAP. XXXVII.

PARISADES

PARISADES, king of Pontus, ufed on different occafions three different dreffes one, when he reviewed his troops, another in time of action and a third, when he was obliged to fly The reafons he affigned for this cuftom were thefe. at a review he wifhed to be known by every individual in his army, in action he wifhed not to be known by the enemy, and when he was obliged to fly, he defired to be known by no one

CHAP. XXXVIII.

SEUTHES.

WHILE the Athenians in petty incurfions ravaged the maritime country at Cherronefus; Seuthes took into pay two thoufand light-armed Getæ whom he ordered, in the face of the enemy, to ravage the country, as they did, wafting it with fire, and attacking with darts and arrows the people on the walls. The Athenians from thofe hoftile motions doubted not, but they were enemies of the Thracians, difembarked in order to join them, and boldly marched up to the walls. Seuthes immediately fallied out of the city againft them: and the

Getæ,

Getæ, advancing as it were to their affiftance, fell upon their rear. Thus attacked on one fide by the Thracians, and by the Getæ on another, they were moft of them cut to pieces.

CHAP. XXXIX.

CHEILES.

CHEILES, with fafety to rid himfelf of three thoufand Perfians, who had been concerned in a revolt, pretended to have received a threatening letter from Seleucus; but told them, by their affiftance he hoped to bring him to reafon. To concert meafures for this purpofe, he propofed to them, to affemble at Randa, a town not far diftant, where he engaged to meet them. In a clofe low way near the town is a lake: where Cheiles pofted three hundred Macedonian and Thracian horfe, and three thoufand heavy-armed troops, whom he ordered, as foon as they faw an iron target thrown up, to fally forth and cut the Perfians to pieces. The Perfians affembled according to appointment and the plan, which Cheiles had laid, was fo effectually executed, that not a man of them efcaped the general maffacre.

CHAP. XL.

BORZUS.

BORZUS, having received information of a confpiracy being formed againft him by three thoufand Perfians, difcharged, and banifhed them to a place in Perfia, called Comaftos; whither they were conducted under a ftrong guard. The country abounded in villages, was very populous, and the roads were well accommodated with inns. In the towns, where

where they were lodged, some taking up their quarters in one inn, and some in another, the inn-keepers were commanded by the guard, that attended them, and who surrounded the towns, every man to kill his lodgers who accordingly made them drunk, and executed their orders. Thus were three thousand murdered in the night, and buried, without tumult or confusion.

CHAP. XLI.

SURENAS.

CRASSUS, after an ignominious defeat he had received from the Parthians, having retreated to the mountains, Surenas general of the Parthians fearing lest he should rally his forces, and in desperation return to the charge, sent a herald to inform him, that the great monarch was ready to enter into a treaty of peace with him, and that having convinced the Romans of the Parthian courage, he was ready now to convince them of their humanity. Crassus suspected design, and was unwilling to treat with him· but the soldiers, whose spirits were depressed and broken, clashing their arms, insisted on his compliance with the Barbarian's proposal. In silent sorrow he accordingly set out for the Parthian camp on foot when Surenas, who affected to treat him with great respect, sent him a horse richly caparisoned; which he was desired to mount The Barbarian groom then gave the horse a prick, which made him spring forwards and he would have run with Crassus, as was intended, into the midst of the Parthian army, had not Octavius, one of his lieutenants, who perceived the design, caught hold on the reins, as did also Petronius a Chiliarch. Octavius immediately drew his sword, and killed the groom on the spot and was himself slain by a Parthian. Another at the same time fell

fell upon Craffus, cut off his head and right hand, and carried them to Herod, the grand monarch of the Parthians. The king was at that time engaged at an entertainment, where Jafon the Trallian was acting the Bacchæ of Euripides. The tragedian had juft repeated this verfe,

' A new fkinned calf we from the mountains bring,
" Bleft fpoil,'—

when they arrived with the head of Craffus, and brought it to the king. All was immediately clapping and acclamation: and Exathres jumping up obferved, the verfe was moft appofite to the occafion. The circumftance gave a new zeft to the royal banquet: the king remunerated the bearer with a handfome prefent, and gave the tragedian a talent.

CHAP. XLII.

THE CELTS.

THE Celts having been engaged in a long war with the Autoriatæ, and nothing decifive effected on either fide, they poifoned their provifions and wine with noxious herbs, and fuddenly in the night left their camp in confufion. The Autoriatæ, fuppofing they had confcious of their inferiority made a precipitate retreat, took poffeffion of their camp, and rioted on the ftores they found there: but were prefently feifed with violent cholics, and in that condition the Celtæ furprifed, and flew them.

CHAP. XLIII.

THE THRACIANS.

THE Thracians engaged the Bœotians at the lake Copais, and were defeated: they then retreated to Helicon, and made a truce with the Bœotians for a certain number of days, to give time for settling the conditions of peace. In reliance on their late victory, and the faith of the truce, the Bœotians celebrated a sacrifice in honour of Minerva Itonia. But at night while intent on their ceremony, and engaged in the entertainment, the Thracians armed, and attacked them; cut many of them to pieces, and took a great number prisoners. The Bœotians afterwards charged them with a breach of the truce: which the Thracians denied, asserting that the terms of the truce expressed a certain number of days, but not a syllable concerning the nights.

CHAP. XLIV.

THE SCYTHIANS.

THE Scythians, previous to an engagement with the Tribali, ordered their husbandmen and horse-keepers, as soon as they saw them engaged, to shew themselves at a distance with as great a number of horses as they could collect. The Tribali on a distant view of such a number of men and horses, and the dust they raised, supposing them a fresh body of Scythians advancing to the assistance of their countrymen, quitted the field, and abandoned themselves to flight.

2. WHILE the Scythians were engaged in the Asiatic war, the women, considering themselves as deserted by their husbands, had children

by their slaves, who, on the return of their masters, determined to dispute with them the property they possessed. They accordingly took the field, and advanced in arms, to give them battle. When a Scythian, fearing left if once engaged desperation might make them brave, advised, that they should lay down their arms and bows, and advance against their slaves with whips in their hands. The idea was embraced: and the slaves, confounded with the consciousness of their servitude, immediately threw down their arms, and fled.

CHAP. XLV.

THE PERSIANS.

THE Persians, suspecting the Samians and Milesians of sinister designs, posted them by themselves on the heights of Mycale, on pretence of their being well acquainted with the country but in reality, to prevent them from infecting the rest of the Greeks

2. WHEN the Persians under Cyrus engaged the Medes, Æbares a satrap of Persia fled the field, and the army followed him. The Persian women, informed of the defeat, marched out in a body, and met the fugitives and, lifting up their robes, called out to them, Whither would you fly? Will ye hide yourselves here, from whence ye came? The women's reproof struck the Persians with conscious shame. They returned to the charge, and defeated the enemy

CHAP. XLVI.

THE TAURI

IT was a cuftom with the Tauri, a people of Scythia, always before a battle to dig ditches, throw up mounds, and render the ground impaffable behind · that confcious of their retreat being thus cut off, they might know no alternative, but victory, or death.

CHAP. XLVII.

THE PALLENIANS.

THE Pallenians, when they failed from Troy on their return home, touched at Phlegra And while the men were engaged in little excurfions in the country, the captive Trojan women, tired with the voyage, and apprehenfive of the ill treatment they might experience from the Græcian dames, at the inftigation of Euthria, the fifter of Priam, fet fire to the fleet. The Græcians, thus become deftitute of fhipping, poffeffed themfelves of the region of Scione: in which they built a city, and inftead of Phlegra called the country Pallene.*

---

* See a fimilar account of another party of Trojans Book VIII Ch. XXV. Strat II. which is noticed by Plutarch and Dionyfius of Halicarnaffus, as this of the Pallenenfes is by Thucydides.

CHAP. XLVIII.

HANNIBAL.

HANNIBAL having laid siege to Salmatis, a great and opulent city in Iberia, agreed with the inhabitants to raise the siege on payment of three hundred talents of silver, and the delivery of three hundred hostages. The Salmatians afterwards refused to make good the terms of their agreement. In consequence of which Hannibal detached a body of troops to plunder the town. The Barbarians then petitioned him for permission to leave the city, with their wives, and only the cloaths they wore; stipulating to leave behind them their slaves, arms, and treasures. The women accordingly marched out with their husbands, each carrying concealed a dagger in her bosom. The soldiers immediately entered the town, and fell to plundering. When the women gave their husbands the daggers, who re-entered the city, and, some of the women with drawn swords attending them, attacked the plunderers, seised some, and drove the rest out of the city. Hannibal, in respect to the resolution of the women, restored to them their hostages, their country, and property.

CHAP. XLIX.

THE TYRRHENIAN WOMEN.

THE Tyrrhenians, who inhabited Lemnos and Imbros, having been expelled from their possessions by the Athenians, landed at Tænarus: and served as auxiliaries to the Spartans in the Eilotic war. For this service they were presented with the freedom of the state, and permission

mission to intermarry with them. But in being excluded from the senate, and all offices of truſt, they were confidered as diſſatisfied, and being afterwards fuſpected of defigns againſt the ſtate, the Lacedæmonians threw them into prifon. Thither their wives repaired, and requeſted leave of the guards to vifit and converfe with their huſbands. They were accordingly admitted: when they changed dreffes with them, and in the evening difguifed in the women's cloaths, the men made their efcape: while the women remained in prifon in their huſband's dreffes, prepared for any event. Nor did the men forget, or defert their wives, but poffeffed themfelves of Taygetus, and engaged the Eilots to a revolt. The Lacedæmonians, apprehenfive that ferious confequences might enfue, fent an embaffy with powers to fettle the controverfy, and reftored to them their wives. They alfo fupplied them with money and ſhips: and fent them out as a Lacedæmonian colony.

CHAP. L.

THE CELTS.

THE Celts, long harraffed with civil wars, had taken the field againſt each other, and were juſt advancing to battle when their wives, ruſhing into the field, threw themfelves between the two armies, and intreated them to lay afide their mutual animofities. At the inftance of the women the battle was fufpended: and the difputes of the different parties in the end were happily and amicably adjuſted. Throughout the towns and villages of the Celts ever after, on any confultation upon peace, or war, concerning either themfelves or their allies, the opinion of the women is always taken. And in their treaties with Hannibal it was fpecified, that if the Celts ſhould
have

have any charge to offer againſt any of the Carthaginians, the diſpute ſhould be referred to their generals and commanders of horſe but if the Carthaginians had any charge to urge againſt any of the Celts, it ſhould be referred to the determination of the Celtic women.

BOOK VIII.

PROOEMIUM.

THIS Eighth Book of Stratagems I addrefs to your moſt ſacred majeſties, Antoninus and Verus And having with it finiſhed the collection I promiſed, I have only to wiſh to you ſuccefs in the wars, in which you are at preſent engaged, equal to your military merits, and to myſelf your favourable opinion, that amidſt my civil employs I have devoted my leiſure hours to ſuch purſuits, as may ſerve the Roman empire, and the Greeks, in conducting wars, and regulating treaties of peace. What is won in the field, muſt be ſecured in the cabinet and he, that excels in both, deſerves immortal glory, and his country's thanks.

CHAP. I.

AMULIUS.

AMULIUS and Numitor were brothers. Amulius the younger kept his brother in captivity, and himſelf mounted the throne of Alba. And to prevent Numitor, who had an only daughter Sylvia, from having any poſterity capable of revenging his uſurpation, he appointed her prieſtefs of Veſta: who in conſequence of that office became devoted to perpetual virginity.

CHAP. II.

NUMITOR.

REMUS and Romulus, sons of Mars and Sylvia, formed a design against Amulius: possessed themselves of the citadel, and from thence attacked the city. Numitor, who was privy to the conspiracy, summoned the citizens: told them the enemy meaned to attack the city, that Amulius had betrayed the interests of it, and fled: but bade them meet him in the market place. The citizens accordingly armed, and assembled: when Remus and Romulus, after having slain Amulius, marched out of the citadel, harangued the citizens, and told them, who they were, how they had been injured, and the resolution they had taken to revenge the injustice that had been done their grandfather. The people applauded the act, and placed Numitor on the throne.

CHAP. III.

ROMULUS.

THE Romans being in want of wives, Romulus ordered proclamation to be made throughout the neighbouring cities, that he intended a sacrifice to Equestrian Neptune, on which occasion he meaned to exhibit sports, and games, and athletic exercises, and to reward the victors with magnificent presents. From the towns adjacent this drew numbers of people of all ranks, men, women, and virgins. Romulus strictly ordered his people to offer no violence either to the men, or matrons, but on a particular signal given to seise the virgins; and that not for purposes of lust, but to contract marriages with them. And from these marriages the first Romans were born.

2. ROMULUS encamped about ten furlongs from the city of the Fidenates, and in the night marched out his forces, forming a narrow front with one half of his troops. and the rest he posted in ambush, having given his orders to the officers, who commanded the ambuscade. As soon as it was light, he advanced with his little army against the gates, which he ordered his pioneers, furnished with hatchets and pickaxes, to break down. The Fidenates, enraged at his presumption and temerity, opened their gates, and without any order rushed out, and attacked the enemy, who slowly and in good order retreated before them. The Fidenates, suspecting nothing of an ambuscade, and despising the paucity of the troops they saw, pressed closely on him, presuming on a cheap and easy victory The commanders of the troops that formed the ambush made their men sit down close, so as not to be discovered by the enemy · while the Roman army continued retreating, and at a little distance wheeled round them, and were pursued by the Fidenates. The ambuscade, as soon as the enemy had passed them, sallied out; and with a great shout fell upon their rear, which, already fatigued by a long pursuit, they engaged with great advantage. and those, who before fled, faced about, snatched the palm of victory from their pursuers, and made themselves masters of the city.

CHAP. IV.

NUMA.

TO form the Romans to the arts of peace, Numa retired into the sacred temple of the nymphs; and there shut himself up alone for several days. And from thence when he returned to the people, he pro-

duced

duced certain oracles, which he said had been delivered to him by the nymphs, and perfuaded them to receive as laws; to which they accordingly paid a moft implicit obfervance. And the body of thofe religious inftitutions, feafts, fupplications, facrifices, and ceremonies, which are at this day in ufe among the Romans, were framed by Numa, and by the people originally received as the inftitutions of the nymphs. And in this device I have always thought he had an eye to Minos and Lycurgus. For of thefe the one from Apollo, and the other from Jove, received, or at leaft profeffed to have received, the laws, which the one prevailed on the Lacedæmonians, and the other on the Cretans, to accept and obferve.

CHAP. V.

TULLUS.

IN the reign of Tullus, an engagement was fought between the Fidenates and the Romans, in which the Albans, who were pofted in the left wing of the Roman army, deferted their poft in the moment of action, and retired to the mountains. A horfeman rode full fpeed up to Tullus, to acquaint him with the treachery of the Albans: who in a loud and refolute tone of voice immediately replied, go back to your poft, what the Albans have done, they have done by my order, with intention to furround the enemy. On hearing this the Romans fet up a loud fhout. Their exultation ftruck terror into the Fidenates, who, fufpecting the movement of the Albans to be in reality what Tullus pretended, a defign to furround them, fought to elude the manœuvre by a precipitate flight.

CHAP.

CHAP. VI.

TARQUINIUS.

TARQUIN tired out with a long war against the Gabii, in the course of which he had besieged their city, but had not been able to carry it, scourged his youngest son Sextus; and sent him over to the enemy in the character of a deserter. Seeing the marks of cruelty and ignominy, that he carried about him, they doubted not his sincerity, but received him as a friend. He made professions to them of great services against his father, and performed some. He ravaged the Roman territories, in frequent skirmishes defeated the enemy, took some prisoners, and returned laden with spoils. The Gabii convinced of his superior valour, made him general of their armies, and commander in chief. Thus invested with power, he privately dispatched a messenger to his father, to enquire what he would have him do. Tarquin, as they were conversing in the garden, struck off the heads of some of the tallest poppies: then turning to the messenger he said, tell my son, I would have him do thus. According to his instructions, Sextus took means to rid himself of the most powerful of the Gabii; and, thus reduced to weakness, and robbed of its natural protectors, to the Romans betrayed the city.

CHAP. VII.

CAMILLUS.

WHEN Camillus commanded against the Falerians; the master, to whose care the instruction of the Falerian boys was committed, led them out of the city, under pretence of exercising them: and delivered

livered them up to the Romans. Camillus, in detestation of the treachery of the pædagogue, ordered his hands to be tied behind him, and thus disgraced directed the boys to conduct him to their parents. The Falerians whipped him to death. and struck with the exemplary regard to justice and duty, which Camillus had displayed, they surrendered themselves to him without risking a battle. Thus did he by an act of generosity subdue those, who had proved themselves invincible by arms

2. THE Gauls, under the conduct of their king Brennus, made themselves masters of Rome, and kept possession of it seven months When Camillus, having collected the forces that were dispersed in different parts of the country, defeated Brennus, and recovered the city. Thirteen years after the Gauls again ventured to invade the Roman territories, and encamped at the river Aniene, not far from the city. Camillus was on this occasion a fifth time created dictator, and took the command of the army. Against the broad swords of the Gauls, with which they aimed their blows at the enemy's head, he made his men wear light helmets, by which the swords were soon blunted, and broken · and the Roman target, which was of wood, not being proof against the stroke, he directed them to border it round with a thin plate of brass. He also taught them the use of the long spear, with which they engaged in close fight, and receiving the blow of the sword on their target, made their thrust with the spear: while the Gallic steel, being soft and ill-tempered, the edge of the sword was by means of the brass plate soon turned, and the weapon became unserviceable. By this advantage in the arms, the Romans obtained a cheap and easy victory, many of the Gauls were cut to pieces, and the rest saved themselves by flight.

CHAP.

CHAP. VIII.

MUCIUS.

IN a war between the Tuscans and Romans, when Porsenna was king of the Tuscans, and Poplicola, then in his third consulship, commanded the Romans; Mucius, a Roman citizen of approved valour, formed a design against the life of Porsenna: and for that purpose entered the Tuscan camp, imitating the Tuscan dialect, and habited in a Tuscan dress. And, while the king was seated on his throne, attended by his officers, Mucius advanced towards it; and, not knowing the king's person plunged his sword in the breast of one who sate near him, whom he mistook for the king. He was instantly seised; and confessed his intention, and who he was: and while the sacrifice, according to immediate orders, was offering for Porsenna's safety, he thrust his errant hand into the fire; and with an intrepid voice, and without emotion, conversed with the king, his hand in the mean time broiling in the flames. On Porsenna expressing his astonishment at the intrepidity he displayed, Mutius bade him not be surprised at any extraordinary resolution he might fancy in him: for, said he, there are at this instant three hundred Romans, possessed of as much courage and resolution as myself, straggling about your camp, and with the same design. The king gave credit to his assertion, and, alarmed for his own safety, immediately put an end to the war.

CHAP. IX.

SYLLA.

IN the social war Aldinus, an officer of rank, and advanced in years, was murthered by some of his own men, who set upon him with stones and clubs. Great as the offence was, Sylla neglected to punish it, on the principle of making them behave with the greater courage in future; observing, that to expiate a great offence, so much greater display of military merit would be necessary; which in the next engagement proved eventually true.

2. In an engagement at Orchomenus with Archelaus general of Mithridates, Sylla, perceiving the Romans give ground, leaped from his horse; and seising a standard, advanced with it through the flying squadrons, and called aloud to them, "My death, O Romans, will be glorious, and when you are asked, where you betrayed Sylla, say at Orchomenus." The reproof so stung the Romans, that they faced about, vigorously attacked the enemy, and changed the fortune of the day.

CHAP. X.

MARIUS.

WHEN the Cimbri and Teutones, a people savage in their manners, of immense stature, with horrid countenances, and a language scarcely human, penetrated into Italy, Marius would not venture at first a close engagement, but ordered his men to advance no farther than the trenches, and within javelin's cast skirmish with them at a distance. The Romans, after having been thus familiarized to their figures, soon learned as favages to defpife them, and defired Marius to lead them out, and give them an opportunity of fignalifing themfelves againft the barbarous invaders. He did fo, and of a hundred thoufand of the enemy few efcaped, the greater part being either taken prifoners, or flain.

2. PREVIOUS to an engagement with the Teutones and Cimbrians, who were advantageoufly pofted on the heights of the mountains, Marius ordered Marcellus with three thoufand heavy-armed troops in the night to take a circuit round the mountains, and endeavour to make good their march over the more inacceffible parts of them, on the enemy's rear. This fervice performed, he commanded the troops, with which he had advanced to the mountains, to fall back, that the enemy prefuming on their inferiority might purfue them, and be thus decoyed into the plain. The manœuvre fucceeded, and Marius attacking them in front, and Marcellus in the rear, obtaining a brilliant victory.

3. MARIUS in his war with the Cimbrians, who came out of a cold country, fenfible that they could bear froft and fnow much better than heat and fun, took the field againft them in the month of Auguft, and harraffed their rear. And when the Barbarians faced about, they met in front not only the enemy, but a hot beaming fun; to fence againft the heat and glare of which, they endeavoured to fhade their faces with their fhields. This left their bodies bare, at which the Romans aimed, flew of them twelve thoufand, and fix thoufand were taken prifoners.

CHAP. XI.

MARCELLUS.

MARCELLUS at the fiege of Syracufe, having been repeatedly beaten off from the walls by the machines of Archimedes, defifted for a time from his attempts to storm the town. Till having taken prisoner Damippus the Spartan, who had sailed from Syracuse, and gained intelligence from him of a particular tower on the walls, capable of containing a great number of men, and carelessly guarded, and that the walls also in that quarter were very accessible, he ordered proper ladders to be made for an escalade, and, while the Syracusans were engaged in celebrating a festival in honour of Diana, and giving a loose to banqueting and merriment, he made himself master of the tower. and lining the parapet with his troops, early in the morning he broke open the gates, and possessed himself of the city. The men, who had behaved with great gallantry, required the city to be given up to them to be plundered. But Marcellus, wishing to preserve from acts of outrage the inhabitants, yet at the same time unwilling to disappoint the soldiery, gave up to them the money and slaves. but forbade any injury being offered to the persons of the freemen and priests.

CHAP. XII.

ATILIUS.

ATILIUS, when a prisoner of the Carthaginians, engaged himself by an oath, if they would give him leave to go on his parole to Rome, to endeavour to persuade the senate, to put an end to the war. and, if he did not succeed in the negociation, to return. As soon as he arrived at Rome, he advised the senate to the direct contrary. he discovered to them the weakness of the Carthaginians, and pointed out to them in what part, and in what manner they were most open to attacks. The senate were convinced of the propriety of his advice, and requested him to remain with them, and consider an oath extorted from him by necessity as no oath at all. To the intreaties of the senate his

wife,

wife, his children, friends, and relations, tenderly embracing him, added theirs. But, deaf to all their pleadings, he difdained to violate his oath, and returned to Carthage where he informed the Carthaginians of the ftratagem he had employed for the fervice of his country, and the determination of the Romans. In refentment of his conduct, they threw him into a dungeon, and after fcourging, and exercifing various cruelties on him, put him to death.

CHAP. XIII.

CAIUS

CAIUS had given expref's orders for every one to continue under arms, and not to ftir out of the camp when, in the heat of the day, his fon led out his horfe to water at a river, that ran clofe by. The father immediately ordered his head to be ftruck off for difobedience of orders thus enforcing difcipline by the facrifice of his fon.

CHAP. XIV.

FABIUS.

FABIUS, when he commanded againft Hannibal, after having been cenfured in the fenate for not bringing the enemy to an engagement, was preffed by his fon to wipe off the afperfion, and proceed to action. Fabius then, leading him through the army, pointed out to him every part of it, and explained the apparent myfterioufnefs of his conduct Obferve, faid he, how many infirm men, how many unfit for action, contribute to form this army. and who would in prudence rifk the hazard of a battle on the prowefs of fuch troops as thefe?

Every man, that has had any experience in military affairs, knows that we can never depend on bringing our whole force into action and if separately attacked, in the parts where those men are posted we must be defeated. For this reason I study to avoid a general action, contenting myself with harrassing the enemy in his march, by securing advantageous posts, and by secret negociations winning over cities to revolt from him. Such his conduct was at first censured as timidity, but afterwards received its full praise. the Romans, after other generals had lost great armies, having recourse to Fabius, whom they appointed general, and afterwards dictator, and also sirnamed MAXIMUS, which in the Greek signifies MEGISTOS.

2. FABIUS having been honoured with the sirname of MAXIMUS, and Scipio only with that of MAGNUS, Scipio, with some degree of pique at the superiour distinction of Fabius, asked him how it was, that he, who had only saved the Roman armies, should be sirnamed MAXIMUS, while himself, who in close action had engaged Hannibal, and beat him, should have no higher distinction than that of MAGNUS. Why, replied Fabius, if I had not preserved the men, you would have had no soldiers, with whom to have fought and conquered him.

3. FABIUS by stratagem made himself master of the city of the Tarentines, then in alliance with Hannibal. In the army of Fabius was a Tarentine, whose sister, a young woman of exquisite beauty in Tarentum, possessed the affections of Abrentius, to whom Hannibal had committed the charge of the walls. Fabius, informed of the circumstance, dispatched the Tarentine into the city, with instructions through his sister to cultivate an acquaintance with Abrentius, and endeavour to bring him over to the interests of the Romans. This he effected, and Abrentius having discovered to him, in what part the walls might be most successfully attacked, Fabius there applied his ladders, and took the town by storm. This exploit gained Fabius great reputation,

in that he had by a ſtratagem got the better of Hannibal, than whom no general had ever employed ſtratagems with greater ſucceſs.

*CHAP. XV.

QUINTUS.

QUINTUS Fabius, when very far advanced in years, in order to get his ſon appointed general, requeſted the Romans not to charge him with the command of their armies which would in effect, ſaid he, be calling me out in extreme old age to attend him. The Romans wiſhed for nothing more, than to have a man of Fabius's experience to ſuperintend the operations of the army, and therefore inveſted the youth with the ſupreme command. But as ſoon as he was appointed, Fabius excuſed himſelf from attending him in the field left his ſuppoſed conſequence ſhould prove a diminution of his ſon's glory.

CHAP. XVI.

SCIPIO

SCIPIO, when in Spain, having received information that the enemy had advanced to action before they had dined, drew up his army againſt them, and amuſed them for ſeven hours with various manœuvres then after they had been thus wearied, and faint for want of refreſhment, he vigorouſly attacked, and eaſily defeated them.

2 Scipio expelled all proſtitutes from the camp bidding them go, and exerciſe their trades in cities, abandoned to eaſe and luxury He

---

* This ... ſhould have made the 4th in the preceding chapter as it refers to Quint... ... other three chapters do. But I follow the Leyden edition of M ſi ... ...dered

ordered also to be sent away all couches, tables, vases, and the whole dinner equipage, except a pot, a spit, and an earthen mug. And if any one defired to be indulged in a filver cup, he limited the fize of it to a pint. The ufe of oils he prohibited, and forbade thofe, who ufed unguents, to be attended by fervants in their frictions, obferving that thofe might be much more ufefully employed in taking care of the cattle. He obliged the army to cold dinners, allowing the preparation of hot meat only for fuppers. He introduced the drefs of the Gallic cloak, and himfelf ufed to wear a black one: and in walking about the camp, if he faw any of the generals reclined on couches, he would lament the luxury of the army, and their love of eafe.

3. Scipio obferving a foldier bending under a huge piece of palifade, called out to him, "Fellow-foldier, you feem over-loaded." "Indeed I am,' replied the man." 'I fee it,' faid he.' and am afraid, you place your hopes of fafety more on your palifades, than your fword."

4. Seeing a foldier very intent on difplaying the elegance of his fhield, "It is a fhame, 'faid Scipio,' for a Roman to pique himfelf more on the ornament of his left hand, than of his right."

5. Scipio, interrupted by a commotion of the people, called aloud to them, "The fhout of an armed foe never terrified me, and the clamour of a mob never fhall, the baftard fpawn of Italy, and not her genuine fons." The refolution, with which he expreffed himfelf, filenced the rioters, and quafhed the commotion.

9. After the taking of Phœniffa, a city in Iberia, they who had the charge of the prifoners brought to Scipio a virgin of extraordinary beauty. He immediately enquired for her father, and reftored to him his daughter. The prefents alfo, which he had brought to purchafe her ranfom, Scipio returned defiring him to accept them in addition to her fortune. And whatever other women were taken, whether the wives or daughters of men of any confequence, he committed them to

the

the care of two grave and aged Romans, with orders that they should be entertained in a manner suitable to their rank. This eminent display of continence in Scipio won over to the Roman interests and alliance a great number of Iberian cities.

7. Scipio, having engaged Syphax king of the Maffæsyllians in an alliance with him, passed over into Sicily. While he was there, Asdrubal, who had a daughter of exquisite beauty, promised her to Syphax, on condition that he would renounce the Roman alliance. The marriage accordingly took place, and Syphax dispatched a letter to Scipio, with information of the connection he had formed, and a prohibition of his intended expedition to Libya. Sensible of the great confidence the Romans placed in the alliance of Syphax, and apprehensive that if apprised of his revolt they would not venture to invade Libya, Scipio summoned a council, and laid before them Syphax's letter, altering the purport of it to the direct contrary of what he had expressed as, that he thereby invited them into Libya, was surprised they had so long deferred their expedition, and observed that treaties of alliance should be briskly executed, or would soon be dissolved. This representation gave new confidence and alacrity to the Romans, who were instant with him to fix a day for their embarkation.

8. Some Carthaginian spies having been apprehended, instead of executing them as the Roman law directed, Scipio ordered them to be conducted through every quarter of the camp. Where after having seen the men some exercised in launching the dart, others in hurling the javelin, some again employed in furbishing their arms, and others in sharpening their swords, they were again introduced to Scipio: who, after having entertained them at dinner, bade them go, and tell their employer all they had seen. The report, which the spies made of the magnanimity of Scipio, and the preparations for war they observed in the

Rom... ... Hannibal ... struck the Carthaginian army
...

CHAP. XVII.

PORCIUS CATO

WHEN Porcius Cato invaded Spain, ambassadors met him from every city, with tenders of submission to him and the Roman people: those he directed within a fixed time to send hostages. And two of these hostages from each place he charged with a letter to their respective cities, directing them all to be delivered on the same day. The purport of the letters was the same. "The moment you receive this, demolish your walls." The orders being immediate gave no time to one city to consult another, and each fearing left, if the rest complied with the orders, and they should not, they might be reduced to a state of slavery, obeyed the mandate: and in one day every city in Iberia razed their walls.

CHAP. XVIII.

FAUNUS

IN honour of Diomede, who died in Italy, Faunus instituted funeral games. On the first day he proposed to the Greeks to form a procession in arms: the next day he commanded the Barbarians to do the same, directing them, for the purpose, to borrow arms of the Greeks with which they were no sooner furnished, than they fell upon the Greeks, and slew them with their own weapons.

CHAP.

CHAP XIX.

TITUS

CLEONYMUS having made Titus prisoner, demanded for his ransom two cities, Epidamnus and Apollonia. The father of Titus refused to give them up to him, bidding him keep his prisoner. Under these circumstances Titus procured a statue to be made of himself in an attitude of sleep, which he placed in his house, and having contrived means, while the centinels were guarding the room where he had placed the statue, to get secretly on board a ship, he made his escape before the deception was discovered.

CHAP. XX.

CAIUS.

WHILE the Carthaginian fleet, consisting of eighty large ships, lay at Tyndarus, Caius with two hundred sail of triremes endeavoured in vain to bring them to an engagement, deterred by the very superiour number of his fleet. Furling therefore the sails of one hundred of his vessels, and setting those of the rest, he concealed one half of his fleet behind the expanded sails of the other half; and, his line thus formed, shewed himself to the enemy: who, supposing the number of his ships to be only in proportion to the number of the sails they saw, advanced against him, determined to hazard a battle. Caius lay by, till they had approached too near him to escape; and then bearing down upon them with all his force obtained an easy victory.

CHAP. XXI.

PINARIUS.

THE Ennæans having determined to renounce the alliance of the Romans demanded of Pinarius, prefect of the guard, the keys of the gates. If, said he, the people will assemble to-morrow, and a publick decree sanction the revolt, I will readily obey it, and give up the keys. The next day they accordingly assembled: but he in the night placed an ambuscade at the fort, and detached different parties, to surround the theatre, post themselves in the narrow streets, and attentively watch the signal that should be given them. The Ennæans assembled, according to their engagement, and passed a decree confirming the revolt. The prefect of the guard then gave the signal: when the men, who were posted on the eminences near the fort, let fly a shower of darts, and those, who were posted in the narrow streets, with drawn swords attacked the people, and such a general carnage prevailed, that none escaped, except some few who let themselves down from the walls, or made their way through subterraneous passages.

CHAP. XXII.

SERTORIUS.

SERTORIUS when in Iberia had a present made him by some huntsmen of a white fawn: which he brought up so tame, that it would follow him wherever he went. When he mounted the tribunal, it mounted it with him, and it would move its mouth to him, before he determined a cause. From hence he took occasion to persuade the
Barbarians,

Barbarians, that it was sacred to Diana, that through it the goddess foretold him all events; and under her auspices he waged, and conducted his wars. And of whatever secrets he possessed himself by his emissaries and spies, he pretended to have been apprised of them by this fawn. Of hostile attacks, ambuscades, and sudden incursions, he gave out that this messenger of the goddess never failed to afford him early notice and his future victories he asserted had by his fawn been revealed to him. Rapt in astonishment the Barbarians paid him abject homage, and resorted to him as a peculiar favourite of Heaven.

CHAP. XXIII.

CÆSAR.

CÆSAR in his voyage to Nicomedia was taken by some Cilician pirates who demanding a very large sum for his ransom, he promised to double it. As soon as they had made Miletum, and landed there; he dispatched Epicrates a Milesian servant to the Milesians, desiring them to lend him the sum he required; which was immediately sent. Epicrates had it also in command from Cæsar, at the time when he brought the money, to bring likewise every preparation for a magnificent entertainment, together with a water-pot filled with swords, and wine with mandrake steeped in it. The double sum according to his engagement Cæsar then paid them, and made them partake of the banquet he had prepared. In high spirits at the large sum they had received, they gave a loose to their appetite, and drank freely of the medicated wine. which presently set them asleep. In that state Cæsar ordered them to be slain, and immediately repaid the money to the Milesians.

2. CÆSAR, when in Gaul, arriving at the foot of the Alps,

found the mountains occupied by the Barbarians, who were prepared to dispute his passage. On a minute investigation of the nature of the place, beneath those mountains he observed a great number of streams, and of considerable depth from whence rising the exhalations, that every morning ascended, formed a thick cloud * Under cover of that, Cæsar with half his army making a circuit round the mountain reached the heights, the enemy for the thickness of the cloud not being able to see his movement, but supposing him still in his camp. As soon as he found himself above the enemy, he set up a loud shout, which was returned by the other half of the army below while the mountains re-echoing on all sides with the sound threw the Barbarians into a general consternation, who precipitately quitted their posts, and fled, leaving Cæsar to pass the Alps without molestation

3 In his war with the Helvetians, who to the number of eighty thousand, twenty thousand of whom bore arms, had penetrated into the Roman territories in Gaul, Cæsar, as in his engagements with the Barbarians was his usual method, the first day retreated before the enemy, suffering a kind of defeat This imaginary success gave them fresh confidence: and they determined to cross the Rhone in pursuit of him, while he encamped some little distance from it The stream was rough, when the Barbarians to the number of about thirty thousand with great difficulty and fatigue passed it the rest of the army waiting to cross it the next day They, who had effected the passage, fatigued with the labour of

---

* Something like the fog, which Cæsar observed to rise in the morning from those streams at the foot of the Alps, seems to have been that heavy mist described by Polybius, as rising from the Thrasymene lake, and supposed to be a principal cause of the defeat of the Roman army by Hannibal Livy too describes it as having been particularly dense on the plain so that the Romans, who were formed in the valley, could see nothing, while the enemy, who were posted on the eminence, had the advantage of a purer air, and a much clearer view.

the

the day, threw themselves down on the banks to rest. when Cæsar in the night attacked, and cut every man to pieces; who had neither time nor opportunity to repass the river.

4. CÆSAR not thinking himself strong enough to engage the Germans, who had offered him battle, contented himself with acting on the defensive till, having learned that their augurs had forbidden them fighting before the new moon, he took the first opportunity to advance and attack them, supposing they would fight with less spirit and alacrity, when contrary to the instructions of their augurs. The event justified his expectations and, by availing himself of an advantageous time for engaging, against every other advantage he gained a compleat victory.

5 CÆSAR's passage over a large river in Britain being disputed by the British king Cassovellaunus, at the head of a strong body of cavalry and a great number of chariots, he ordered an elephant, an animal till then unknown to the Britons, mailed in scales of iron, with a tower on his back, on which archers and slingers were stationed, to enter the river first If the Britons were terrified at so extraordinary a spectacle, what shall I say of their horses? Among the Greeks, the horses fly at the sight of a naked elephant· but armed, and with a tower on its back, from which darts and stones are continually hurled, it is a sight too formidable to be borne The Britons accordingly with their cavalry and chariots abandoned themselves to flight, leaving the Romans to pass the river unmolested, the enemy thus routed by the appearance of a single beast.

6. CÆSAR having received intelligence, that Cicero, who was besieged by the Gauls, would be reduced to a capitulation, if not speedily relieved, dispatched a soldier with orders in the night to hurl a javelin over the walls with a letter tied to it The letter as soon as discovered by the guards was carried to Cicero: the contents of which were these; " Cæsar bids Cicero hold out. Expect assistance." Very soon after

a cloud

a cloud of smoak and dust was seen, the harbinger of his approach, who wasted the country as he advanced. The siege was immediately raised and Cicero had the satisfaction not only to find himself relieved, but to see his besiegers defeated.

7. ADVANCING with an army of seven thousand men against the Gauls, to make his force appear to the enemy less than it really was, Cæsar fixed his camp on a confined spot of ground and with a considerable detachment posted himself on an eminence, covered with wood, and there lay concealed. A small body of cavalry marched out of the camp, and skirmished with the enemy who in confidence of their superiority pursued them to their trenches, and begun, some to fill the fosse, and others pull down the palisades. In the mean time a sudden charge was sounded, the foot in an entire body sallied out of the camp, the ambuscade poured down from the eminences, where they had been posted, on the enemy's rear, while the Barbarians, thus vigorously attacked on all sides, were most of them cut to pieces.

8. CÆSAR had laid close siege to a citadel in Gaul, which the Barbarians with great resolution defended. But a heavy storm of rain and hail happening to fall, Cæsar observed the guards to have been driven by it from the walls and battlements, availed himself of the moment, and ordered his men instantly to arm, and mount the walls which they found undefended, and without loss made themselves masters of the place.

9. CÆSAR having undertaken an expedition against Gergobia, the largest city in Gaul, Vercingetorix, king of the Gauls, took the field, and encamped against him. Between the two armies ran a large navigable river, which it was impracticable to ford. Convinced of this, Cæsar made no open attempt to cross it, which drew on him the contempt of the Barbarians, and gave them confidence on presumption of their security. But in the night, he detached into some thick woods

two

two legions, who, while Cæsar amused the Gauls, marched up the river and finding the old piles, on which a bridge had been formerly constructed, they expeditiously cut down a quantity of timber from the wood where they had been posted, which they threw over the remains of the old bridge, that were left, and over this temporary bridge effected a safe passage When advancing immediately against the Gauls, they easily routed them, astonished at the unexpected approach of an enemy, and unprepared to receive them. Cæsar with the rest of his army effected a passage by the same way, and by his resolution and address, and the rapidity of this movement, struck terror into all Gaul

10. CÆSAR, having advanced to the siege of Gergobia, found it strongly fortified both by art and nature. The city was situated on a steep hill, that had a flat top. The left side of the hill was covered with thick trees and underwood, the right was too steep to admit access. and one narrow pass led to it, which the Gergobians with a powerful force commanded. Some of the most active and resolute men, he could pick out, Cæsar armed, and in the night secretly posted in the wood equipping them with short javelins, and such small swords as might not incommode them, by being entangled among the trees, and ordering them not to attempt to advance upright, but to observe all possible silence and creep upon their hands and knees By break of day they had made good their passage through the wood, and reached the summit of the hill Cæsar then advanced with the rest of his army against the right side, and drew thither the attention of the Barbarians: while the ambuscade from the woods formed in good order, and made themselves masters of the hill.

11. WHEN Cæsar lay before Alæsia, the Gauls advanced against him with an army of two hundred and five thousand men. In the night he detached three thousand heavy-armed infantry, and all his cavalry, directing them to take different routs, and about two o'clock the next day

to

to fall upon the enemy's rear, and bring them to an engagement. Himself, as soon as it was light, drew up his army, and offered them battle a challenge, which the Barbarians, relying on their numbers, treated with ridicule and contempt But the detachments appearing in their rear, and advancing with a shout of exultation, struck them with terror and consternation, on seeing their retreat thus cut off: and the greatest carnage ensued, the Gauls till then had ever experienced.

12. CÆSAR formed a design to possess himself of Dyrracchium, then in the interests of Pompey, and protected by a powerful body of cavalry. But great as their force was, Cæsar found means to baffle it with a handful of men, and a happy stratagem He ordered a small body of cavalry on a handsome gallop to attack them, having detached three companies of foot before them, with orders to regard nothing but to raise as great a dust with their feet as they possibly could. The immense cloud of dust that was raised, and the confidence with which the horse seemed to advance to the attack, impressed the enemy with an opinion that they were in great force and struck with a sudden and general alarm they immediately fled.

13. CÆSAR obliged to retreat through a narrow defile had a lake on his left, and on his right the sea The enemy hung upon his rear, whom by occasional halts, quick evolutions, and sudden sallies he without much loss repulsed But on the sea side Pompey's fleet, that attended him in his march, with their darts and javelins heavily galled him. Against this attack Cæsar ordered his men to carry their shields on their right hands. which had the desired effect.

14. WHEN Cæsar and Pompey were in Thessaly, the latter well supplied with provision declined coming to an action, while Cæsar, who was short of it, was proportionably anxious to engage. Cæsar used every expedient to irritate the enemy, sometimes shifting his camp, to procure forage, and sometimes retreating. Pompey's army,

taking

taking those frequent movements for signs of timidity, scarcely contained themselves, and were instant with Pompey to lead them against the foe. Cæsar continued to retreat before them, till he had drawn them into an open plain. then facing about, fought them gallantly, and obtained a victory.

15. On a sedition, which appeared to be forming in the camp, the soldiers clamorously insisting on being discharged from service, Cæsar with a composed and chearful air went into the midst of them, "And what is it, 'said he,' my fellow-soldiers, that you want?'" "To be discharged from service," replied they. "Very well, 'said he.' but be advised then, citizens, and refrain from sedition." Piqued at being stiled citizens, and not fellow-soldiers, they were more clamorous than before, altering their cry of grievance, and saying their title was not citizens, but fellow-soldiers. Cæsar with a smile replied, "If we are fellow-soldiers then, let us fight together."

16. In an engagement with the younger Pompey, Cæsar, seeing his men give way, jumped from his horse, and called aloud "For shame, my fellow-soldiers you will not fly, and leave me in the hands of the enemy." The troops felt the reproof, rallied, and renewed the charge.

17. Cæsar ordered his men to be always in readiness, as in the midst of a festival, or of a storm, by night, or by day, if occasion required, he might at an hour's notice march them out. and therefore never fixed for his movements any distant period, or future day.

18. Cæsar's practice was to make his sallies on full speed. thereby never giving the enemy time to insult his rear.

19. Whenever Cæsar saw his men under apprehensions of the enemy's superiority of force, he never endeavoured to diminish, but on the contrary exaggerated their strength. that the greater the force

of the enemy, his army might fee the greater neceffity for a vigorous exertion

20. CÆSAR encouraged his men in having their arms richly ornamented with gold and filver, not only for the fake of a fplendid appearance, but becaufe the more valuable they were, their owners would the more reluctantly part with them.

21. CÆSAR was not very nice in obferving, or fcrupulous in punifhing, petty offences in his men, fuppofing that to overlook, or pardon a fault, would be a fpur to valour But any one, who was a principal in a fedition, or had deferted his ranks, was fure not to go unpunifhed.

22 CÆSAR ufed always to ftile his foldiers, fellow-foldiers. rendering them by that equality of title more ready to face dangers, and execute his commands.

23. ON receiving intelligence, that fome troops had been butchered in Gaul, Cæfar made a vow not to fhave his face, till he had taken fatisfaction on their murtherers A difplay this of his fenfibility, that won him univerfal efteem.

24. CÆSAR, when in diftrefs for provifions, diftributed to his men loaves, which were made of herbs. One of thofe loaves fell into Pompey's hands, who was then engaged in war againft him which he concealed, unwilling to produce to his own troops fo ftrong an inftance of the refolution and continence of the enemy, with whom they were engaged

25. IN the battle fought between Cæfar and Pompey on the plains of Pharfalia, Cæfar knowing that there were in the enemy's army a great number of elegant young men, who valued themfelves on their perfonal attractions, ordered his men not to aim their fpears and javelins at the bodies of their enemy, but at their faces. The dread of

being

being disfigured drove those from the field, and contributed not a little to the success of the day

26. AFTER the defeat at Dyrrachium, Cæsar's men surrendered themselves up to be decimated a punishment however, which he would not suffer to be inflicted, but exhorted them by their future behaviour to retrieve the honour and advantages they had lost. They accordingly in every future engagement, though with superiour force, bore away the palm of victory.

27. WHILE Pompey declared, that he considered all, who attached themselves to neither party, as his enemies; Cæsar on the contrary ordered it to be reported, that all, who did not appear in arms against him, he esteemed his friends.

28. CÆSAR, when he commanded in Iberia, made a truce with the enemy notwithstanding which they exercised hostilities, and cut many of his men to pieces. Instead of retaliating, some prisoners which he had of theirs he set at liberty, and by that act of humanity much ingratiated himself with the foe

29. CÆSAR, after he saw the fortune of the day at Pharsalia decisive in his favour, called aloud to his men, who he thought did not use their victory with sufficient moderation, "Spare the flying foe."

30. AFTER Cæsar had seen all his enemies subdued, he empowered every one of his soldiers to save the life of any Roman he pleased. By this act of beneficence and humanity he ingratiated himself with his soldiers, and restored her exiled citizens to Rome.

31. THE statues of Pompey and Sylla, which by their enemies had been demolished, Cæsar ordered to be replaced: an act of moderation that, which gained him much esteem.

32. WHEN the auguries were pronounced adverse, to keep up the spirits of his men, Cæsar used to say, he could render them auspicious whenever he pleased.

33. A VICTIM having been offered, in which no heart was found: "And where is the wonder, 'cried Cæsar,' that a brute animal should be found without a heart?" His men, who had been alarmed at the inauspicious appearance of the sacrifice, recovered their spirits on the ludicrous turn he gave to it.

CHAP. XXIV.

AUGUSTUS.

THOSE, who in battle evaded action, Augustus did not order to a general execution; but punished them with decimation.

2 To those, who through cowardice suffered themselves to be left behind, he ordered barley to be distributed instead of wheat

3 IN exposure of those, who in the army had committed offences, he ordered them to be stationed before the general's pavilion on their knees; and sometimes, to be employed for a whole day in carrying bricks

4 AUGUSTUS directed his generals always to act with caution and was continually repeating to them FESTINA LENTE, be active, but not rash; for a general had better be too cautious, than too confident.

5 THOSE, who had performed any signal exploit, Augustus never suffered to go unrewarded

6 IN respect to those, who without some good purpose wantonly exposed themselves to danger, Augustus used to say, it was like fishing with a golden hook

7 AUGUSTUS, in his war with Brutus and Cassius, had occasion to cross the Adriatic when the enemy's fleet under the command of Mucius was stationed at an island near Brundysium, ready to dispute his passage Augustus advanced in line of battle, directing his course along the coast of Italy on the right of the Adriatic, as if

his

towards the ifland, and with intention to give Mucius battle, and on the fhips of burden he erected his towers and machines Mucius from thofe preparations for action concluded his intention to fight, and therefore ftretched out into the open fea, where he might have room to form his line. But Auguftus, inftead of engaging, flipped into the port, which Mucius had left While he, having no other port at hand where he could lie fafe from ftorms, was obliged to fail forward to Thefprotis leaving Auguftus to crofs the Adriatic without rifk, who from thence paffed over into Macedonia.

CHAP. XXV.

THE ROMANS.

AFTER the Celts had made themfelves mafters of the city, they concluded a treaty with the Romans on the following conditions: that they fhould pay them tribute, leave a gate at all times open, and give them a portion of land to cultivate Thefe terms acceded to, the Celts fixed their camp and the Romans treating them as friends fent them various prefents, and fupplied them with plenty of wine The Barbarians (for the Celts in particular are ftrongly addicted to liquor) fo freely indulged in the wine, that there was fcarcely a man amongft them who could ftand upright. In that condition the Romans attacked them, and cut every man to pieces And that they might in effect appear to have fulfilled the conditions of the treaty, they conftructed a gate which was left open on an inacceffible rock

2. THE Trojans, who had furvived the conflagration of Troy, under the conduct of Æneas anchored at the mouth of the Tyber, and landing there, in detached parties went up into the country In their abfence the women held a confultation: when the Trojan Rhome thus addreffed

addressed them · "Whither are we wandering? How long are we to be tossed on the sea? Come on, let us burn the ships, and thereby reduce our husbands to the necessity of establishing themselves here." Having thus said, she instantly lighted a torch, and set one of the ships on fire the rest of the women followed her example, and demolished the whole fleet Thus destitute of shipping, the Trojans through necessity fixed themselves in Italy.

3 CORIOLANUS, after he had been banished Rome, offered his services to the Tuscans, which they accepted, afterwards constituted him general of their forces, and under his conduct in various engagements defeated the Romans At last he advanced against Rome, determined to storm the city A procession of Roman matrons, with Veturia the mother of Coriolanus at their head, advanced to meet the exasperated foe, and to try the force of entreaties to win him from his purpose. They prostrated themselves before him, and embraced his knees, Veturia thus concluding their supplications "If however you are determined not to spare your country, first slay your mother, and this venerable band of Roman matrons" Coriolanus moved with compassion, dropped a tear, and retreated · affording an eminent instance of filial duty, but fatal to himself. For the Tuscans by a publick decree sentenced him to death, for breach of trust in desisting to prosecute a victory which he had in his hands.

CHAP. XXVI.

SEMIRAMIS

SEMIRAMIS when in the bath received intelligence of the revolt of the Siracians, and, without waiting to have her sandals put on, or her hair dressed immediately left it, and took the field. Her exploits are

are recorded on pillars, in thefe words. NATURE MADE ME A WO-
MAN, BUT I HAVE RAISED MYSELF TO A DEGREE OF RIVALRY
WITH THE GREATEST MEN. I SWAYED THE SCEPTRE OF NINOS
AND EXTENDED MY DOMINIONS TO THE RIVER HINAMEMES EAST-
WARD, ON THE SOUTH TO THE COUNTRY, FRAGRANT WITH THE
PRODUCTION OF FRANKINCENSE AND MYRRH, AND NORTHWARD
TO THE SACCÆ AND THE SOGDIANS No ASSYRIAN BEFORE ME
EVER SAW THE SEA BUT, DISTANT AS THE SEAS ARE FROM HENCE,
I HAVE SEEN FOUR. AND TO THEIR PROUD WAVES WHO CAN SET
BOUNDS? I HAVE DIRECTED THE COURSES OF RIVERS AT MY WILL·
AND MY WILL HATH DIRECTED THEM WHERE THEY MIGHT PROVE
USEFUL I HAVE MADE A BARREN LAND PRODUCE PLENTY, AND
FERTILISED IT WITH MY RIVERS. I HAVE BUILT WALLS THAT
ARE IMPREGNABLE AND WITH IRON FORCED A WAY THROUGH
INACCESSIBLE ROCKS. AT GREAT EXPENCES I HAVE FORMED
ROADS IN PLACES, WHICH BEFORE NOT EVEN THE WILD BEAST
COULD TRAVERSE AND GREAT AND VARIOUS AS MY EXPLOITS
HAVE BEEN, I HAVE ALWAYS FOUND LEISURE HOURS, WITH WHICH
TO INDULGE MYSELF AND FRIENDS

CHAP. XXVII.

RHODOGUNE.

RHODOGUNE juft coming out of the bath, her hair yet un-
drefled, received intelligence of the revolt of a fubjugated nation
Without waiting to have her hair dreffed, fhe mounted her horfe, and
put herfelf at the head of her army at the fame time vowing never
to have her hair dreffed, till fhe had fubdued the revolters, which not
till after a tedious war fhe accomplifhed. She then bathed, and had
her

her hair dressed from which circumstance the royal arms of Persia bear on them Rhodogune with dishevelled hair

CHAP. XXVIII.

TOMYRIS.

CYRUS advancing against the Massagetæ, Tomyris their Queen retreated before him. The Persian army closely pursued her, entered, and plundered, her camp where they found great plenty of wine, and all sorts of provision, on which they immoderately indulged, revelling all night, as if they had obtained a victory. In that situation Tomyris attacked them, and cut them to pieces, being partly buried in sleep, and partly so drenched with wine, and surfeited with banqueting, that they could scarcely stand upright and Cyrus himself was slain.

CHAP. XXIX.

NITETIS.

CYRUS king of Persia demanded of Amasis king of Ægypt his daughter in marriage. But, instead of his own, he sent him Nitetis the daughter of king Apria, whose death he had effected, and mounted his throne. Nitetis had long passed for the daughter of Amasis, after she had cohabited with Cyrus. But after having borne him children, and made herself mistress of his affections, she informed him, who she was, that Apria was her father, the king and master of Amasis. And now, said she, since Amasis is dead, it will be a generous act to revenge the injury of my family on Psammetichus his son. Cyrus consented. but died before the expedition took place. His son Cambyses however

however was prevailed on by his mother to undertake it which he finifhed fuccefsfully, and transferred the Ægyptian fceptre once more into the hands of the family of Apria.

CHAP. XXX.

PHILOTIS.

THE Latins under the command of Pofthumus made war upon the Romans at the fame time offering to form an alliance with them, if they would give them their daughters in marriage, thereby cementing the two nations, as they had themfelves done in the cafe of the Sabines The Romans were at that time in no condition to engage in a war, and yet were unwilling to part with their daughters. When Philotis, a young and handfome flave, propofed to them to drefs her, and fuch other good-looking flaves as they could pick out, and fend them to the Latins in place of their daughters, at the fame time engaging to let them know by lighting a torch, at what time in the night the Latins went to reft. Accordingly as foon as with their new brides they had retired to repofe, Philotis lighted the torch, and the Romans furprifed the Latins in bed, and flew them.

CHAP. XXXI.

CLOELIA.

THE Romans concluded a treaty with the Tyrrhenians, and fent as hoftages for the obfervance of it the daughters of fome of the firft families in Rome Thofe young women ufed frequently to retire to the Tyber to bathe when Clœlia, who was one of them, propofed to
the

the rest to tie their cloaths about their heads, and swim over the river. The Romans admired their resolution; but agreeably to the faith of the treaty sent them all back to the Tyrrhenians. Porsenna king of Tuscany, on their being introduced to him, asked who was the proposer of so daring an act. To which Clœlia undauntedly replied, she was. Porsenna pleased with her manly spirit, presented her with a horse richly caparisoned, and with just encomiums on their fortitude sent her and the rest of her companions back to Rome.

CHAP. XXXII.

PORCIA

PORCIA, the daughter of Cato, and wife of Brutus, suspecting her husband entertained some designs against Cæsar, which he would not venture to communicate to her, cut her thigh with a razor: thus giving him proof of the resolution, with which she could inflict the wound, and bear the pain. Brutus no longer hesitated to discover to her the conspiracy: when carrying her own dress to him, he found a sword privately concealed in it. This Brutus used, when with the rest of the conspirators he murdered Cæsar. And when afterwards, in conjunction with Cassius, he engaged, and was defeated by, Augustus, and fell upon his own sword. Porcia first endeavoured to starve herself. But not being able to effect that by the interposition of her relations and domestics, she ordered some fire to be brought to her, under pretence of using some unguents; and seising the burning coals in her hands, she swallowed them, before any body that was present had time to prevent it. Thus died Porcia, a memorable instance of resolution and fortitude, and of conjugal affection.

CHAP. XXXIII.

TELESILLA.

CLEOMENES king of Sparta having defeated the Argives, of whom more than seven thousand were left dead on the field, directed his march to Argos, in hopes of making himself master of the city. When Telesilla, a musician, put herself at the head of the Argive women: who armed, and so successfully defended the walls, that they repulsed Cleomenes, and the other king Damaratus, and saved the city. In memory of this exploit of the women the Argives every month celebrate the festival of the Numenia: when the women wear the tunic and robe, and the men the woman's gown.

CHAP. XXXIV.

CHILONIS.

CHILONIS, the daughter of Cleades, and wife of Theopompus, learning that her husband was made prisoner by the Arcadians, travelled into Arcadia to see him. The Arcadians, in consideration of the affection she had displayed, gave her leave to visit him in prison: when she changed dresses with him, and he by that means effected his escape, she in his stead remaining in prison. Theopompus ere long watched an opportunity, and seised a priestess of Diana, as she was celebrating a procession at Pheneus. and for her the Tegeatæ exchanged Chilonis.

CHAP. XXXV.

PIERIA

A confiderable body of the Ionians, that inhabited Miletum, on a fedition that was formed againft the pofterity of Neleus, feparated and eftablifhed themfelves at Myuntes and there lived in a ftate of hoftility with their old countrymen, though not in actual war, but ufed to meet them on feftivals, and public occafions On the celebration of a folemn feftival called NELEIDES, Pieria, daughter of Pythu a man of eminence, went to Miletum where Phrygius, one of the pofterity of Neleus, met her, and becoming enamoured of the girl, afked how he could moft agreeably ferve her. By giving me an opportunity, replied the maid, of coming hither frequently, and with as much company as I pleafe Phrygius underftood her meaning, effected a permanent peace, and a re-eftablifhment of the union of the two ftates. Famous ever after in the annals of the Milefian hiftory became the love of Phrygius and Pieria.

CHAP XXXVI.

POLYCRETE.

THE Milefians, affifted by the Erythræans, made war on the Naxians and Diognetus general of the Milefians ravaged their country, and brought off confiderable booty, befides a number of women, and among them Polycrete, of whom he became enamoured, and cohabited with her not on the terms of a flave, but as his wife. In the Milefian camp was celebrated a folemn feftival, which by the Milefians

fians is univerfally obferved. Polycrete requefted Diognetus's permiffion to fend her brothers a fmall prefent of the fumptuous fare that was prepared and in a cake moulded up a piece of lead, ordering the bearer to tell her brothers, that it was intended only for their ufe. On the lead fhe infcribed, that if they would attack the Milefian camp, they might furprife the enemy in a ftate of intoxication and fleep. The Naxian generals accordingly made the attack, and fucceeded. Polycrete for her fervice was highly honoured by her citizens, who at her inftance preferved Diognetus, and his fortunes.

CHAP. XXXVII

THE PHOCÆANS.

THE Phocæans under the command of Phoxus marched to the affiftance of Mandron, king of the Bebracians, who was attacked by the neighbouring Barbarians. Mandron for their fervice appointed to the Phocæans a part of the country, and city, and invited them to fettle there. By their courage and conduct they had obtained many victories, and enriched themfelves with great fpoils; which fo drew upon them the envy of the Bebricians, that, in the abfence of Mandron, they formed a refolution to maffacre them. But Lampface, the daughter of Mandron, having got information of the defign, as fhe could not prevent it, privately difcovered it to the Greeks who prepared a magnificent facrifice in the fuburbs, and invited the Barbarians to partake of it. The Phocenfians then divided themfelves into two bodies one of which fecured the walls, and the other flew the banqueters, and made themfelves mafters of the city. Lampface they afterwards honourably rewarded, and from her named the city Lampfacum.

CHAP. XXXVIII.

ARETAPHILA.

NICOCRATES, tyrant of the Cirenenſians, among a number of other oppreſſive and atrocious acts, with his own hands ſlew Melanippus, prieſt of Apollo, and married Aretaphila his wife, a woman of exquiſite beauty. She endeavoured by poiſon, and various methods, to revenge on the tyrant her diſtreſſed country, and her huſband's death: for which ſhe was accuſed, and tried. But, notwithſtanding the tortures to which ſhe was expoſed, ſhe confeſſed nothing, but that ſhe had adminiſtered to him a love-potion, in order to fix his affections. By the tyrant's order ſhe was finally acquitted; and on ſuppoſition that ſhe had ſuffered innocently, he afterwards treated her with marks of greater attention and affection. Having a daughter, who was extremely beautiful, ſhe introduced her to Leander, the tyrant's brother, who became enamoured of her, and with the conſent of Nicocrates married her. Influenced by the frequent remonſtrances of his mother-in-law, Leander formed a reſolution to free his country by the tyrant's death: which, after much difficulty he found means to effect by the aſſiſtance of the groom of his chamber.

CHAP. XXXIX.

CAMMA.

SINORIX and Sinatus were poſſeſſed of Tetrarchies in Gaul. Camma, the wife of Sinatus, was eſteemed as virtuous, as fair: and was prieſteſs of Diana, an office of the higheſt rank that a woman can hold in Gaul. Sinorix conceived a paffion for her, which he defpaired of gratifying either by force, or entreaties, while her hufband was alive. Sinatus therefore he procured to be affaffinated: and not long after paid his addreffes to Camma, who repeatedly rejected his pretenfions. At laft however at the preffing folicitation of her friends and acquaintance fhe pretended to confent and the day of marriage was fixed. When Sinorix, attended by a great number of Gauls, both men and women, waited on her who with blandifhments and tendernefs accompanied him to the altar There from a golden cup fhe drank to him, and bade him partake with her in the draught. He received it with pleafure, as a token of bridal love, and drank it off But the bridal cup was a potion of ftrong poifon As foon as fhe faw, that he had drank it, falling down on her knees, fhe with a loud voice exclaimed "I thank thee, venerable Diana, for granting me in this thy temple a glorious revenge for my murdered hufband" This faid, fhe dropped down, and expired and the bridegroom at the altar of the goddefs expired with her.

CHAP. XL.

TIMOCLEA.

TIMOCLEA was fifter of Theagnes the Theban: that Theagnes, who fought Philip at Chæronea, when he called out, whither would you purfue me? and was anfwered, even into Macedonia. After his death, when Alexander facked Thebes, and fome were plundering the city in one part, and fome in another. a certain Thracian, named Hipparchus, entered the houfe of Timoclea, after fupper forced her to his bed, and alfo infifted on her telling him, where fhe had depofited her treafures. She acknowledged, fhe had vafes, cups, and other pieces of

orna-

ornamental furniture, which on the city being taken she said she had deposited in a dry well. The Thracian pressed her immediately to attend him, and shew him the place; which she accordingly did, conducting him through the garden and bringing him to the well. Fearing lest any one should be beforehand with him, he eagerly entered it: but instead of a treasure, found a shower of stones, which Timoclea and her servants discharged upon him, and buried him under the pile. The Macedonians getting intelligence of the transaction, seised her, and carried her before Alexander. When she confessed the fact, and said, no terrors would make her repent of having so gloriously revenged the brutal violence that the Barbarian had offered to her, Alexander applauded her spirit, and excepted from the publick calamity not only her, but all who could prove any relation to her.

CHAP. XLI.

ERYXO

LEARCHUS was declared regent of the Cyrenensians, during the minority of Battus son of Arcesilaus: but intoxicated with power, soon became not only a king, but a tyrant, exercising upon the citizens the most atrocious acts of cruelty and injustice. The mother of Battus was Eryxo, a woman of great modesty and exemplary virtue; for whom Learchus conceived a violent passion, and made her proposals of marriage; on which subject she referred him to her brothers. They, as it had been concerted between them and their sister, demurring upon it, she sent a servant to Learchus, acquainting him that her brothers seemed to disapprove of it: but if he would give them a meeting at her house, a conference she apprehended might remove their present objections. So fair an opening seemed to him to promise a favourable
issue.

issue At night he repaired to Eryxo's house without a guard. and on entering found there Polyarchus her eldest brother, attended by two youths, armed, and in waiting to receive him, who immediately fell upon him, and slew him. They then proclaimed Battus king, and restored to the Cyrenensians their antient form of government

CHAP. XLII

PYTHOPOLIS.

PYTHES, in his dominions having discovered some gold mines, set all his men at work in digging, searching for, and cleaning the ore no business but that was carried on either by land or sea The people were all uneasy at the land being suffered to lie uncultivated as in the mean time there was likely to be had no corn, no fruits, nor any thing for the purposes of life. The women entreated the wife of Pithes to use her influence with her husband on this subject of general complaint. She bade them not be uneasy, and assured them she would. Accordingly sending for some goldsmiths, she ordered them to make her in gold fish, ripe fruits, cakes, and meats of various kind Pythes, on his return from a journey, asked if supper was ready When a golden table was placed before him, covered with the resemblance of various eatables, all worked up in gold Pythes much admired the workmanship then ordered them to be taken away, and the supper to be brought Other dishes were accordingly served up. and others after them · but in all were served up only the resemblance of viands in gold Pythes in a rage desired her to have done with her shew, and let him have his supper, for he was fatigued and hungry. You do not consider, replied his wife, that victuals are scarce to be procured The whole country is employed in ransacking the bowels of the earth for gold and unless we can eat it,

we

we muſt all ſoon ſtarve. Pythes, convinced of the propriety of this remonſtrance, ordered the people from the mines, and directed them to employ themſelves in huſbandry, and other uſeful occupations.

CHAP. XLIII.

CHRYSAME.

CNOPUS, deſcended from the family of the Codridæ, made war on an Ionian colony, that had been planted at Erythra. And having been directed by the oracle to commit the conduct of the expedition to a Theſſalian prieſteſs of Hecate, he ſent an embaſſy to the Theſſalians, informing them of the declaration of the oracle, which returned with the prieſteſs Chryſame. Poſſeſſed of great ſkill in the occult qualities of herbs, ſhe choſe out of the herd a large and beautiful bull, gilded his horns, decorated him with garlands, and purple ribbands embroidered with gold, and mixing in his fodder a medicinal herb that will excite madneſs, ordered him to be kept in the ſtall and fed upon it. The efficacy of this medicine was ſuch, that not only the beaſt that eat it was ſeiſed with madneſs, but all, who eat of the fleſh of it, when in ſuch a ſtate, were ſeiſed with the ſame diſeaſe. The enemy having encamped againſt her, ſhe directed an altar to be raiſed in ſight of them, and, every preparation for a ſacrifice being made, the bull was brought out when, the medicine operating, he broke looſe, and run wild into the plain, roaring, and tilting at every thing he met. The Erythræans ſeeing the victim, intended for the enemy's ſacrifice, running towards their camp, conſidered it as a happy omen, ſeiſed the beaſt, and offered him up in ſacrifice to their gods · every one, in participation of the ſacrifice, eating a piece of the fleſh. The whole army was ſoon after ſeiſed with madneſs, and exhibited the ſame marks of wildneſs and frenzy

the

the bull had done. Chryfame, obferving this, directed Cnopus immediately to draw out his forces, and charge the enemy. Incapable of making any defence, the Erythræans were cut to pieces; and Cnopus made himfelf mafter of Erythra, a great and flourifhing city.

CHAP. XLIV.

POLYCLEA.

ÆATUS the fon of Philip had an only fifter named Polyclea, defcended with him from the Heraclidæ. The oracle having declared, that whichever of the family fhould firft crofs the Achelous, fhould poffefs the city, and enjoy the throne, while he was engaged in a war with the Bœotians, who had formerly fettled themfelves in Theffaly, and the army was preparing to pafs the Achelous, Polyclea bound up her foot, pretending to have hurt it, and requefted her brother to carry her acrofs the river. With her defire, fufpecting no defign, he readily complied, gave his fhield to his armour-bearer, and took his fifter on his fhoulders who, as he approached the oppofite bank, leaped from him on fhore, and turning to Æatus, "Remember, ' faid fhe,' the oracle, by whofe declaration the kingdom is mine. for I firft reached the fhore." Æatus, pleafed with the device, and captivated with the girl's addrefs, married, and fhared the kingdom with her. The product of the marriage was a fon, whofe name was Theffalus, from whom the city was afterwards called Theffalia.

CHAP. XLV.

LEÆNA

HOW Aristogiton and Harmodius delivered Athens from the tyrant's yoke, is known to every Greek. Aristogiton had a mistress, whose name was Leæna. Hippias ordered her to be examined by torture, as to what she knew of the conspiracy: having with great resolution long borne the various cruelties that had been exercised on her, lest the further increase of pain should extort from her any discovery, she with her own hand cut out her tongue. The Athenians in memory of her erected in the vestibule of the tower the statue of a lioness in brass, without a tongue.

CHAP. XLVI.

THEMISTO

PHILO the son of Phricodemus the tyrant became enamoured of Themisto, daughter of Critho the OEanthian. The tyrant demanded her for his son in marriage, and was by her father refused. In resentment of the affront, Phricodemus ordered Critho's sons to be exposed to wild beasts before the eyes of their father and mother: then seised the daughter, and gave her in marriage to his son. Themisto, thus forced to his embraces, under her robe concealed a sword, with which in the night, while the bridegroom was asleep, she so secretly dispatched him, that not the least noise was heard. She then found means to escape out of the house, and fled to the shore, where she found a boat, went into it, and committing herself to the mercy of the wind and
waves,

waves, was carried to a city of Achaia, in which was a temple of Neptune where she took refuge. Thither Phricodemus sent his other son Heracontes, the brother of him that had been murthered, to demand the girl of the Elicensians; who, in conformity with the tyrant's requisitions, delivered her up. But the ship had scarce got under sail, when a violent storm arose, which drove them to Rhium a town in Achaia: where two Acarnanian vessels, the Acarnanians being at that time at open war with the tyrant, made prize of the ship, and carried it to Acarnania. The people there, as soon as they were informed of the transaction, bound Heracontes, and delivered him up to the disposal of the girl. The tyrant then sent an embassy to her, requesting his son; whom she promised to give up, after she had received her parents. Phricodemus accordingly sent her parents; but the Acarnanians notwithstanding would not deliver up Heracontes, but scourged him, and afterwards put him to death. The tyrant himself not many days afterwards fell by the hand of his citizens. And, what is remarkable, the inhabitants of Elice with their city were not long afterwards ingulphed in the sea, which swelled over them by an earthquake. Neptune thus seeming to have revenged himself on them for the indignity they had offered him, in delivering up a fugitive, that had fled for refuge to his shrine.

CHAP. XLVII.

PHERETIMA.

ARCESILAUS son of Battus king of the Cyrenians by a sedition of the people was driven from his kingdom. when his mother Pheretima sailed to Cyprus, to supplicate the assistance of Euelthon king of Salamis. The Cyprian however was deaf to her entreaties. and Arcesilaus

silaus at laſt entered into the ſervice of Greece, where he acquired great wealth, and recovered his kingdom. But being too ſevere in the puniſhments he exacted on ſome of his enemies, he was ſlain by the neighbouring Barbarians. Amidſt all theſe calamities Pheretima did not loſe her ſpirit, but applied to Aryandes an Ægyptian prince, and repeating ſome obligations ſhe had formerly an opportunity of conferring on Cambyſes, ſhe was ſupplied with a powerful force: with which ſhe attacked the Cyrenians both by ſea and land, revenged the death of her ſon, and re-inſtated her family on the throne.

CHAP. XLVIII.

AXIOTHEA

PTOLEMY king of Ægypt having ſent a powerful force to diſpoſſeſs Nicocles of his kingdom, both he and his brothers, rather than ſubmit to ſlavery, fell by their own hands. Axiothea the wife of Nicocles, emulous of the glorious reſolution of the deceaſed, aſſembled their ſiſters, mothers, and wives, and exhorted them not to ſubmit to any thing unworthy of their family. Accordingly barring the doors of the women's apartments, while the citizens were crowding into the palace, with their children in their arms they ſet fire to the houſe. Some diſpatched themſelves with the ſword, and others reſolutely leaped into the flames. Axiothea, who was the promoter of the enterpriſe, after ſhe had ſeen them all thus gloriouſly fall, firſt ſtabbed, and then threw herſelf into the fire, to preſerve even her dead body from falling into the hands of the enemy.

CHAP. XLIX.

ARCHIDAMIS.

PYRRHUS king of Epire in a bloody battle having defeated the Lacedæmonians, marched against the city when they came to a resolution to convey their wives and children to Crete, and themselves to try the fortune of another battle determined either to obtain the victory, or at a dear price to fell their lives But Archidamis the daughter of king Cleades rejected the proposal, alledging that Spartan women ought with their husbands to live, and die They therefore insisted on sharing in the operations of war. some fetched the tools, others dug in the fosse, some again were employed in sharpening the arms, and others assisted in dressing the wounded. The spirit of the women gave new resolution to the Spartans: who again took the field, engaged Pyrrhus, and defeated him.

CHAP. L.

PANARISTES.

ANTIOCHUS, sirnamed Deus, married Laodice his sister by the father's's side, and had by her Seleucus He also afterwards married Berenice, daughter of king Ptolemy, by whom he had likewise a son. and dying, while he was in his infancy, he left his kingdom to Seleucus. Laodice not thinking her son secure on the throne, while the son of Berenice was living, sought means to procure his death. Berenice invoked the pity and assistance of her husband's subjects. but too late. The assassins however exhibited to the people a child very like him, they

had

had murthered, declared him to be the royal infant, whom they had spared, and a guard was appointed for his person. Berenice had also a guard of Gallic mercenaries, and a fortified citadel appointed for her residence: and the people swore allegiance to her. By the suggestions of Aristarchus her physician, she now conceived herself perfectly secure, and hoped to reconcile to her all who had before been inimical to her pretensions. But their object in the oath they had taken to her was only to throw her off her guard which effected, she was privately assassinated. And several of the women, who were about her, fell in attempting to save her. Panariste however, Mania, and Gethosyne buried the body of Berenice, and in the bed on which she had been murthered, placed another woman in her stead, pretending she was still living, and likely to recover of the wound she had received. And of this they persuaded her subjects, till Ptolemy the father of the deceased arrived, who dispatched letters into the countries round in the names of his daughter and her son, as if still alive: and by this stratagem of Panariste secured to himself without a single engagement the whole country from Taurus to India.

CHAP. LI.

THEANO.

THEANO the mother of Pausanias, after he had been convicted of a design to betray the city to the Medes, and had taken refuge in the temple of Minerva Chalciæca, from whence the law strictly forbids to force the suppliant, thither immediately repaired, and laid a brick, she carried with her, at the door. The Lacedæmonians, in admiration of her prompt thought and resolution, carried also every one a brick to the door of the temple. And the door way thus blocked up, without forc-

ing

ing the suppliant from the altar, the traitor perished by being blocked up in the temple.

CHAP. LII.

DEIDAMEIA.

DEIDAMEIA, the daughter of Pyrrhus, attacked and took Ambracia, to revenge the death of Ptolemy. And on the Epirots suppliantly suing for peace, she granted it only on condition of their acknowledging her hereditary rights, and the honours of her ancestors. This they engaged to do, without any intention to observe their engagement. For some of them immediately formed a design against her life, and bribed Nestor one of Alexander's guards to murther her: who, struck with her majestic dignity, fixed his eyes on the ground as in meditation, and returned without accomplishing his purpose. She then withdrew to the temple of Diana Hegemone, where Milo, who had been guilty of parricide, with a drawn sword pursued her. She had just time to call out, to him,

"Slaughter, thou matricide, on slaughter raise."

When Milo aimed a blow, and slew her in the temple.

CHAP. LIII.

ARTEMISIA.

ARTEMISIA in the naval battle at Salamis finding the Persians defeated, and herself near falling into the hands of the Greeks, ordered the Persian colours to be taken down, and the master of the ship to bear down upon, and attack a Persian vessel, that was passing by her. The Greeks, seeing this, supposed her to be one of their allies, drew off,

off, and left her, directing their forces against other parts of the Persian fleet. Artemisia in the mean time sheered off, and escaped safe to Caria.

2. ARTEMISIA, the daughter of Lygdamis, sunk a ship of the Calyndensian allies, which was commanded by Damasithymus. The king in acknowledgment of her gallantry sent her a compleat suit of Græcian armour, and presented the captain of the ship with a distaff and spindle.

3. ARTEMISIA always chose a long ship, and carried on board with her Græcian, as well as Barbarian, colours. And when she chased a Græcian ship, she hoisted Barbarian colours, but when chased by a Græcian ship, she hoisted Græcian colours, that the enemy might mistake her for a Greek, and give up the pursuit.

4. ARTEMISIA planted an ambuscade near Latmus; and herself with a numerous train of women, eunuchs, and musicians, celebrated a sacrifice at the grove of the mother of the gods, distant about seven miles from the city. The Latmians came out to see the magnificent procession; when the ambuscade entered, and took possession of the city. Thus did Artemisia by flutes and cymbals possess herself of what she had in vain endeavoured by force of arms to obtain.

5. ARTEMISIA, queen of Caria, fought as an ally to Xerxes against the Greeks. And at the famous battle of Salamis, the king acknowledged her to have signalised herself above all the officers in the fleet. And even in the heat of the action observing the manner, in which she distinguished herself, he exclaimed "O Jupiter, surely of man's materials you have formed women, and of woman's men."

CHAP.

CHAP. LIV.

TANIA.

TANIA the wife of Zenis, prince of Dardania, after the death of her hufband, with the affiftance of Pharnabazus governed the realm Drawn in a chariot, fhe always went to battle, gave her orders at the time of action, formed her lines, and rewarded every man who behaved well, as fhe faw he deferved And, what has fcarcely happened to any general except herfelf, fhe never fuffered a defeat But Medius, who had married her daughter, and from that near relation might have been fuppofed faithful to her, fecretly entered her apartments, and murthered her.

CHAP. LV.

TIRGATAO.

TIRGATAO, of Mæotis, married Hecatæus king of the Sinti, a people who inhabit a little above the Bofphorus. He had been expelled his kingdom, but was reinftated in his throne by Satyrus, tyrant of the Bofphorus: who gave him his daughter in marriage, but enjoined him to kill his former wife. As he paffionately loved the Mæotian, he could not think of killing her, but confined her in a ftrong caftle: from whence however fhe found means to make her efcape. In fear left fhe fhould excite the Mæotians to war, Hecatæus and Satyrus made ftrict fearch after her. which fhe happily eluded, travelling through lonely and defert ways; hiding herfelf in the woods in the day, and purfuing her journey in the night. At laft fhe reached the

country

country of the Ixomatæ, where her own family possessed the throne. Her father was dead, and his successor in the kingdom she afterwards married. She then excited the Ixomatæ to war, and engaged many warlike nations about the Mæotis to join the alliance. When the confederates first invaded the country of Hecatæus, and afterwards ravaged the dominions of Satyrus. Harrassed by a war, in which they found themselves inferior to the enemy, they sent an embassy to sue for peace, accompanied by Metrodorus son of Satyrus, who was offered as a hostage. Thus on stipulated terms she granted, to the observance of which they engaged themselves by oath. But no sooner had they made the oath, than they planned schemes to break it. Satyrus prevailed on two of his friends, to revolt to her, and put themselves under her protection, the more easily to find an opportunity to assassinate her. On their revolt Satyrus wrote a letter, to demand them: which she answered, by alledging the law of nations justified her in protecting those, who had placed themselves under her protection. The two revolters one day requesting an audience of her, while one was entertaining her with a pretended matter of importance, the other with a drawn sword levelled a blow at her, which fell upon her girdle, and the guards immediately seised, and secured them. They were afterwards examined by torture, and confessed the whole plot. When Tirgatao ordered the hostage to execution, and with fire and sword laid waste the territories of Satyrus. Stung with remorse and sorrow for the calamities he had brought upon himself and country, he died in the midst of an unsuccessful war: leaving his son Gorgippus to succeed him in the throne. Abjuring his father's proceedings, he sued to her for peace, which on payment of a tribute she granted, and put an end to the war.

CHAP. LVI.

AMAGE.

AMAGE the wife of Medofaccus king of the Sarmatians, who inhabit the maritime parts of Pontica, observing her husband to be totally given up to luxury, took the reins of government into her own hands. She determined causes, stationed her garrisons, repulsed the invasions of enemies, and directed every thing with so great ability, that her fame extended through all Scythia. The Cherrhonesites, who inhabit Taurica, and had been much harrassed by a king of the adjacent Scythians, had heard of Amage's fame, and requested an alliance with her. In consequence of a treaty formed between the two nations, she wrote to the Scythian prince, not to repeat his ravages in the Cherronese. who treated her prohibition with contempt. When with a hundred and twenty men of tried courage, and extraordinary strength, each of them provided with three horses, in one night and day she stretched a march of twelve hundred furlongs, and unexpectedly arriving at the palace, slew all the guard. And while the Scythians, confounded as in a moment of imminent danger, conceived her force to be much greater than it really was, Amage rushing into the palace, where she had made her first attack, slew the Scythian, his friends, and relations; and put the Cherronesites in free possession of their country. To the son of the Scythian prince she gave his hereditary dominions. cautioning him to take warning by his father's death, and not intrench upon the territories of his neighbours.

CHAP. LVII.

ARSINOE.

ARSINOE, after the death of her husband Lysimachus, while the city of Ephesus remained distracted with seditions, and the faction in the interests of Seleucus threw the Lysimachians from the walls, and set open the gates, placed a slave in the royal bed-chamber, whom she dressed in her own robes, and posted a strong guard at the door. Then dressing herself in ragged cloaths, and disfiguring her face, she passed through a private door, run to the ships, and going on board immediately weighed anchor and made her escape. Menecrates in the mean time, one of the adverse generals, forced his way into the bed-chamber, and slew the servant she had left there, mistaking her for Arsinoe.

CHAP. LVIII.

CRATESIPOLIS.

CRATESIPOLIS, who had long sought in vain for an opportunity of betraying the Acrocorinthus to Ptolemy, having been repeatedly assured by the mercenaries, who composed the guard, that the place was tenable, applauded their fidelity and bravery. however, said she, it may not be improper to send for a re-inforcement form Sicyon. For this purpose, she openly sent a letter of request to the Sicyonians; and privately an invitation to Ptolemy whose troops were dispatched in the night, admitted as the Sicyonian allies, and without the concurrence or privity of the guards put in possession of the Acrocorinthus.

CHAP. LVIII.

THE PRIESTESS.

DURING the siege of Pellene, which was carried on by the Ætolians, from a high hill, opposite to the tower where the Pellenensians used to arm, on the festival of Minerva the priestess of that goddess, who was the tallest and handsomest virgin that could be picked out, according to annual custom, in a full suit of elegant armour and a three-plumed helmet led the procession of the day. The Ætolians seeing a virgin come out in arms from the temple of Minerva, and advance at the head of the armed citizens, supposed it was the goddess herself, who was come to their protection, and immediately raised the siege. In their retreat the Pellenensians pursued, and made no small havock amongst them.

CHAP. XVI.

CYNANE.

CYNANE, the daughter of Philip, was famous for her military knowledge. She conducted armies, and in the field charged at the head of them. In an engagement with the Illyrians, she with her own hand slew Cæria their queen, and with great slaughter defeated the Illyrian army. She married Amyntas, son of Perdiccas, and, soon after losing him, never would take a second husband. By Amyntas she had an only daughter named Eurydice: to whom she gave a military education, and instructed her in the science of war. Upon Alexander's death, in exclusion of the royal family, his generals parcelling out his dominions among themselves, she crossed the Strymon; forcing her way in the face

face of Antipater, who disputed her passage over it. She then passed the Hellespont, to meet the Macedonian army, when Alcetas with a powerful force advanced to give her battle. The Macedonians at first paused at the sight of Philip's daughter, and the sister of Alexander; while after reproaching Alcetas with ingratitude, undaunted at the number of his forces, and his formidable preparations for battle, she bravely engaged him; resolved upon a glorious death, rather than, stripped of her dominions, accept a private life, unworthy the daughter of Philip.

CHAP. LXI.

PYSTA

PYSTA the wife of Seleucus, firnamed Callinicus, when he was defeated by the Gauls at Ancyra, falling into the hands of the enemy, threw aside her royal robe, put on the ragged dress of an inferiour servant, and as such was sold among the prisoners. After having been conveyed amongst the rest of the slaves to Rhodes, she there made a discovery of herself. The Rhodians immediately re-purchased her of the buyer, habited her in a manner suitable to her rank, and conducted her to Antiochia.

CHAP. LXII.

EPICHARIS.

PISO and Seneca were accused of a conspiracy against Nero; and Mellas, a brother of Seneca, having a mistress whose name was Epicharis, Nero examined her by torture, concerning what she might know of the plot: which she resolutely bore without making any discovery.

She

She was therefore for the present dismissed; but three days afterwards was ordered to be brought again in a litter, in which as she was carried, she pulled off her girdle, and strangled herself with it. As soon as the men, who had the charge of the litter, had brought it to the place of torture, they set it down, and bade Epicharis come forth; but on examining the litter, they found only a dead corpse. The circumstance exceedingly irritated the tyrant, finding himself thus over-reached by a prostitute.

CHAP. LXIII.

THE MILESIAN WOMEN.

A GENERAL despondency once possessed the young women of Miletum: many of whom for no visible reason destroyed themselves. A Milesian woman at last advised, that those, who were guilty of suicide, should be dragged through the forum. The advice was followed, and had its desired effect for dread of the ignominy, that would attend their bodies after death, rivetted them to a life, which the horrors of death itself could not effect.

CHAP. LXIV.

THE MELIAN WOMEN.

AFTER the Melians under the conduct of Symphæus had established themselves in Caria, the Carians, who were settled at Cryasus, grew jealous of their consequence, and anxious to get rid of them. With that view, they made a publick entertainment, and invited the Melians to partake of it. But a Carian virgin, who had conceived a passion for Symphæus,

Symphæus, discovered to him their design. He then returned answer to the invitation of the Carians, that it was the custom of the Greeks to attend no entertainments without their wives. They were therefore desired to bring their wives with them. The Melians accordingly went, in their tunics, and unarmed but their wives, every one carried a sword in her bosom, and placed herself by her husband. In the midst of the entertainment, observing a Carian give a signal, the women instantly opened their bosoms, and gave every man his sword: who falling upon the Barbarians, cut them to pieces, and took possession of their city and domains.

CHAP. LXV.

THE PHOCÆAN WOMEN.

IN a war, that was carried on with so great animosity between the Phocæans and Thessalians, that the latter had made a resolution to give no quarter to any Phocæan that bore arms, and to reduce their wives and children to slavery, the Phocæan women previous to the battle collected a great quantity of wood, which they piled up, and mounted it with their children; vowing, as soon as they saw their husbands defeated, to set fire to the pile, and expire in the flames. This resolution of the women produced correspondent bravery in the men: who fought obstinately, and obtained the victory.

CHAP. LXVI.

THE CHIAN WOMEN.

THE Chians and Erythræans had been long at war about the possession of Leuconia, when the Chians, finding the enemy too powerful for them, demanded a truce, and engaged to evacuate the place, taking with them only their cloak and tunic. The Chian women were enraged at the terms, and pressed the men not to relinquish their arms. The men told them, they had engaged by oath to do it. The women persisted in their advice, by no means to part with their arms, and proposed to them, in observance of their oath to say, by their cloak and tunic they meaned their spear and shield, it being the custom of their country to call their spear a cloak, and their sword a tunic. The Chians followed the women's advice; and, by thus shewing their determination to defend themselves, became afterwards more formidable to the Erythræans.

CHAP. LXVII.

THE THASIAN WOMEN.

THE Thasians closely besieged, and in want of cords to tie together the machines, which against the enemy's works they erected on their walls; the women shaved their heads, and twisting their hair, made it into bands, which were used in framing their machines.

CHAP. LXVIII.

THE ARGIVE WOMEN.

PYRRHUS, king of Epire, having on the invitation of Aristæus the Argive undertaken an expedition against Argos, the Argives assembled in arms at the forum while the women from the house tops with stones and bricks attacked the Epirots, and obliged them to retreat, and Pyrrhus himself was killed in the attack, by the discharge of a brick, which struck him on the temples. The Argive women on this occasion obtained immortal reputation in the conquest and death of Philip, the most warlike prince of the age.

CHAP. LXIX.

THE ACARNANIAN WOMEN.

THE Ætolians after a long war with the Acarnanians, were at last introduced into the city by treachery. The Acarnanians in the hour of danger fought bravely, but were overpowered. The women got upon the tops of the houses, and from thence discharging stones and bricks, killed many of the enemy; and by exhortations, remonstrances, and supplications, when the men before superiour numbers were obliged to retreat, they rallied them, and brought them back to the charge. And at last, when every effort failed, and those who survived the carnage were taken, the women clinging to them, whether their husbands, parents, or brothers, held so close, that the enemy unable to separate them, were forced to kill both men and women together.

CHAP. LXX.

THE CYRENIAN WOMEN.

PTOLEMY having made war on the Cyrenians, they committed to Lycopus an Ætolian general the whole conduct of the war. And while the men engaged in the field, the women also took their share of duty: they made the palisades, dug the trench, supplied the men with darts, took care of the wounded, and prepared their provisions. The men at length being most of them cut off, Lycopus changed the constitution into a monarchy: for which the women so persecuted him with their reproaches, that he ordered many of them to execution, to which they chearfully and gladly ran.

CHAP. LXXI.

THE LACEDÆMONIAN WOMEN.

THE daughters of the Lacedæmonians married the Minyans, who were descended from the Argonauts. And in consequence of these marriages, they were by the Lacedæmonians admitted to a share of the government. But not contented with that, they attempted to make themselves absolute. The Spartans thereupon seised them, and threw them into prison. Their daughters——

[*So far Polyænus. The remainder of the Stratagem is wanting: but may however be thus supplied from the fourth Book of Herodotus.*]

THE

The wives of the Minyans, and daughters of the principal Lacedæmonians, entreated permission to visit their husbands in the prison the night before their intended execution. which was accordingly granted. And in the prison they exchanged dresses with their husbands: who thus furnished made their escape in women's disguise They afterwards posted themselves on mount Taygetus; and by the intervention of Thera had their wives restored to them, with free permission to remove, and settle themselves wherever they pleased.

FINIS.

Lightning Source UK Ltd.
Milton Keynes UK
UKHW021839191221
395946UK00003B/13